D0984433

The Folklore of
Leicestershire and Rutland

Wishing well at Ashwell. The inscription reads: '*All ye who hither come to drink Rest not your thoughts below Look at that sacred sign and think Whence living waters flow*'.

"The Spring"
Built over by a rector Rev. Jones

Roy Palmer

The Folklore of Leicestershire and Rutland

SYCAMORE PRESS LTD
WYMONDHAM

Designed by Sue Steel
Photoset by Parker Typesetting Service, Leicester
Process by Planit Litho Ltd., Leicester
Printed and bound by Woolnoughs of Wellingborough

Contents

By the same author:
Room for Company, 1971
Songs of the Midlands, 1972
The Painful Plough, 1972
The Valiant Sailor, 1973
Love is Pleasing, 1974
A Touch on the Times, 1974
Poverty Knock, 1974
The Folklore of Warwickshire, 1976
The Rigs of the Fair (with Jon Raven), 1976
The Rambling Soldier, 1977
Feasts and Seasons (with Anthony Adams
and Robert Leach), 4 vols, 1977–8
Strike the Bell, 1978
Folk Music in School (with Robert Leach), 1978
A Ballad History of England, 1979
Everyman's Book of English Country Songs, 1979
Birmingham Ballads, 1979
Everyman's Book of British Ballads, 1980
Manchester Ballads (with Harry Boardman), 1983
Folk Songs Collected by Ralph Vaughan Williams, 1983

 Introduction

The central counties, Leicestershire and Rutland, which I still think of as separate although they have been administratively one since 1974, seem to have been neglected by folklorists. The only major work on the folklore of the two counties is Charles Billson's 153–page study, published in 1895, which was drawn almost entirely from printed sources. Yet interest in the subject is probably greater now than ever before, and there is no shortage of pamphlets, articles and newspaper stories. The time seems opportune for the first comprehensive survey of the folklore of Leicestershire and Rutland, using both printed and oral sources.

The *Oxford English Dictionary* defines folklore as 'the traditional beliefs, legends and customs current among the common people'. Like languages, the subject should perhaps be divided into the dead and the living. Some folklore is dead in the sense that certain sayings, stories, beliefs are no longer current, no longer passed on to a child on its mother's knee, at the fireside, at a family gathering, or even in the street or playground. In some cases beliefs and customs have been swept away by social change such as industrial development, population movement, technical innovation. In other cases folklore was systematically attacked on moral, religious, educational or organisational grounds. A relatively recent example which combined all these was the suppression by Leicester Council in 1904 after a fifteen-year campaign of the Humberstone Gate Fairs.

The climate of opinion has now changed, and many of the forces once ranged against folklore now support it. Enlightened clergymen once opposed village feasts and hiring fairs, and these have disappeared; but their successors often regard themselves as guardians of parish customs such as hay-strewing in churches or blessing the plough. Local authorities preserve in their archives and museums photographs, artefacts and documents concerning folklore as part of their heritage. Teachers see the songs and tales, beliefs and practices of the past not only as local social history but as cultural material with an interest and a message for today.

Yet folklore is far from being a dead language or an archaeological study. On the contrary, it clings doggedly, obstinately, tenaciously to life. Few people are entirely without some superstition, local saying or traditional story. One ghost story, that of Lady Aslin at Whitwick, is still current after over 600 years. Buildings like ancient houses and churches, features of the landscape such as hills, wood and streams still have their attendant tales. Institutions like markets and fairs survive the centuries, often on the same spot and on the same date. Customs hold, sometimes unobtrusively, sometimes spectacularly, as in the case of the bottle-kicking and hare-pie scramble at Hallaton, which now has national fame.

Not even the Hallaton custom, though, is unique. It has affinities with analogous events in other parts of the country, and in a similar way the folklore of Leicestershire and Rutland is the local shape of a national, and even international pattern. It is a shape which is remarkably full and varied. My own roots reach into it. I was born at Markfield, and lived in Leicestershire and Rutland until I was eighteen. I went to school at Newtown Linford and Coalville; and later married a fellow-pupil from 'off the Forest'. Many years later I was one of the main contributors to the Reader's Digest book, *Folklore, Myths and Legends of Britain* (1973), and wrote *The Folklore of Warwickshire* (1976). I am delighted now to have had the opportunity of writing about the counties of my youth. Members of my family, most of whom still live in Leicestershire, have provided me with a great deal of information, but strangers also have gone out of their way to help, as I acknowledge on page 279. In the final analysis, the future of folklore in Leicestershire and Rutland is in the hands of these strangers and brothers, and that is where it should be.

Site of the Battle of Loosecoat Field, Pickworth, viewed from the A1

1. Beginnings and battles

There is a story that Leicester was founded by Llyr, a sea-god, who called it Llyrcester. Llyr married an earth-woman, and they had three children. The oldest, Bran, was brave and good; the youngest, Eynissyen, ugly and evil. These were boys, and in between was their sister, Branwen, who was fair and gentle. An Irish king, having heard of her beauty, travelled to Leicester with an escort of eight hundred men to ask for her hand in marriage. A wedding was arranged, but on the night before it was due to take place Eynissyen mutilated the Irishmen's horses by cropping their manes, ears and tails. The Irish were understandably enraged but, although he suspected Eynissyen, Llyr made amends by presenting fresh horses and gifts, including a huge bronze cauldron which had the power to restore life. If warriors killed in battle were placed inside overnight they would arise fit and strong the next morning. The marriage was duly celebrated, and Branwen left for Ireland.

Soon afterwards, on the death of his wife, Llyr told his sons that he must return to his ocean kingdom. He left Leicester to his older son, exhorting him to rule wisely. Bran followed his father's advice, and prospered, but eventually became so exasperated with Eynissyen's constant plotting and mischief-making that he banished him from the town. Eynissyen therefore went to visit his sister and her husband in Ireland. He was welcomed, but soon grew jealous of his sister's good fortune and the king's power and wealth. He was fascinated by the bronze cauldron, and one night crept in and closed the huge lid. When he found himself unable to open it again he frantically battered on the sides. The cauldron disintegrated, and in so doing, killed him.

The Irish king was furious at the loss of the cauldron, and assumed that Bran had sent Eynissyen to destroy it. Despite Branwen's entreaties he set off with his army for Leicester. At the end of a bloody campaign Leicester was devastated, but he and most of his followers were dead. When the news reached Branwen she died of a broken heart. Bran, who had received a mortal wound in the conflict, called on his people to take his body to a sea-cliff overlooking his father's kingdom, and to bury it upright, with the dead eyes looking towards the waters. As long as Bran remains undisturbed in his burial-place the city of Leicester and the land of England will never be destroyed. Such a prophecy must often have reassured the anxious.

An alternative claim to be the founder of Leicester is made for Leir, son of Bladud and grandson of Lud, who ruled the whole of Britain for sixty years. Geoffrey of Monmouth, reporting a tradition already some two thousand years old in about 1136, when he wrote *The History of the Kings of Britain*, said that it was Leir 'who built the city of the River Soar which is called Kaerleir after him in the British tongue, its Saxon name being Leicester'. As an old man, Leir proposed to divide his kingdom amongst his three daughters, Goneril, Regan and Cordelia. The older two made gushing protestations of love for him, but the youngest, Cordelia, refused to profess anything more than the love she already felt. As a result Leir gave her nothing, but divided the whole country between Goneril and Regan. The sorry sequel was ingratitude, dissension, war and heartbreak. Leir's death was saddened by the tardy realisation that Cordelia's love for him was genuine.

Shakespeare had the story from Geoffrey of Monmouth, via Holinshed's *Chronicles*, and we know it best from the play, *King Lear*. There is a tradition that Shakespeare visited Leicester as an actor in the Earl of Leicester's company in 1585 or soon afterwards, when he picked up stories not only about Leir but also Richard III. In addition, he is said to have been inspired by the wild scenery of Charnwood Forest when writing of Lear's wanderings in the storm.

We read in Geoffrey of Monmouth that Leir was buried by Cordelia 'in a certain underground chamber which she had ordered to be dug beneath the River Soar, some way downstream from Leicester'. Geoffrey studied at Oxford, and it is possible that he might have visited Leicester and seen some ceremony, perhaps at the Jewry Wall, for he adds: 'This underground chamber was dedicated to the two-faced Janus; and when the feast-day of the god came round, all the craftsmen in the town used to perform there the first act of labour in whatever enterprise they were planning to undertake during the coming year'. No firm identification of this site has been made, though a cave which once existed in New Parks was pointed out as a place where Leir had hidden from his enemies.

If the story of Leir is to be believed, the pedigree of Leicester is even longer than that of Rome, though some sober etymologists suggest that the ending of the name indicates a town which had originally been a Roman station, and therefore much younger than Rome itself. The first written mention was in 803. Leicester was occupied by the Danes in 920 after the death of King Alfred, but was later re-taken by his daughter, Ethelfleda, Lady of Mercia. It is she who is reputed to have built the first castle at Leicester and also the nearby church of St Mary de Castro. Edwin, grandson of Lady Godiva, was Earl of Leicester in 1066. He met his death at the hands of the Normans, who sacked both the castle and the church. Fourteen years later William the Conqueror granted the town to Hugo de

Grantmeisnel, who set about repairs. A tradition remained that evil would follow any king of England who feasted in Leicester Castle.

The first written record of Rutland occurred, as 'Roteland', in 863, but the county did not properly exist until over three hundred years later, when it was constituted out of two wapentakes detached from the sheriffdom of Nottingham and part of Northamptonshire. The resulting county was presented by King John to Queen Isabella. The old Roteland had previously belonged to other royal ladies, first to the mother of Ethelred the Unready, then to his queen, Emma. The village of Edith Weston still bears the name of Queen Edith, who received Roteland as a gift from her husband, Edward the Confessor.

The history of Rutland has been peaceful, but in the course of a single battle fought in the county during the Wars of the Roses ten thousand men are said to have died. The Battle of Loosecoat Field took place near Pickworth, not far from the Great North Road, in 1470. The spot to this day is called Bloody Oaks. The Lancastrians were defeated, and the Lincolnshire and Rutland men who had been fighting on the losing side under the Pickworth squire, Sir John Hussey, fled through the village. As they ran, they tore off their coats which bore his colours, and in so doing, provided the name by which the battle has been called ever since. There was fighting in the village, which was partly destroyed as a result. Just one arch now remains of the church of that time as a visual reminder. Workmen digging nearby in the 1970s found a mass grave containing the skeletons of many young men.

The last battle of the Wars of the Roses was fought on Redmoor Plain, near Market Bosworth in Leicestershire, on 22 August, 1485. It decided the fate of a dynasty, and perhaps of a whole country. Stories have been told about the battle and the dead King Richard for five hundred years, and the scene of the fighting is now a major attraction for tourists.

On his way to meet the rebellious Henry Tudor and his army, Richard III travelled from Nottingham to Leicester, where he put up at one of the principal inns of the town, the White Boar, which stood in the High Street at the corner of the lane that led to the Guildhall. The white boar was Richard's own emblem, which might have determined his choice. According to tradition, the innkeeper promptly changed the name to the Blue Boar after the battle, to favour the badge of the Earl of Oxford, one of the supporters of Henry Tudor. The street is still called Blue Boar Lane, though the old inn building was demolished in 1838.

On Sunday, 21 August, Richard set out from the inn. No doubt he expected to return, since he left behind his own bedstead, which was found many years afterwards to contain a large sum of gold (see page 195). He rode down Westgate and crossed the first arm of the River Soar by the West Bridge, where a blind beggar predicted his doom. Then he

The arch at Pickworth

took Bow Bridge over a second arm of the river. As he passed over one of his spurs struck a coping stone on the low parapet. A woman, some later said Black Annis herself, recognised a clear omen when she saw one, and foretold that his head would strike at the same place on his return to Leicester. In another version of the story the prophecy was made by an old blind beggarman, a wheelwright by trade. It was conditional on the moon's changing twice that day. The second change came about when a nobleman whose colours bore an image of the moon defected from Richard to Henry.

The opposing armies were ready for battle, but Richard refused to engage on a Sunday. One tradition holds that he spent that night in Elmesthorpe Church, another that he remained in a tent on Ambion Hill, thus fulfilling two prophecies. The first was that if he fought where many placenames ended in *ton* he would 'come to great distress'; and the neighbouring villages included Sibston, Upton, Shenton, Sutton Cheney, Peckleton, Stapleton, Dadlington, Fenny Drayton and Atherton. The second said that if the place at which he fought began and ended in the syllable *an* he would lose the battle to expiate the murder of his former wife, Anne; and Ambion could be spelled 'Anbian'.

On the same evening before the battle a youth of sixteen, called Richard, whom the king had summoned from London, was shown into the royal tent. To his amazement the king invited him to watch the battle on the morrow, and told him of a safe vantage point. Then he ordered him to return to see him after the battle. Finally, lest the outcome should be adverse, the king gave him a purse of gold and told him that he was his bastard son, Richard Plantagenet. Until then the boy had been ignorant of his origins, though he had received an excellent education in London, paid for by unknown patrons.

King Richard did not sleep well. During the night 'there appeared about him divers fearful ghosts, running about him, not suffering him to take any rest, still crying revenge'. Next morning he heard mass at Sutton Cheney. A different tale says that he went the rounds of his outposts, found a sentry asleep, and buried a dagger in his heart, remarking: 'I found him asleep, and I left him as I found him'. One wonders at such a story. Perhaps it was put about after Richard's death as part of the new regime's big campaign to discredit him. At all events, it stuck, as did his celebrated cry of anguish on becoming unseated during the fighting: 'A horse, a horse. My kingdom for a horse'. In default of a horse Richard dashed into the melee on foot, and was overwhelmed. Some said that he received his mortal wound from one of his own followers. His mangled body was stripped and ignominiously thrown over a horse, to be conveyed to Leicester. According to one story Richard Plantagenent saw his father's body as it was carried in this fashion. Another account suggests that when he saw from his vantage point that the battle was lost he immediately set off for London. He could expect no mercy

13

if Henry VII became aware of his existence, so he went to ground by using his father's money to apprentice himself to a bricklayer. He told all this many years later to Sir Thomas Moyle at Eastwell Hall in Kent. In about 1546 when alterations were being made to the house Sir Thomas noticed that during every break from work the foreman bricklayer took out a book to read. His curiosity became particularly keen when he saw that the books were in Latin, and asked how the bricklayer had received his education. Sir Thomas found him work at Eastwell House until his death at the age of 81. The church register for 1550 has the entry that 'Richard Plantagenet was buryed the 22nd daye of December', and the grave can still be seen in the churchyard.

Back at Bosworth Field, King Richard's crown was found in a thorn bush near Stoke Golding by a soldier, or perhaps deposited there by him when he realised that he could not get away with so conspicuous an item of

The Blue Boar Inn, from Kelly's *Royal Progresses*

booty. The place is still called Crown Hill, though the site of the bush is now occupied by a Victorian house. Sir Reginald Bray, who claimed to have found the crown, was granted the right to show a thorn bush in his coat of arms ever afterwards. Henry triumphantly put on the crown, and made a victory speech to his jubilant followers.

Richard's body came back over Bow Bridge, and as it did so the dead head swung against the parapet, thus fulfilling the prophecy. The body was exposed for two days at the Collegiate Church of the Newarke, then interred 'without any pompe or solemne funeral' in the monastery church of the Grey Friars, which stood between St Martin's and the present Friar

Bow Bridge in the mid-nineteenth century, from Kelly's *Royal Progresses*

Lane. Ten years later, by order of Henry VII, a monument was erected there, but Richard's humiliations were still not over. When the religious houses were dissolved, under Henry VIII, the monument was defaced, and Richard's bones were taken from his stone coffin and thrown into the river from Bow Bridge. The coffin was removed to the White Horse in Gallowtree Gate, where for the next two hundred years it served as a drinking trough for horses. Celia Fiennes heard the story when she visited Leicester in 1697, though she placed the coffin elsewhere: 'The stone he struck his heel at, and against which his head was struck at his return when brought athwart the horse dead, I could not see, it being removed, but I saw a piece of his tombstone he lay in, which was cut out in exact form for his body to lye in, that remains to be seen at the Grey-hound in Lecester but is partly broken'. A further report says that parts of the coffin were used to make cellar steps, but it has been suggested that the coffin is still intact, and that Richard's skull also survives, having been found by a surveyor and identified by its slashed cranium when the present Bow Bridge was built. Photographs of both objects appeared in the *Leicester Mercury* in 1983, though their whereabouts was not revealed.

The death of a king in battle is remembered in Leicestershire; so is the death of a young queen on the scaffold. Lady Jane Grey lived at Bradgate House, near the village of Newtown Linford. One evening she was riding home through the forest with a young man, Francis Beaumont, of Grace

15

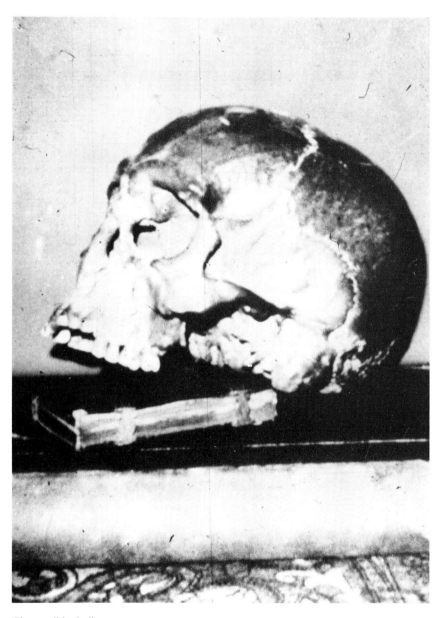

The possible skull . . .

Dieu. Near Benscliffe they saw a huge wolf, the last ever to be encountered in Charnwood. It was carrying a little child in its jaws. Although they were poorly armed, Francis Beaumont attacked the wolf with a small knife, and Lady Jane Grey wielded a large stone. They were successful in killing it, and in restoring the injured but living child to its mother, a forester's wife called Jane Hardy. The final outcome was unfortunate, however. Lady Jane's father, the Marquis of Dorset, was alarmed not only by the adventure but by the thought that Beaumont might become fond of his daughter, and wish to marry her. He therefore swore an oath that Jane, with her royal blood – she was the grand-daughter of Mary Tudor, Henry VIII's sister – should never marry a commoner.

At the age of sixteen Jane married a nobleman, Lord Guilford Dudley. Shortly afterwards, on the death of Edward VI in July, 1553, she was proclaimed queen. She reigned for only thirteen days, though for some reason she is known as the Nine Days' Queen: perhaps they did not count weekends. Then she was deposed, and subsequently beheaded on Tower Hill by order of another Mary Tudor, Henry VIII's daughter, who was later to be known as 'Bloody' Mary. According to a local tradition still

... and coffin of Richard III
(Photographs by courtesy of *Leicester Mercury*)

17

current in Newtown Linford when I was a boy, all the oak trees in Bradgate Park were pollarded as a sign of mourning when Jane was executed.

Lady Jane Grey

Charles I was another monarch who met his death on the scaffold. One of the steps which led him there was his defeat at Naseby, near Market Harborough but just over the Northamptonshire border. Before the battle the royal forces besieged Leicester, then took and sacked the town. Their outrages included the burning of Leicester Abbey. Oral tradition relates that a number of people were driven out of St Martin's and killed in the churchyard. It is supported by a record in the accounts for 1645 of three shillings 'paid Francis Motley for mendinge the locks of the church doors broke by the kings army'.

Charles spent the night before the Battle of Naseby at Thorpe Lubenham Hall, now part of the building called the Tower House. The chair in which he is said to have sat to eat his supper is still kept in the church at Lubenham. During the night he was awakened and went to Market Harborough for a council of war, then on to Naseby. After being defeated by Cromwell he made his way to Hereford, via Leicester, Ashby-de-la-Zouch, Lichfield and Bewdley. There is a story, told to me by Mr Bill Measures, who was an apprentice butcher at Lubenham in the 1920s, that immediately after the battle Charles and a few followers fled on horseback to the hall, which is four miles from Naseby, closely pursued through the thickly-wooded country by a party of Cromwell's troopers. The royal group dashed into the hall and barricaded the doors. Hot on their heels, their pursuers arrived and started to batter a way in, but in the meantime Charles and his men were escaping through a tunnel which led to the church, 150 yards away. Fresh horses were waiting there, which enabled Charles to get away. At some stage he visited Tur Langton, where he watered his horse at what is still called King Charles' Well. (This was once the only source of water in the area, and even during the drought of 1976

18

it did not run dry). At Belton Charles rested on a stone, now incorporated in the war memorial and known as the King's Stone. At Wistow he stayed with Sir Richard Halford, who was later sentenced to death for his trouble by Parliament, but reprieved on payment of a ransom.

Of Charles' opponent, Cromwell, there are also many traditions. He is said to have spent the night at a house in Horn Lane, Uppingham, which until recently was called Cromwell House, and to have battered down Essendine Castle with cannon, the stone of which was later used to build the present church. Cannonball Lane at South Luffenham takes its name from the recollection that Cromwell's soldiers set up artillery there to fire at North Luffenham.

The Magazine Gateway

In the year of the Siege of Leicester and the Battle of Naseby, Garendon Pool, which was on land near Shepshed owned by the Duke of Buckingham, turned red, as if with blood. Local people reacted with consternation, and the news spread as far as London, where it was thought that 'perchance in this miraculous appearance is to be read the immediate anger of God, in great characters of blood'. Eventually the pool was drained. A few fish were found, but nothing else, and the mystery remained without explanation.

Some two hundred years later there was another battle in Leicestershire, but this time there were no fatal casualties, merely some wounded and prisoners. This was the Battle of Saxby, an extraordinary series of brawls, both physical and legal, which went on for three years. It began with the decision by the Eastern Counties Railway Company to build a line from Syston to Peterborough which would cross land at the village of Saxby, near Melton Mowbray. The owner of the land happened to be Lord Harborough, who virulently opposed the railway scheme since he thought it would damage the trade of the Melton to Oakham canal, in which he had an interest.

In November, 1844, surveyors were ordered off the land, and when they declined to move they were unceremoniously bundled away by gamekeepers. The next day they returned with reinforcements in the shape of a gang of navvies and three Nottingham prize-fighters. The earl had a defence force of between thirty and forty men, and in addition a large crowd had gathered to see the fun. The police were also on the scene, and a warning was issued that any man committing an assault would be arrested, so weapons were put aside and the leaders decided that the outcome could be settled by a pushing match. A large-scale scrummage ensued. The railway side lost, and retired from the field.

A few days later they returned and created a diversion to draw the defence force away, thus opening the ground to surveyors. They had not reckoned with what might be called Harborough's cavalry, for the earl had indeed organised a mounted troop. A free-for-all began, with staves being liberally used, and the railway forces were not only routed, but some of their number were arraigned for riot at the next assizes in March, 1845. They were found guilty, and sentenced to a month's imprisonment. Three months later the company was successful in having its parliamentary act for the line passed, but the earl's supporters had manoeuvred it into permitting the insertion of a clause by which his lordship's consent was required before any of his land might be taken. The act was therefore as good as a dead letter.

Hoping to succeed by an oblique approach, the company then purchased the Oakham Canal, but the earl remained unmoved. There was more fighting in November, 1845, when surveyors again attempted to do their work. As a result the earl was charged by the company with conspiracy to prevent its officials from carrying out their duties, and also with assault. At Nottingham in July, 1846, he was triumphantly acquitted.

Next, the company obtained an act authorising it to drive a tunnel. Boring started, but the workings were too shallow, and collapsed. Some sixty trees were brought down, and the earl obtained an injunction forbidding any further uprooting, which effectively stopped the tunnelling. In the end, the company was compelled to take the line round the earl's land, and it procured the necessary act in July, 1847. The deviation was known as Lord Harborough's curve, and the first through train from Leicester to Peterborough negotiated it on 1 May, 1848. Peace hath her victories . . .

2. Places and people

People once had – often still do have – a tremendous loyalty to their own locality, sometimes with the corollary of fierce antagonism towards other places. Pride and prejudice of this kind were often expressed in nicknames, sayings and rhymes. The inhabitants of both counties had standard nicknames, by which they were widely known. Michael Drayton quotes them in his massive verse travelogue, *Polyolbion*, which was published between 1612 and 1622:

Bean belly, Lestershire, her attribute doth bear.
And *Bells and Bagpipes* next, belong to *Lincolnshire*.
Of *Malt-horse, Bedfordshire* long since the Blazon wan.
And little *Rutlandshire* is termèd *Raddleman*.

Raddle or ruddle was the colouring used to make an identifying mark on sheep, and the sobriquet no doubt shows the importance of sheep in Rutland farming. Similarly, beans were widely grown in Leicestershire. The mayor was once chosen at Leicester, or so the story goes, by a sow. The candidates sat each with a hat full of beans in his lap, and the one from whose hat the sow first ate was thereby selected as mayor. There was a saying that if you shook a Leicestershire man by the collar you would hear the beans rattle in his belly. The classic rejoinder was: 'Yoi, lad, but ew doo'st?' ('Yes, lad, but who does so?') Neither expostulation nor reply is heard any more, though one village is still called Barton-in-the Beans.

To use the nickname of a place gives a sense of superiority over those not in the know, and can also express affectionate familiarity. To many people, 'Niffy' merely means 'smelly', but to the inhabitants of Countesthorpe it means home. Wigston is known as 'Two Steeples' from its two churches, and also as 'Tangletown', which is less clear. Anstey is 'Nookery', Loughborough, 'Bell 'op', and Church Langton, 'Sing-song'. Moira's nickname, 'Whom', is probably from the way the locals pronounce the word, 'home'. The epithet in 'Tinhat Hinckley' puzzles many. One explanation is that it refers to the great helmet worn in the town's Whitsuntide procession by the effigy of Hugo Grantemeisnel, Baron of Hinckley in the time of William Rufus. Another story, still current, is that the baron once set up a pole with a helmet on top in the centre of the town and made all the people who passed bow to it.

Whatever the reason, Hinckley people are still known as 'tinhats'. Another collective nickname, 'Anstey Neddoes', may date from the days of Ned Ludd (page 90). The people of Lyddington, itself known as 'Long Lyddington', are called 'Lithers'. Those of Carlton Curlieu took their name of 'Carlton Wharlers' from the habit they once had of gargling the letter 'r' at the back of their throats. 'Braunston Turks' was an allusion to the alleged pugnacity of the Rutland villagers.

The names of some places appear in set expressions. 'Then I'll thatch Groby Pool with pancakes' was used to indicate incredulity when an earlier speaker had boasted or suggested doing something unlikely. 'He's gone over Asfordby bridge backwards' originally meant that someone was past learning, but later evolved to indicate that he or she had put the cart before the horse. 'Put up your pipes, and go to Lockington Wake' in modern vernacular would be: 'get lost', Lockington being a village in a remote corner of Leicestershire. A put-off to someone enquiring where a person was going was: 'I'm going to Huncote on a pig'. 'In and out like Billesdon, I wot' was a simile inspired by the scattered nature of the village mentioned. Another version was self-explanatory: 'In and out like Billesdon brook'.

The Cuckoo Inn at Wing

Many rhymes categorised a village or a group of villages, while often revealing bias or rivalry. The allegiance of the speaker is fairly clear here:

Mountsorrel is a stony place;
Sileby it be sandy.
Rothley has the Half-way House;
Quorndon is the dandy.

Other verses positively glow with pride:

I've explored the tiny county, but I'll not have had my fill
Till I've had a look at Egleton, near Burley-on-the-Hill.

Or:

In Rutland, old Rutland, as I can recall,
The village of Barley is the best place of all.
The girls of old Barley are the plagues of our lives,
But when they are married they make excellent wives.

Another rhyme perhaps reflects Rutland's ancient connection with Nottinghamshire:

Nottingham where they knock 'em;
Oakham where they catch 'em.
Bringhurst where they bury 'em,
And Cottesmore where they cry.

The allusions here are not very obvious but another apparently obscure rhyme becomes clear when one realises that it refers to the quality of the church bells. The last village mentioned is Burton Lazars:

Brentingby pancheons
And Wyfordby pans,
Stapleford organs
And Burton tingtangs.

Local trades and characteristics are often mentioned. Market Bosworth and some neighbouring villages appear here:

Sutton for mutton,
Bosworth for beef;
Carlton the pretty boy,
Coton the thief.

Hinckley had a deserved reputation for its beer:

Higham on the hill,
Stoke in the dale;
Wykin for buttermilk,
Hinckley for ale.

However, there was a challenge from Ratby:

Markfield on the hill,
Newtown in the vale;
Groby for silly buggers
And Ratby for ale.

Putting the pig on the wall at Countesthorpe
(Photograph by courtesy of *Leicester Mercury*)

At times the verses make a frontal attack. Odstone's name lends itself readily to the joker:

Odstone of all places most odd,
With ne'er a beer-house nor yet a house of God;
On the top of a hill, not in a hole,
Neither good for your body nor good for your soul.

The village of Hose also calls for a pun, and receives it in the saying: 'There are more whores in Hose than honest women in Long Clawson', which can be taken at face value or as meaning: 'There are more whores wearing hose than honest women with long clothes on'. 'Bread for borough men; at Great Glen there are more dogs than honest men' is taken to be a reference to the large numbers who once lived in the village workhouse. Other jibes are more direct, such as 'Stretton on the [Ermine] Street, where shrews meet', and 'In Cawcott [Caldecott] the folk are awk'ard'.

Alliteration comes in useful in 'Grievous Greetham where they pine 'em', which means either that the parson was so badly paid that he starved or that the villagers grieved because they were so poor. Neither explanation reflects very well on the place. 'Tit tattling Teigh' is clear enough, though the village has a much better claim to fame: it is the only one in Rutland to which all the inhabitants involved in the Great War, eleven

24

men and two women, returned safely. Willesley in Leicestershire has a similar distinction, though only three men were concerned there.

'The folk of Wing tried to hedge the cuckoo in', says another pithy jingle. The implication is that the foolish people of Wing, like the wise men of Gotham, built a hedge to keep the cuckoo in so as not to fail to hear its song. Perhaps the Wing people were not so foolish after all, for the reference could be to the Cuckoo Inn, which still stands in the village. Yet again, the name of the inn could have been chosen to reflect the rhyme, thus showing that Wing people can laugh at themselves. People do seem to delight in suggesting that others are less clever than they. The story goes that in at least five Leicestershire villages, Countesthorpe, Huncote, Moira, Sapcote and Stoney Stanton, local people put a pig on the wall to see the band go by, thus showing their stupidity. An alternative suggestion at Moira is that the pig got up of its own accord to hear the music. Either way, the local miners had a pig as a mascot, and carried it, bedecked with ribbons, at the local gala until the 1960s.

Three other villages, Debdale, Foxton and Glooston, are said to have treacle mines. Mocking outsiders use the assertion to imply laziness, since working in treacle mines cannot be very hard; poverty, shown by living on bread and treacle; luxury, with treacle as a symbol of the sweet life; or just plain daftness. Insiders can use it to mystify, or to suggest exclusiveness; outsiders can use it as a reproach or to pull the legs of insiders. In short, treacle mines are a fruitful source of jokes and verbal jousting.

The names of some places have inspired popular explanations. Hugglescote is said to derive from 'huddle coat', which in turn comes from people huddling in their coats in bad weather or possibly from a man's taking off his coat and wielding it against an attacking wolf. Etymologists will have no truck with such tales, but they continue to be told. Belgrave is said to derive from the occasion when a bell was being moved from one place to another, and could be carried no further. Better-known is the story that, for a wager, a giant named Bel set out to reach Leicester by three jumps of his horse. He mounted his sorrel at Mountsorrel. In his first leap he reached Wanlip, and in his second, Birstall, where he burst all: his harness, his horse and himself. He made a third leap in a desperate atempt to reach his goal, but fell dead with his charger at Red Hill, a mile and a half short of Leicester. He was buried where he fell, and the place became known as Belgrave:

Mountsorrel he mounted at,
Rothley he rode by,
Wanlip he leaped o'er,
Birstall he burst his gall,
At Belgrave he was buried at.

As well as names of places, features of the landscape aroused curiosity, and sometimes anxiety. They gave rise to stories or occasioned beliefs. Earthworks made in ancient times were thought to be the grave of a giant, as at Charley, in Charnwood Forest, or of some great captain, as at Shipley Hill, Cossington. A mound of Roman origin in a meadow near Hoby is known as Robin Hood's Barn. Lud, the grandfather of King Leir, was thought to be responsible for earthworks at Saltby, Stathern and Stonesby.

A huge granite stone some six feet wide and twelve high once stood in a hollow on the top of an eminence at Humberstone. It was variously called the Hoston, Hostin, Holly, Holy or even Hell Stone, and gave its name to the village, though the official derivation is from Hunbeort's Stan [Stone]. Geologically, the stone is an erratic, which was carried to the spot by glacial activity, but there were notions that it was dropped by a god, and frequented by fairies. In the eighteenth century the farmer on whose land it stood had the upper parts of the stone broken off, and the hollow levelled for the plough. For meddling with the stone he was soon reduced from being the owner of 120 acres to penury, and six years later he died in the workhouse. The remnant of the stone can still be seen. In the same locality there was a plot of land called Hell-hole Furlong, and also the traditional site of a nunnery which was reputed to be connected by an underground passage to Leicester Abbey, two miles away.

In the Abbey Fields at Leicester there was once a seven-foot stone, called St John's Stone. Its site is now in the middle of the Stadium Housing Estate. It was the custom for people to visit it on St John's Day (24 June). Children sometimes played round it, but were always careful to leave before nightfall, when the fairies came out. Mill Hill at Stoney Stanton, so called from a post-mill which once stood on its summit, was once famous for its fairy-rings and fairy-dances. As a rhyme put it: 'Hand in hand we'll dance around Because this place is fairy ground'. A good fairy called Hob lived at Breedon and willingly helped with any housework, until he was offended, and went off to live in a cave in the parish.

About two miles from Shepshed, between the hills of Lubcloud and Ives Head the Grey Hangman's Stone can be found. The story is that a local poacher, John of Oxley, was out one night and shot a deer – with an arrow, which gives some idea of the age of the tale. He hoisted the carcase over his shoulders and made for home. On the way, he leaned against the stone to rest, with the deer still on his back. He did not reach home, and was discovered several days later by a swineherd, dead. As a poem on the subject says:

All was clear. There was Oxley on one side of the stone,
On the other the down-hanging deer;
The burden had slipped, and his neck it had nipped;
He was hanged by his prize – all was clear.

The Moody Bush Stone can be seen in Moody Bush Field, off Ridgemere Road, between Syston and South Croxton. One rather curious tradition says that people used to bring a turf and leave it on the stone. The Hundred Court of Goscote probably met there, and its name may be a corruption of Moot Stone. A huge stone at the bottom of Main Street, Thringstone, was known as the 'Council Stone', and was a recognised meeting place for people who wanted to engage in discussion and debate on an informal basis.

One of the great landmarks of Leicester was not a stone but a cave, situated on the Dane Hills, off Glenfield Road. It was known as Black Annis' Bower, after its mythical occupant, a savage hag with long teeth and nails who relished human flesh. She came to be largely a means of frightening children into good behaviour, under threat of having their blood sucked and their skins hung out on a tree near the cave, though she was once much more than that (see page 219).

Wells and springs were another important physical feature, both for the vital water they supplied and for the legends which seemed to grow round them. In Old English 'wella' could mean well, spring or stream, and the names of at least six villages in Leicestershire and three in Rutland have the suffix, 'well'. At Ashwell there is still a wishing well, and at Whitwell ('white well') a stream can be heard running beneath the chancel of the church in times of heavy rain. At Sketchley there was a well whose water was thought to sharpen the wits, giving rise to the expressions: 'Go to Sketchley' for someone who was dull, or: 'Oh, you've been to Sketchley', for the unduly smart.

Many wells were thought to have special powers. The waters of Ratby's Holy Well were anti-scorbutic, which would have been very useful in

Remains of the Humber Stone, near Thurmaston

winter when fresh vegetables were in short supply. Other holy wells were at or near Ab Kettleby, Ashby-de-la-Zouch, Beeby, Bescaby, Bradley, Claybrooke, Garendon, Nanpantan and Shawell. At Hinckley's Holy Well six fine gold coins from the time of Edward III were found in 1755, which must have added to its prestige. A writer of 1831, pointing out that it was 'on the entrance into the town, on the London road', remarked that the water was 'exquisitely clear and good'. Holy Well Field was used for gatherings of townspeople.

Pilgrims were attracted in medieval times to Lady's Well at Oakham, in a field near the Odd House Inn. It was still renowned for healing powers in the Victorian era, and its water was applied to the eyes for soreness, always provided that a pin had first been thrown into the well. The water of the nearby Chrisswell also had curative properties. It is said that during the first world war a Belgian refugee took his sick cow to drink, and she recovered.

TRADE DEPRESSION

No Work, No Bread, No Hope!

A

MEETING

OF THE

INHABITANTS OF HINCKLEY

WILL BE HELD

NEAR THE HOLY WELL,

ON TUESDAY EVENING, JUNE 28, 1842,

AT SEVEN O'CLOCK:

To consider and to adopt such Resolutions as are required by the present times, in which the Hosier has little Trade and no Profit; the Landlord no Rent; the Shop-keeper no Custom; the Stockinger neither Bread nor Hope; and in which the heavy Poor-Rates are involving the Householder and the neighbouring Farmer in one Common Ruin.

Handbill from Pickering's *Hosiery Trade*
(By permission of Ferry Pickering Group)

28

Holywell Haw, now a farmhouse but previously a hermitage, stands on the edge of Charnwood Forest. Its name comes from the well which stood close by. Some five hundred years ago one of the ladies of Groby Castle, Agnes, the daughter of Lord Ferrers, was desired by Lord Comyn of Whitwick, a huge, violent man. Under threat of being abducted, Lady Agnes left the castle with the intention of seeking sanctuary at Grace Dieu Priory. She took a circuitous route through Charnwood, pursued by Comyn's men, but she became lost in the forest. She might well have died, had she not stumbled upon the Holy Well, where the monks of the hermitage gave her assistance. She escaped Comyn, and when she later married Edward Grey the couple went back to the hermitage after their wedding at Ulverscroft to thank the monks and to make an endowment of two hides of land and three fallow deer annually.

At the risk of spoiling a good story one should point out that it was Elizabeth Ferrers, not Agnes, who married Sir Edward Grey (in 1446). Grey took the title of Lord Ferrers of Groby *de iure uxoris*, that is, though his wife, there being no male heir to the Ferrers title. He died in 1457, and three years later his widow married King Edward IV. In 1463 her oldest surviving son was made Marquis of Dorset, and he was an ancestor of Lady Jane Grey. So do legend and history interweave.

Four centuries ago crops, cattle and people round the village of Prestwold were threatened by a three-month drought. A maiden lady, Gertrude Lacey, who lived at neighbouring Hoton, dreamed one night that she had found a spring. The location was precise: in Langdale Field beyond Gorse Farm, about half-way between Hoton Hill and Wymeswold. To make the water gush forth, a wand brought from the Holy Land would have to be pushed into the ground. Gertrude's sister, Grace, was sceptical when told the story, but after Gertrude had dreamed the same thing three times in a single night it was agreed that they should go in search of the spring. One drawback was the wand, but the villagers managed to unearth a staff which had been brought back from Canaan by a pilgrim. The staff, duly inserted at the spot shown in Gertrude's dream, tapped a supply of water which has never since run dry. It is known as the Sisters' Well. Local tradition states that two unidentified female effigies in Prestwold Church, dating from about 1520, portray the sisters, and that originally a wand was shown between them, though this no longer exists

At Griffydam an old well beside the road is said to have been taken over at one time by a griffin, a beast which is half lion and half eagle. The villagers were obliged to travel two miles to fetch water from another spring, until a knight happened to ride by and ask for water for himself and his horse. When he heard the problem he killed the griffin by an arrow through the neck, and the villagers' well was restored to them. There is a column in Breedon Church carved with the griffin's shape, and

29

The two sisters at Prestwold Church

it is said that the skin was hung in the church and that every bride passes beneath it on her wedding day.

The ecclesiastical reformer, John Wycliffe, was Rector of Lutterworth during the last years of his life. He died in 1384, and was buried in the chancel of the church. Even after his death he was hated by establishment figures in the church for his reforming ideas, though he was revered by ordinary people: 'You could hardly see two persons upon the high road but one of them was a follower of Wicklif', wrote Henry of Knighton,

Canon of Leicester Abbey. At that time Leicestershire was in the Diocese of Lincoln and in 1428 a mob sent by the Bishop of Lincoln removed Wycliffe's bones from their resting place, and took them to a waiting hand-cart through a door called 'Wycliffe's Door' ever since. The bones were conveyed to the bank of the River Swift by the present bridge, where there was once a ford. They were burned, and the ashes thrown into the river, dispersing themselves – like Wycliffe's teachings, said his followers – throughout the world. On the way to the river one of the bones fell from the cart, and a spring of healing water immediately gushed forth. Another story is that one of the mob picked up a bone, then immediately fell and dashed his brains out at the spot, where a spring emerged. It was known as St John's Well. It still flows in the grounds of the house which today stands on the site, at the bottom of Lutterworth on the London Road. It is called The Springs. A picture showing the burning of Wycliffe's bones can be seen in the church.

St Tibba, niece of King Penda of Mercia, and her cousin, St Eabba, are said to have lived at Ryhall in the seventh century. At first they were 'wild hunting girls', but later became holy hermits. The present church at Ryhall is said to have been built over the cell of St Tibba, who, because of

The site of Tibba's Well, near Ryhall

31

her early love of the chase, is the patroness of falconers and wildfowlers. She was buried at Ryhall, but in 936 her body was transferred to Peterborough. A tradition which has lived for more than a thousand years in the village is that she used to walk up a hill to wash at the spring which was called after her. The spring in turn gave its name to the hill, but over the years this became garbled, first to Tibb's-well-hill, then to Stibbal's-well-hill. On the brow of the hill, near the spring, is Halegreen. 'Hale' was the Saxon word for gatherings held in the fields to honour saints, and Halegreen was the place where such meetings were held on St Tibba's Day (14 December).

St Tibba's cousin, St Eabba, also had her spring, near the River Gwash. St Eabba's Well is now called Shepherd's Jacob's Well. The ford on the river nearby, originally St Eabba's-well-ford, is now Stableford, or rather Stableford Bridge, since the ford is no longer used.

3. Churches

A church usually occupies a prominent position, reflecting its importance in the life and history of a community. Breedon Church stands on a high hill, with the village at its foot. Building originally began where the village is, but each night doves carried to the top of the hill all the stones which had been laid during the day, until the people accepted that their church should be at the new site. At Fleckney the church was originally to have been about a mile west of the present village. Oral tradition says that the little folk demolished each night what had been built and threw the materials into the stream where, in time, they became lodged near to the present church. The builders decided to abandon the original site, and follow the wishes of the little folk. A more scientific suggestion is that the first site represents early medieval settlement, the current site being later, but no explanation for the change is offered. The church-builders at Tilton-on-the-Hill also, apparently, has second thoughts because of supernatural intervention.

'The church that died of shame' might serve to describe the parish church of St Mary-in-Arden at Market Harborough. Apparently it acquired an unpleasant reputation 'on account of the many clandestine marriages that were celebrated within its sanctuary, and the questionable character of those who performed the matrimonial ceremonies'. Eventually, 'it became necessary to annul its privileges; the tower, as was said at the time, being no longer able to hold up its head, fell with a crash upon the main body of the church, and reduced it to ruins'. Only a small fragment remained, together with a circular-headed doorway which forms the porch to the mortuary chapel at the present cemetery

Conversely, the tower of about 1444 at St Margaret's Church at Leicester must have meant a great deal to all the parishoners, since it was built from the proceeds of a farthing tax levied on every hearth, the Smoke Farthing. The church is now almost an island, surrounded by fast roads. A truncated steeple at the village of Beeby is called Beeby's Tub. It is the work of two brothers, masons who had built the beautiful needle-spire at Queniborough. While building at Beeby they quarrelled over costs, and also over the ability of the tower to bear the steeple's weight. One day their anger led to a scuffle, during the course of which they both plunged from the tower to their deaths. The spire,

Beeby Church

barely begun, remains a stump to this day. As the rhyme puts it:
  Beeby Tub was to have been a spire.
  Two brothers fought and broke their backs,
  And so 'twas built no higher.
Many of the objects preserved in churches either illustrate or give rise to
tales and legends. The Norman font at Thorpe Arnold shows St George
and two dragons, while the tympanum at Hallaton portrays St Michael
slaying the dragon. An iron-bound chest at Seaton is said to have been
made to receive contributions for the crusade of Richard Coeur de Lion.
At Theddingworth an almsbox bears this inscription:

If aught thou hast to give or lend,
This ancient British church befriend;
If poor but still in spirit willing,
Out with thy purse and give a shilling;
But if its depths should be profound,
Out with thy purse and give a pound.
Look for no record to be given
But trust to thy reward in Heaven.

Horseshoes on the south door at Ashby Folville Church

The south door at Ashby Folville bears two mysterious horseshoes, far too large for any horse. Shepshed, formerly called Sheepshead, has a sheep's head carved on a stone in the gallery wall of the church, and Braunston a two-thousand year-old Celtic earth mother close to the north wall of the churchyard. Carvings in wood and stone often had a musical theme, reflecting what went on in church and was expected to continue in heaven. The connection between the two was sometimes the church roof, where at Burton Lazars there are ten figures with musical instruments, and at Kegworth fourteen others with either instruments or shields. A musical steeplejack who repaired the spire at Kegworth is said to have celebrated by sitting on the top and playing a tune on the horn. Musical instruments are preserved in the churches at Ridlington, Prestwold and Seagrave where they were played until supplanted by the organ, a development which was not pleasing to local players of the kind in Thomas Hardy's *Under the Greenwood Tree*.

Serpent and ophicleide at Seagrave . . .

A kind of medieval strip-cartoon is shown on carved capitals at Tilton-on-the-Hill and Oakham. At Tilton a fox is seen running away with a goose held by the neck in his jaws, and half-flung over his back. A monkey is also in attendance. The scene is clearer at Oakham, where a similar fox and goose (perhaps the origin of the inn sign) are being pursued by a woman with a distaff. A monkey is also running away from her. The ecclesiastical explanation is that the carvings depict the Abbot of Westminster in the guise of the fox, running away with the great tithes, the goose. The local clergy follow, as the monkey with the collar, and finally the abbot sweeps up and makes amends by building a Trinity

36

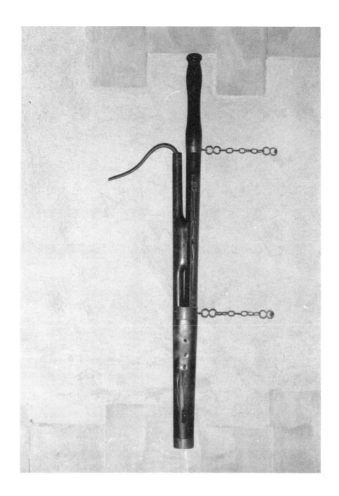

. . . and bassoon at Prestwold

Chapel, as the figure not with a distaff but with a broom. The theory is ingenious, but the more likely origin of the carvings is the story already at least two hundred years old in about 1390 when Chaucer used it in his *Nun's Priest's Tale*. It is still well-known as the doings of Reynard the Fox and Chanticleer the Cock. Medieval sculptors often substituted a goose, in view of its reputation for silliness, for the cockerel. The pursuing woman is Dame Malkin. There is no monkey in Chaucer's version of the story, but sculptors liked to introduce the animal because of its reputation for cunning. At Oakham it was no doubt helping the fox to steal.

Messages in churches are often a good deal more sombre, as might be expected. A fresco at Lutterworth has a *memento mori* in the shape of three dead kings and three skeletons. The story attached is that the three kings, in all their finery, were out hunting when they met the three skeletons, who gave them a forceful reminder of their mortality.

William Staresmore, formerly the rector, has a tomb in the church at Swinford. He was a very mean man, who locked up his servants at night and protected the apple trees from pilferers by having a bulldog attached to each one when the fruit was ripening. In 1747 a pack of his dogs jumped up to greet him and caused him to fall backwards into his own pond, where he drowned, since the servants were unable to get out in time to assist him. He was found to have left 100 pairs of breeches, 500 pairs of boots and shoes, 240 razors and 200 pickaxes.

More pleasantly eccentric was Sir Joseph Danvers, who died in 1753. His epitaph at Swithland reads:

When young I sailed to India, east and west,
But aged in this port must lye at rest.
Be cheerful, O man, and labour to live,
The merciful God a blessing will give.

Danvers wished his favourite dog to lie by his side, but knew that the animal could not be buried in consecrated ground. He therefore arranged for a tomb to be buried partly within the churchyard, partly without, so that they could both be accommodated.

A violent end is commemorated by the tombstone of Richard Smith at Hinckley, which is said to sweat blood on 12 April, the anniversary of his death. Smith, a saddler, was killed in 1727 by a recruiting sergeant who took exception to his jokes. The stone, which can still be seen, reads:

A fatal halbert this body slew,
The murdering hand God's vengeance will pursue;
From shades terrene though Justice took her flight,
Shall not the Judge of all the World do right?
Each age and sex his innocence bemoans,
And with sad sighs lament his dying moans.

What Nikolaus Pevsner describes as the 'effigy of a knight, badly decayed' at Ashby Folville is locally known as 'Old Folville'. Tradition says that Eustace de Folville met Lord Roger Beler in a duel over the disputed ownership of some land. A stone cross was thought to commemorate the spot where they fought, at a crossroads between Ashby Folville and Kirkby Bellars. Folville killed Beler, but, having established his title to the land by force of arms, died of his wounds, and left it to his son, Euchre. The church effigy shows him with a wound in his left breast.

It seems, however, that Folville died of natural causes, and that Beler was not killed in a duel, but murdered. A duel would have been unlikely between a very young man, Folville, and a very old one, Beler. Whereas Beler died in 1326, Folville survived for twenty-one years afterwards. In fact, Folville and his two brothers were indicted for Beler's murder. The outcome of the case is not known, but some Folville land at Rearsby was seized by Edward II, and not returned.

There is a wealth of interest in epitaphs, many of which followed traditional lines. Sometimes they expressed tenderness, as on the brass tablet on the south wall at Castle Donington, to William Fox and Helen, his wife, 'both buried here the XXth day of July, 1585':

The fatal scyth which cuts in two
Most nuptiall knots this closer drew;
Life made them one, death left them so,
And love more constant who can show?

A poignant tablet at Church Langton commemorates Thomas Watts, who died in 1770 at the age of nine:

Our lives are like a summer's day,
Some only break their fast, and then away;
Others stay dinner, and depart full fed;
The deepest age but sups, and goes to bed,
They're most in debt who linger out the day –
Who die betimes have less and less to pay.

At Lockington Church an alabaster panel shows William Bainbridge, who died in 1614, together with his wife and thirteen children. The epitaph reads:

A peerless payr lies here beneath
Linkt long in love and now in death
Foure times ten years and somewhat more
One soul in bodies twain they bore
Which multiplied its own perfection
To thirteen payres of chaste affection.

A rather less chaste form of affection was shown by King Richard I to a lady friend whom he installed in a hunting lodge at Blaston which he visited when he was staying at Rockingham Castle. He had two chapels built at Blaston in about 1190, one dedicated to St Giles and the other, now in ruins, to St Michael. The boundaries between two ecclesiastical jurisdictions ran between the two places of worship, and if the priests on one side became too critical of his conduct Richard could move to the other.

From time to time epitaphs have details of occupations. Samuel Pears of Wymondham, who died in 1809 at the age of 91, addresses the passer-by:

I in my time did gather rags
And many a time I filled my bags,
Altho it was a ragged trade
My rags are sold and debts are paid.
Therefore go on dont waste your time
On bad biography and bitter rhyme

39

For what I am this cumbrous clay assures
And what I was is no concern of yours.
There is a verse almost exactly identical at West Down, Devon, which shows that such things were often traditional rather than individual. The epitaph at Aston Flamville of William Hames, who died in 1814, is often found elsewhere:
This world's a city full of crooked streets,
Death is the Market-place where all men meet;
If life was merchandise that men could buy,
The rich would live, the poor might die.
Another widely-used verse appears on the tombstone of William Adcock of Melton Mowbray, a blacksmith who died in 1786:
My sledge and hammer lie reclined,
My bellows, too, have lost their wind;
My fire's exhausted, forge decayed,
And in the dust my vice is laid;
My coal is spent, and I am gone.
My last nail's drove, my work is done.
The fate of Samuel Grangers, run over by his own wagon in 1787, was used as a lesson for others. His body was brought back from Hertfordshire for burial at Slawston. The tombstone is no longer visible, but the verse was reproduced on the stone of another Samuel Grangers who died almost a hundred years later:
Oh sudden change! I in a moment fell
And had not time to bid my friends farewell;
There's nothing strange; death happens to us all.
My lot today; tomorrow you must fall.
Other inscriptions are much more laconic. One at Old Dalby reads: '1835 Henry Wells who was killed'. Another at Burton Overy on two young men who were drowned says:
As they are gone, for want of room,
I must have done. 1721.
A sombre, moralising tone is sometimes adopted by those apparently wishing to address the living from beyond the grave. John Stephens of Hinckley, who died in 1721 at the age of 38, is made to say:
You readers all both old and young,
Your time on earth will not be long;
For Death shall come, and die thou must,
And like to me return to dust.
Amidst the gloom there are attempts at humour. John Morris of Asfordby died on 14 February, 1687:
Here lies his dust, who living had the love
Of all that knew him here, of God above,

Whose soul with too much virtue was array'd
In this world's pest-house to be longer stay'd
And therefore to secure his innocence,
He bade adieu from hence,
Ascending to the court of power divine,
To chuse his Saviour for a Valentine.

Mrs Stone of Melton Mowbray cannot resist a pun:

Curious enough, we all must say,
That what was stone must now be clay;
Most curious still, to own we must,
That what was stone must soon be dust.

Even more elaborately, Mr Theophilus Cave points out at Barrow-on-Soar:

Here in this Grave there lyes a Cave,
We call a Cave a Grave,
If Cave be grave and Grave be Cave,
Then reader judge I crave
Whether doth Cave lye in Grave
Or Grave lye here in Cave?
If Grave in Cave here buried lye
Then Grave where is thy victorie?
Goe reader and report here lyes a Cave
Who conquers death and buries his own Grave.

In a small way Mr Cave has indeed conquered death, for people are still talking of him over three hundred years later. The same might be said of Cardinal Wolsey, who died at Leicester Abbey in 1530 while on his way south to appear before the king, Henry VIII. A gravestone was laid for him in the ruins of the abbey in 1936, engraved with a line from Shakespeare's play, *Henry VIII*: 'Give him a little earth for charity'. A little earth is always to be found on the flat stone, thrown by the charitable in memory of Wolsey.

Acts of charity and munificence are often recorded in churches, though sometimes they are remembered through customs and traditions. One-armed twin sisters at Ayston are said to have made enough money by their industrious spinning to be able to buy a field, which they left to the poor of Uppingham. Their effigy stands in Ayston Church, though it has been suggested that it shows two priests, rather than the two sisters. There is no trace of their field at Uppingham; perhaps it is the local recreation ground, Todd's Piece, which takes its name from a mower called Todd, who undertook to mow the whole of it with his scythe within a very short space of time, for a wager. Although the feat was considered impossible, he accomplished it, won his bet, then dropped dead.

A field at South Luffenham was donated to the church by a woman who had been lost on the heath near the village and had been literally saved by the bell, probably the curfew bell which was rung at nightfall from the Norman Conquest until, in some cases, the twentieth century. The field, opposite the Halfway House Inn on the Morcott Road, had various names in succession: Fraser's Field, Bellringer's Field, Feast Field and Bell Field. The income was used to pay the sexton to ring a bell to guide travellers from March until October at 5 a.m. and 8 p.m., and the practice continued until 1914. The annual rental of sixteen shillings from a field at Blaby was also devoted to paying for a bell in winter to guide travellers. At Market Harborough, too, a traveller left a grateful tribute for being guided out of the Welland marshes in 1500 by the ringing of a bell. The curfew bell at St Helen's Parish Church at Ashby-de-la-Zouch once guided a traveller benighted in the wilds of Moira, and in gratitude he paid for the building of the 'day bell' houses in his native town.

A bell was once rung to give the news of a death in the parish. It was called the Passing Bell, since it was rung, not after the person's death, but while he or she lay dying. This was the case at Melton Mowbray until 1708, when the ringing changed to after death, and was called the Funeral Bell. The practice continued until 1939. At Langham the tenor bell tolled three times three for a man and twice three for a woman. At Frisby each bell rang three times for a man and twice for a woman then the big bell and then the small bell each chimed as many times as the number of years the person had lived.

At Belton there was a 5 a.m. bell for the start of work and a 1 p.m. bell for 'dinner-time'. The curfew bell appears to have been rung at only a few places in Rutland: Langham, Oakham, South Luffenham and Teigh. In Leicestershire it was heard much more widely, but a list dating from 1876 shows the custom falling into decay: 'Barrow-on-Soar, Belgrave (in winter), Bottesford (excepting during Whitsun week), Burbage (in winter), Burton Overy, Claybrook (discontinued), Glen Magna (discontinued), Hinckley (winter), Kegworth (winter), St Martin's, Leicester, St Mary's, Leicester (discontinued), Lockington (winter), All Saints, Loughborough, Lutterworth, Market Harborough (discontinued), Melton Mowbray (from Michaelmas to Lady Day), Rotherby (discontinued), Shepshed (winter), Sheepy Magna (winter, except during the interval between the death and burial of any parishioner), Sibson (winter), Stoke Golding (formerly), Waltham-on-the-Wolds, Whetstone (discontinued)'.

During the year bells pealed out on certain special occasions. Over seventy villages had a Pancake Bell at noon on Shrove Tuesday. Vera Wright, born in 1907 at Frisby-on-the-Wreake, remembered: 'There was great excitement on Shrove Tuesday when the pancake bell was rung at midday, for then we all ran home from school in great glee to eat our

Melton Mowbray Church

43

pancakes which, by the way, were a luxury. The rest of the day was a holiday'.

During harvest time a bell was rung to show gleaners when they might enter and leave the fields. This seems to have been fairly uncommon in Leicestershire, with only Waltham-on-the-Wolds and Wymondham apparently having followed the custom in relatively recent times. In Rutland, however, over twenty villages had such a bell. Until 1914 it was rung at Ketton at 9 a.m. and 5 p.m. Gleaning, which was restricted to women and children, was not allowed outside those hours, and not at all while a single stook remained in a field. There were similar arrangements at Langham, except that the morning bell went at 8. Langham also had a half-yearly bell which reminded tenants that the steward was to call for the rents. Payments of over £20 a year were made annually at Christmas or Big Rent Day, which culminated in a dinner, followed by Rum Shrub (a potent hot drink), songs and toasts.

The discovery of the Gunpowder Plot was celebrated by a peal a Morcott on 5 November, and Oakham rang the Devil's Knell on Christmas Day. The New Year was rung in everywhere, as it still is.

The sound of bells does not please everyone. After objections to the Friday night practice at Empingham in 1952 the belfry windows were boarded up to reduce the sound, whereupon the ringers went on strike. There was once a full-time bellman at Loughborough, whose duties were set out in a document dating from the time of Edward VI. To say the least they were extensive:

These duties following belong to the bellman's office in the church Item, first to lie in the church and to come at eight of the clock at night in winter and summer to ring curfew and then go to bed. And every Sunday and holy day bid forth to ring at seven of the clock at night Also the bellman to light the candles in the church every holy day as custom has been used. Also to blow the organ at matins, mass and evensong as of custom afore time. Also to help to ring the service if need be. Also to sweep the church through and to clean every seventh day and every Halloweve. Also to sweep the pillars to the end of the church as high as he can reach with a long banner pole and where cobwebs and dust does hang. Also to go every Friday about the town to bid the parishioners pray for all Christian souls as of custom has been used at six of the clock in summer at seven of the clock in winter. Also to prepare and set in order the hearse of every corpse.

(The hearse at that time was simply a framework on which candles were placed).

Some church officials enjoyed certain perquisites. Until 1900 the clerk at Barrowden was unpaid, but was allowed to collect from all parishioners in Easter Week. The larger farmers gave a shilling and a dozen eggs and the smaller, sixpence and half-a-dozen eggs. Other parishioners simply gave a few eggs. After 1900 the clerk was given a salary, supplemented by gifts from just a few people, including the doctor and the rector, but after 1928 the perquisites were discontinued. At one time he had the hay from the Clerk's Acre, as it was called, in addition.

At Hinckley the sexton had the 'ancient privilege' on Shrove Tuesday of 'admitting as many persons as he pleases on the leads and battlements, and to examine the bells; which is considered as an annual holiday to the children of the town'. Children were allowed to play in the church itself at Exton on Innocents' Day (28 December).

The floors of houses and churches were once as a matter of course strewn with hay or rushes, which were periodically renewed. In churches the practice was often supported by benefactions, as at Ashby Folville, where the floor was spread with hay or rushes from the first Sunday in August until Christmas. The crop came from a piece of land one rood (a quarter-acre) in extent which was donated by two benighted ladies who had found their way to safety by hearing the bells. They marked the precise spot at which they had been lost by dropping a handkerchief, and

General view of Langham Church

bought this piece for the church. It was known as the Bartlemews, and lay between Ashby Pastures and Thorpe Trussels. Later the land was let to a tenant, then sold. Although the proceeds were spent on repairing the church windows the custom was extinguished.

A favourite time for hay strewing, mainly because hay was available then, was the end of June or the beginning of July. Many village feasts and wakes, like hay-strewing, were connected with St Peter's Day (29 June). At Medbourne the practice was discontinued in the 1780s. At Wymondham until the nineteenth century rushes were strewn on the first Sunday after St Peter's Day, and at Glenfield until the field was sold in 1936, on the second Sunday. At Barrowden rushes from the Church Field, as it is called, near to the River Welland, were spread in the church not only on Feast Sunday, the first after 29 June, but on the preceding five Sundays also. The custom continues, but only on Feast Sunday.

On the same day similar ceremonies take place at Langham and Braunstone. The parishioners at Langham still own a field which produces the hay needed. At Braunstone, Hay Sunday is also kept up. The story is that the daughter of the lord of Glenfield Manor was lost in the forest after running away to escape from some outlaws. She was found and rescued by the parish clerk of Braunstone, and her father dedicated one of his meadows to the church in gratitude. On the Thursday before the wake the clerk used to go and fetch a small load of hay, and spread it on the church floor with his own hands. Now, the hay is donated by parishioners. The Gas Board, which built a gas-works on the traditional field, contributes a token payment of £1 per annum to the hay-strewing, and through it the thanks of the long-dead father and daughter are still expressed.

4. Ages and stages

'One for sorrow, two for mirth', says the rhyme; 'three for a wedding, four for a birth'. Like other climactic events in life, birth was surrounded by customs and beliefs which reflected the hopes and fears attached to it. A bird entering a bedroom was considered to be a sign of a coming birth. Another indication was if one person were pouring out tea and another took over the pot to finish doing so. The caul or membrane surrounding the head of some babies when they are born was very highly prized. It was considered a good omen for the child, and was also thought to have the power of saving a sailor from drowning. Cauls were occasionally sought or offered in newspaper advertisements. Old-fashioned midwives would nevertheless usually burn the caul on the fire, together with the placenta. I have recently heard of one Leicester woman who, after giving birth in hospital, insisted on taking her placenta home, with the intention of cooking and eating it.

When a baby first left its mother's room it had to go up before going down. If this were not easily possible someone would mount a chair while holding the child, otherwise it would never rise in the world. Weighing babies was considered unlucky: at worst it might cause them to die, and at best not to thrive. Cats should be kept away from babies for fear of killing them by sucking their breath. Moonlight should not be allowed to fall on a sleeping child, since it would cause nightmares. It was believed unlucky to to allow a baby to see itself in a mirror before it was twelve months old. Its milk teeth should be burnt and its nails bitten, rather than cut. The first time a baby went on a visit with its mother the hosts would present an egg, a pound of salt and a bundle of matches. These symbolised respectively life, immortality and light and warmth.

As they begin to grow up, children need control. Various traditional mechanisms were used by parents, starting with lullabies which often implied disaster if babies refused to go to sleep: 'Down will come baby, cradle and all'. Crying was reproved by the rhyme: 'Croy, beeby, croy, Put its finger in its oye'. Sulking seldom long resisted the repetition of this monotonous but derisive chant':

Cross patch
Draw the latch,
Sit by the fire and spin.
Take a cup

And drink it up,
And call the neighbours in.
When my sister and I quarrelled my mother, in a voice heavy with
reproach, would utter these lines:

Let dogs delight to bark and bite,
For God hath made them so,
But O it is a wicked sight
To see young children fall out and fight.

Many years later I found that they derived from a poem entitled 'Against
Quarrelling and Fighting' by the eighteenth century hymn-writer, Isaac
Watts.

Certain vague terrors were used as threats to children. They were
probably more effective for being left vague, since the imagination could
get to work on them. The bogey man was commonly mentioned; he might
emerge in some houses, so parents said, from a dark cupboard kept for
odds-and-ends, called the bogey-hole. By far the most widely-used threat
was that of the nine o'clock horses which would mangle young children
who were out too late, or even staying up too late. In some places they
were called bell horses, which might indicate that the fear was originally
connected with the curfew bell, which once rang at nine o'clock. Most
children imagined them as real horses, ridden by Cossack-like horsemen.
One associated them with the horses that pulled the night-soil carts.
Another heard the screams of their victims, but later realised that he had
been hearing train whistles. Mr Ken Bell of Burbage remembers lingering
at play one summers's evening early this century, to the fury of his
mother, who shouted: 'I'll give you the nine o'clock horses'. At that very
moment the horse-drawn fire-brigade came galloping through the village, and young Ken was in bed and under the blankets before the last
hoofbeats had died away.

Children out too late near Kilby, if they passed Lady Denby's Spinney
after dark might find that the lady's spirit was throwing out black stockings, or so they were told. An even more powerful threat in Leicester was
that of Black Annis (see page 27), who ate naughty children, and even
good ones if they were out too late.

Some games played by children allowed them to retaliate against adults.
'Spirit rapping' or 'pin and button' consisted of pinning to a window
frame a thread with a button attached. When the thread was repeatedly
tugged and released the button would tap against the window, and it was
some time before those in the house could trace the source of the noise. A
more straightforward annoyance was the self-explanatory 'knock and
run'. A variant of this, remembered at Braunston, was known as 'Kick
blind horse'. A boy, blindfolded, would be led to a door and told to kick it,
as the others ran away. In the same village the boys liked to play a trick on

48

the blacksmith: they would spit on the striker's hammer, which would make it fly in the air when it came into contact with a hot shoe. The smithy also attracted practical jokes at Barrowden, where a plough was once placed on the chimney. A handcart belonging to a wheelright there was hidden in a hayrick, and not discovered for months. Rather a neat trick at Belton was to throw a handful of maize at a window and smash a bottle at exactly the same moment. James Buchan has described how during the 1920s in the north Leicestershire village which he disguises by the name of 'Overton' practical jokes often centred on outdoor lavatories which had box-like wooden seats with removable metal pans beneath. Placing a bunch of thorn twigs in the pan, projecting just far enough upwards, was considered great fun. Another jape was to put in carbide, normally used for bicycle lamps, since it would bubble and hiss in contact with the liquid. It would also produce volatile gas, and on one occasion a man lit his pipe and dropped the match into the pan. There was a small explosion, and he ran out with blue flames playing round his bare posterior, remarking: 'Ooh yer bugger. 'Oo's bin pissin' paraffin?'

Children had formulae which could avert certain misfortunes. 'If you see an ambulance, hold your collar and don't swallow till you see a dog', said a Loughbrough girl. Only a few miles away at Coalville it was: 'Cross your fingers till you see a dog'. This would either avert one's own illness or prevent the death of the person in the ambulance. Good fortune would follow if, on sighting a flock of birds, one crossed one's legs and wished, or so said a Langham girl. A 'bus ticket could be used to foretell the future. The digits in the serial number were added together, then divided by seven, after which the number left over was applied to this rhyme:

One for sorrow,
Two for joy,
Three for a letter,
Four for a boy,
Five for silver,
Six for gold,
Seven for a secret that's never been told.

A simpler method of finding the significant number was to count the prickles on a holly leaf picked up at random, or of counting the prune stones left on one's plate. These could also be used for 'He loves me, He loves me not' if the girl had the name of a boy in mind, or for 'Tinker, tailor', and so on, if not. Finally, cracks in the pavements had to be avoided, since: 'If you tread on a crack You'll break your back'. There was an element of Catch 22, however, because: 'If you tread on a stone You'll break a bone'. No doubt this was the lesser evil.

Once they went to school children's contact with traditional lore intensified, not in the classroom, but in the playground, through riddles, rhymes, nicknames, games and stories. One soon learned that 'Pinch me' was not the correct answer to the conundrum: 'Adam and Eve and Pinch me went down to the river to bathe. Adam and Eve got drownded, who do you think got saved?' Exchanges of property were ratified by this solemn declaration: 'Chiff chaff, never change again, As long as the world stands. Amen'. Some of the many games played, both in and out of school, are described in Chapter 7.

At the secondary school there were rites of passage, both on entering and leaving. As a new boy at Coalville Grammar School, over forty years ago, I was given the bumps on my first day. This privilege, also conferred on birthdays, consisted of being held by the four limbs and repeatedly raised in the air and lowered, more or less hard, on to the backside. Another way of greeting the tyro was to ask him: 'What happens when a ship enters port?' While he fumbled for the answer it was crisply supplied: 'It ties up'. At the same time his tie was vigorously flipped up into the air.

The bumps are still administered today, through rather more with consenting victims than used to be the case. Leaving school now attracts more attention than starting, and, to the chagrin of teachers and parents, there are sometimes outbreaks of mutual dousing with flour and eggs as the pupils stream away from school for the last time. Bystanders sometimes become unwitting targets, but those participating are usually doing so willingly. More mild is the practice of autographing the shirts and blouses of leavers, and sometimes of ritually destroying their blazers.

There are now few traditional breaks in the school routine other than those enjoyed by society as a whole. In the past pupils were customarily given a holiday from school as soon as the Pancake Bell rang on Shrove Tuesday at noon. Certain schools had a tradition which gave the pupils licence, once a year, to arrive before the teacher and bar him out, whereupon they were granted a holiday. The practice could get out of hand, and in 1618–9 there is a record in Leicester Corporation accounts of the expenditure of two shillings and eight pence paid to men 'for watchinge the Schoole howsse for to prevent the Scholers from shuttinge out there Masters untymelie and from the breakinge of the Schoole howse wyndowes.' Barring out took place on St Andrew's Day (30 November) at Hallaton, where 'the children locked the master out of the belfry and jangled the bells' before being given a holiday. The practice was discontinued in the 1840s 'upon the death of the then aged master'. On Shrove Tuesday at Frisby-on-the-Wreake the schoolmaster was enticed out on some pretext, then asked in set form for a holiday:

Pardon, master, pardon,
Pardon in a pin;
If you don't give a holiday
We won't let you in.

Sensibly bowing to tradition, the master would then grant their wish.

In other traditional rhymes pupils expressed their views of teachers. I remember 'Daddy Hill Ate a pill Twice as big As Bardon Hill' and an end-of-term exhortation:

Build a bonfire, build a bonfire,
Put the teachers on the top;
Put the prefects round the bottom
And then burn the bloody lot.

Particular subjects are sometimes mentioned, as in 'No more Latin, no more French, No more sitting on the old school bench' and the classic:

Multiplication is vexation,
Division is as bad;
The Rule of Three it puzzles me,
And practice drives me mad.

Often beginning during schooldays is another important stage in life, courtship. A young woman would know that her true love was thinking of her if her apron-strings became untied. Her garters could indicate the waxing or waning of love: 'If the garter tightens the love heightens, If the garter slackens the love backens'. If a woman wished to find the identity of her future husband she could resort to all kinds of different expedients. If she looked in a mirror while holding a piece of wedding cake in her hand she would see his reflection next to hers. She could make herself dream of him by cutting her finger-nails and placing the parings under the pillow, or by sleeping for three nights with a piece of wedding cake beneath her pillow. Another possibility was for her to put her shoes at night to form a T, and say:

I set my shoes in the form of a T,
Hoping to dream who my true love's to be;
The shape of his body, the colour of his hair,
The Sunday clothes that he does wear.

It was even simpler to write the names of four possible candidates on a laurel leaf, then steep it overnight in water. The name which was the most legible next morning would be that of the future husband. Alternatively the initial letter of his name would be formed if any apple were peeled in a continuous strip, the paring swung three times round the head, then thrown over the left shoulder. On second thoughts this was perhaps not so simple after all, but it was considered to be most efficacious if done on St Agnes' Day (21 January).

Divination on the same day is mentioned by Robert Burton, a Leicestershire man, in his *Anatomy of Melancholy*, published in 1621. He was born at Lindley Hall near Higham-on-the-Hill, and buried at Seagrave, where he was rector. St Agnes was sentenced to death in Rome for her faith, and it was ordered that before execution she should be 'debauched in the public stews'. Her virginity was miraculously preserved by divine thunder and lighting which frightened off the potential debauchers. On St Agnes' Eve a young woman could make sure she dreamed of her future husband by taking a row of pins and sticking them in her sleeve while reciting the Lord's Prayer; or she could go into a private place, take her right-leg stocking and twist her left garter round it while saying:

I knit this knot, this knot I knit,
To know the thing I know not yet,
That I may see
The man that shall my husband be,
Not in his best or worst array,
But what he weareth every day,
That I tomorrow may him ken
From among all other men.

Then she had to go to sleep on her back with her hands under her head, and her future husband would appear in a dream and kiss her.

Another opportunity occurred on Midsummer's Eve (23 June). If a woman went round the churchyard at midnight scattering hempseed and repeated the words, 'Hempseed, hempseed, here I sow, Let my true love come after me and mow', she would hear he future husband behind her reaping if she were to be married. It must have taken a bold spirit to do this. At least one old lady, born in the 1820s, reported that her grandmother had followed the ritual and had felt her lover's scythe so close at her heels that she was afraid her feet would be cut off.

A procedure which a woman could follow at home on the same day was to pluck a sage leaf at each stroke of midnight, after which a vision of her future partner would appear. If she were not to be married a coffin would be seen instead. A cook and a housemaid once tried the charm. The latter saw a coffin, and indeed did not marry. The cook saw the man she loved. He came to her at five o'clock the next morning and told her that he had not been able to sleep, and had felt a compulsion to go and see her as soon as it was light.

Still on Midsummer's Eve, a woman could lay a table for twelve guests and invite ten of her friends, the twelfth chair therefore being left empty. The eleven young women would sit silent, their eyes fixed to their plates. The house doors were left wide open. As the clock struck twelve the future husband's apparition would take the vacant seat. Instead, however, a funeral procession could materialise; the corpse would then take the seat, which would mean that the woman would die within the year. One lady at Woodhouse Eaves tried it with her friends. As the clock struck twelve they heard feet approaching, but took to their heels in fear.

Most charms seem to have been intended to identify a future husband, but some also applied to a future wife. A drug called dragon's blood could be sprinkled on the fire at midnight to produce the desired image. One girl tried it and saw the figure of a man appear, then fade. She was terrified, but later did marry the man she had seen. The same substance, mixed with quicksilver, could be used by a woman to regain a man's affection if it were lost. She simply threw the mixture into the fire at midnight, while making the necessary wish, and he would return to her. Many people deeply believed in the power of such practices. One man felt drawn so irresistibly to his sweetheart's house on one occasion that he accused her of 'trying a charm'. She indignantly denied it. 'You must have done so', he insisted, 'for not all the powers of hell could have kept me from you tonight'.

Another method of divination available to both sexes was by Bible and key. The wards of the key had to be placed over the verse in Chapter 8 of 'The Song of Solomon' beginning: 'Many waters cannot quench love, neither can the floods drown it'. The book was then closed, leaving the ring of the key projecting at the top, and the right-leg garter was tied round to hold it firm. The ring of the key was then supported on either side by the third finger of each hand, and the words of the text were repeated. If the Bible remained stationary the holder would remain single. If it turned, he or she would marry. After this, if the Bible and key were placed under the pillow the sleeper would dream of the future partner. Finally, the first letter of his or her name could be obtained by holding the Bible and key again and progressing through the alphabet a letter at a time while repeating the formula: 'If my true love's name begins with A (and so on), turn, Bible, turn, key'. At the significant letter the Bible and key would turn. Such practices were once illegal. In 1624 Anne Garland was examined before Leicester magistrates for telling Robert Roberts 'what was become of a peece of gould which he had lost' by repeating part of the fiftieth psalm (which deals with God judging his people) and using a hollow key. The outcome of the case is not known. Abbot Sadyngton is said to have discovered the thief of a silver plate at Leicester Abbey in the 1430s. He oiled a boy's thumbnail and after uttering incantations asked him whose reflection he saw in it. The boy named a canon who later confessed to the crime.

Obstacles which had to be avoided if a woman wished to marry included taking the last item of food from a plate and wearing a wedding ring on her finger while she was single. Being a bridesmaid was fine, but 'three times a bridesmaid, never a bride'. The imminence of a wedding was indicated by certain signs such as two spoons found in one saucer, though this had the alternative meaning of two husbands. To dream of a death meant a wedding, and the reverse was also true. Other signs were falling upstairs, seeing a live coal fall out of the fire near one's foot, or if four people met and in greeting one another, crossed hands to shake hands.

Two dishes were offered to people curious about their marriage prospects. One was a large mince pie – this was at Woodhouse – containing a wedding ring and a button. The person receiving the wedding ring in his or her portion would be the first of the company to marry. The recipient of the button would remain unmarried. The other dish was called a fortune trifle. It contained a ring, a silver thimble and a threepenny piece. Whoever found the ring would marry within the year. The thimble indicated an old maid and the threepenny piece, a bachelor.

The time of marriage could be shown from stones left on a plate after eating jam or stewed fruit, or by successively removing tufts of grass from a stalk. The formula to be repeated as many times as necessary was: 'This year, next year, sometime, never'. After established the time of the marriage a woman could go on to establish her future husband's position ('rich man, poor man, beggarman, thief'), trade ('tinker, tailor, soldier, sailor'), and in addition what she would wear ('silk, satin, muslin, rags') and which conveyance would take her to church ('coach, carriage, wheelbarrow, cart').

A drunken husband was ordained for a woman who got her clothes excessively wet when she was washing. The duration of a marriage could be found, before the days of tea-bags, if a piece of stalk were found floating on top of a cup of tea. The stalk was removed and placed on top of the closed fingers of the left hand. It was then repeatedly pressed with the closed right fist, little finger downwards, with these words spoken in synchronisation: 'This year, next year, sometime, never'. The point at which the stalk adhered to the right hand foretold the end or otherwise of the marriage.

An unusual way of choosing a wife was adopted in 1773 by a tailor. He walked into a harvest field at Wigston where women were tying up sheaves and offered himself as a husband for anyone who would have him. One of them looked up and said: 'I'll have thee'. The marriage lasted fifty years. The man died in 1823, at the age of 96, and his wife, Elizabeth Smith, four years later, at the age of 86. Although the couple had moved as far away as Parsonby in Cumberland their story was reported in the *Leicester Chronicle*.

Normally the timing of a wedding was very carefully considered. Among the months, May was to be avoided: 'Marry in May, you'll rue the day'. Of the days, Friday was particularly inauspicious; indeed, no enterprise should begin on the day of the crucifixion:

Monday for health,
Tuesday for wealth,
Wednesday best day of all;
Thursday for losses,
Friday for crosses,
Saturday no day at all.

It was unlucky for the bride to wear red, black or green. She should ideally wear, in the time-honoured formula, 'Something old, something new, Something borrowed, something blue'. The groom should not see the wedding dress before the day, nor the bride on the day until she arrived in church. Once she set out from her father's house the bride should on no account turn back. My wife was ignorant of this belief, and did turn back to the consternation of the watching neighbours who all shouted: 'Don't turn back, don't turn back'. She did not realise until too late what they were trying to tell her, but in our case not much harm seems to have been done, since at the time of writing we are in our thirty-first year of marriage.

Although such things are no longer part of normal dress a traditionally-minded bride still wears at least one garter, which she may be willing to display to guests. This is a faint echo of the custom which once apper-tained of young men's obligingly removing the bride's garters, amidst a great deal of horseplay, before she went to bed with her husband for the first time.

Ideally the bride will not have married a man whose surname begins with the same letter as her own: 'Change the name and not the letter, Change for the worse and not the better'. During the ceremony the groom will have avoided dropping the ring, since this is particularly unlucky. Shoes once played a part in the wedding ritual, and still do, in that they are often tied to the going-away car. Shoes were once thrown after a person going to be married, or after servants seeking or entering new posts. In the case of a bride the gesture is said to have been a mark of the renunciation of authority over her by her parent or guardian. It also brought luck, both to the bride and others. One account of a Leices-tershire wedding, which points out in passing that the celebrations lasted a week, says that 'the lucky missile was an old hob-nailed boot, cast away by some tramp, and found in the road by one of the bride's brothers'. The passage, which was written in 1868, continues: 'It was said that the young lady who would retrieve it would be married next, and the brother threw it clear over the carriage into a large clump of rhododendrons on the lawn, and into this the bridesmaids plunged, in all their bridal gear, and one emerged, holding the trophy in triumph over her head. The boot was afterwards suspended by a white satin ribbon from a beam in the hall'. A more recent way of finding the next to be married was by the bride's throwing her bouquet for the young women to scramble for.

The wedding feast is still customarily provided by the bride's parents. Formerly, if people could not afford a proper celebration a 'Bride Ale' was arranged to raise funds. Among the places at which this occurred was Teigh, where they also had Church Ales, for church funds, Clerk Ales, to pay the salary of the parish clerk, and Bid Ales, to help the needy.

Frisby-on-the-Wreake was once called the Gretna Green of Leicestershire, a sobriquet earned by the willingness of the local parson, William Brecknock Ragg, to marry any couple on demand. He was eventually tried, and sentenced to fourteen years' transportation, but the punishment was set aside because of his advanced age. However, he was unfrocked, but the family connection with the parish continued, since his daughter married the next incumbent.

Another clergyman, the Reverend Aulay Macaulay, wrote a classic book about his village, Claybrook, which has now not only changed its spelling but divided into Claybrooke Magna and Claybrooke Parva. In *The History and Antiquities of Claybrook*, published in 1791, Macaulay tells of men being forced to marry women they had made pregnant, though he puts it in these terms: 'We frequently see the bridegroom reluctantly dragged to the altar, guarded like a felon by the parish officers, and compelled to give his hand to a licentious and abandoned woman'. He also describes a more pleasant wedding custom, known as 'riding for the bride-cake', which took place when the bride was brought to her new home:

A pole was erected in front of the house, three or four yards high, with the cake stuck upon the top of it; on the instant that the bride set out from her old habitation, a company of young men started off on horseback; and he who was fortunate enough to reach the pole first, and knock down the cake with his stick, had the honour of receiving it from the hands of the damsel on the point of a wooden sword; and with this trophy he returned in triumph to meet the bride and her attendants, who, upon their arrival in the village, were met by a party whose office it was to adorn their horses' heads with garlands, and to present the bride with a posy.

Sometimes people on foot tried for the cake by hurling heavy bars into the air to dislodge it, in which case the practice was called 'throwing the quintal'. Both versions of the custom died out, Macaulay tells us, sixty or seventy years before he was writing, but another ritual lingered: that of sending the disappointed suitor after the wedding a garland of willow and also sometimes a pair of gloves, a white handkerchief and 'a smelling-bottle'.

In the parish register of St Martin's, Leicester, there is a curious note on the wedding of Thomas Tilsye and Ursula Russel, which took place in 1576. The groom was deaf and dumb, so he was obliged to convey his wishes by signs. He showed his love by 'laying his hande upon his hearte, and holding up his handes toward heaven'; 'and to show his continuance to dwell with her till his lyves end, he did it by closing his eyes, and digging out of the earth with his foot, and pulling as though he would ring a bell'. It is not known whether Thomas and Ursula had a happy marriage; one hopes that they did. Local communities did not hesitate to apply pressure if things went badly wrong between a married couple. Chaff strewn on the doorstep was a sign of strong disapproval. A house at Glenfield had its garden almost filled with chaff on one occasion in the mid-nineteenth century when the man of the house was known to be ill-treating and beating his wife. The ceremony of rough music was an even more powerful form of censure: 'Pokers and tongs, marrow-bones and cleavers, warming pans and tin kettles, cherry clacks and whistles, constable's rattles and bladders with peas in them, cow's horns and tea-trays were all pressed in to service, and the programme generally included a choice selection of recitative with choruses of yells and whistles'. Thus reported a book on Leicestershire dialect published in 1881. The authors added: 'The treatment was frequently successful in driving the offender from the neighbourhood, but it is now seldom resorted to in Leicestershire'.

In Rutland, however, the practice continued until the twentieth century. At Belton, where it was called 'tin-panning', the last case remembered was in 1905, 'when the village turned out to bang on dustbin lids outside two houses whose occupants had been wife-swapping'. It is a surprise to find the suburban chic of the 1970s in the rural Rutland of seventy years earlier. 'Tin-panning' was also the term used at Edith Weston, though 'horn fair' was also employed. The ritual was more elaborate. On three consecutive nights villagers would stand outside the house of a guilty party, banging on tin trays and pans, and blowing trumpets, whistles and mouth organs. Then the offender was burnt in effigy. This went on until the 1880s. An attempt was made to revive the custom in 1909, but the village constable intervened to stop it.

There are reports of similar ceremonies at Melton Mowbray in the 1870s. In March, 1871, 'large numbers of boys and other persons assembled in Nottingham Street, creating a great noise and making demonstrations, known popularly by the term "Horn Fair". The object of these demonstrations had been to express disapproval and indignation at the conduct of a groom, who it was stated had been beating his wife. The street was kept in an uproar for several hours, with horns and hideous noises which were created by them'. Later there was another Horn Fair in Church Lane, where a man had been ill-treating his wife. Not only were there 'musicians, so called, with horns, tin pans, buckets, pot lids, etc., of corresponding harmony, combined with a number of vocalists with wide throats', but the offending man was burnt in effigy before his house.

A drastic response to marital incompatibility was for the husband to sell his wife. The full ritual for this was for him to take her to market with a halter round her neck and to dispose of her by auction or private treaty. Such a transaction seems degrading to say the least, but in fact the wife was normally a consenting party, the purchaser was chosen by her, and the proceedings amounted to a form of popular divorce. Cases have been documented at Lutterworth, Cottesmore, Anstey and Ashby-de-la-Zouch. In August, 1791, the *Leicester and Nottingham Journal* reported:

On Thursday the 4th instant, William Paine, of Bitteswell, in this county, sold his wife to Joseph Stain, of the same parish, for the sum of Half-a-Crown, the purchaser receiving One shilling again. She was publickly delivered in a halter at twelve o'clock the said day, in the market at Lutterworth, amidst a concourse of many hundreds of people. Each party seemed perfectly satisfied, and after regaling themselves at the Angel Inn, retired in perfect peace and unanimity.

Such occurrences were by no means everyday events, as in seen by the degree of interest aroused. A divorce obtained in this way had no legal standing, and the parties could fall foul of the law, as happened at Cottesmore where Richard Hack, formerly of Clipsham, was living in 1818 with Lucy Garfitt. As a result he was indicted at Rutland Quarter Sessions on the charge that 'he did unlawfully indecently wickedly and

Part of the indictment against Richard Hack, from Rutland Quarter Session Minute Book, 14 January 1819
(By permission of Leicestershire Record Office)

wilfully apply to request and persuade one Charles Garfitt to sell and dispose of and to be cause to be delivered to him the said Richard Hack one Lucy Garfitt then and still being the wife of him the said Charles Garfitt for filthy Lucre and gain to wit the price or sum of Ten Pounds'. In addition, by living together at Cottesmore after the transaction 'the said Richard Hack did then and there Commit Adultery and Fornication with the said Lucy Garfitt to the great Scandall and Subversion of the Holy State of Matrimony and of Religion decency and Morality and good Order to the great Corruption of the Morals and Manners of his Majestys liege subjects'. Richard Hack decided to plead not guilty, and was remanded to the next sessions, but then changed his plea to one of guilty. In April, 1819, he was fined one shilling, which seems a small sum in view of the indictment. Perhaps his public humiliation was considered to be a punishment in itself. His subsequent history and that of Lucy Garfitt have not been recorded.

At Anstey it was the old partner, not the new, who was arrested. He had sold his wife for a few shillings in 1829, and 'the bargain had been drawn up and signed by the respective parties'. However, a few weeks later he had become jealous. He saw his wife though the window of her new home, sitting at her stocking-frame. He was in the act of levelling a gun at her when he was seen and overpowered by a passerby, later being committed to the county bridewell. Again, the sequel is not known. No doubt the man was released on giving assurances of future good behaviour, and his wife continued in her new ménage.

The law again intervened at Ashby, as the *Leicester Chronicle* reported in June, 1830. The account shows in its patronising way that there was a good deal of opposition by women to the proposed sale:

On Saturday last a potter took his wife to Ashby-de-la-Zouche market, to dispose of her to the best bidder, but the circumstances having become known to the police they were taken into custody, and consigned to the black hole, or prison of that place, where they were kept together, – but whether in soft or endearing embrace, or otherwise, our informant sayeth not – till the close of the day. An immense crowd of spectators had assembled in the Market-place, to witness the disgraceful scene, and it is thought, that had not the Magistrates ordered the parties into Custody, a breach of the public peace would have followed, such was the excited feeling that seemed to be manifested by some of the females present. It is said that the purchaser, that was to have been is a nailer of the neighbourhood and the Sum to be given for her 5s.

Whether before marriage or after it, life was often precarious, and surrounded by a host of superstitious beliefs. Many of these are still held, and there are few people who can honestly say that they have no superstitions at all. To sweep dust straight out of the house, as opposed to sweeping it up then carrying it out, is to sweep luck out. Similarly, a visitor should leave through the door by which he or she entered, so as to avoid letting the luck out of a house. It is unlucky to turn back after setting out, but if this is unavoidable one should remain for a time before going out again, or one should sit down and cross and uncross the legs three times. To bring in or take out eggs after dark is unlucky. At any time it is unlucky to bring in feathers, especially those of the peacock, may-blossom, lilac or holly (except at Christmas). Picking up flowers which have been dropped is unlucky, in view of the adage: 'Pick up flowers, pick up sickness', or even, 'drop down dead'.

It is unlucky to trip on entering a house, but the evil can be averted by kissing one's thumb. It is lucky to stumble when going upstairs but unluckly to pass a person going the opposite way on the stairs. An umbrella should not be opened in the house. Elder wood should not be burnt on the fire, or even on a bonfire in the garden. The tree was unlucky because Judas was thought to have hanged himself from it. Putting on one's left shoe first in the morning means bad news before the night. Wearing green is unlucky, since black (mourning) follows green. Taking off a garment accidentally put on inside out takes away the luck. Folding up one's clothes at night after taking them off is to be avoided since this keeps the day's sins in them.

Turning the bed on Sunday brings bad luck for a week, and if a bed has to be moved it is unlucky to do so without first dismantling it. It is unlucky to put new shoes on a table, or to leave a white tablecloth on overnight. To help to salt means to help to sorrow, and even passing the salt from hand to hand, as opposed to placing it on the table for someone to pick up, is unlucky. Spilling salt is even worse, but throwing a pinch of it over the left shoulder averts the ill-luck. To boast is to tempt providence, but the offence can be expiated by knocking on wood, underneath the table. The habit, beloved by some small boys, of eating while sitting on the lavatory means 'feeding the devil and starving the lord'.

Cutting one's nails needs to be carefully managed, in line with these recommendations:

Cut them on Monday, cut them for health.
Cut them on Tuesday, cut them for wealth.
Cut them on Wednesday, cut them for news.
Cut them on Thursday, cut them for new shoes.
Cut them on Friday, cut them for sorrow.
Cut them on Saturday, see your true love tomorrow.
Cut them on Sunday, you'll have the devil all the week.

Even an itch can be significant. In the nose it is a sign of vexation, in the feet, of forthcoming travel, in the left hand, of money to be lost, and in the right hand, of money to be gained. In the last case the procedure should be:

Rub it on brick, it's sure to come quick.
Rub it on wood, it's sure to come good.
Rub it on steel, it's sure to be real.
Rub it on iron, it's sure to be mine.

Hair should be cut at the waxing of the moon, since this will bring vigorous growth. The clippings should be burnt, or sickness will ensue. Turning the money in one's pocket on seeing the new moon brings luck, but seeing the new moon first through glass is unlucky, and will cause the person to break some crockery. Breaking a mirror brings seven years' bad luck, but this can be averted by carefully collecting all the pieces and burying them. Seeing a white horse without spitting three times brings ill-luck, as does seeing a solitary crow: 'One crow, sorrow, Two crows, joy; Three crows, a letter, Four crows, a boy'. A single magpie is particularly unlucky, unless one raises one's hat to it or makes the sign of the cross on the ground with one's foot. More than one is a different matter:

One for sorrow,
Two for mirth,
Three for a wedding,
Four for a birth,
Five for silver,
Six for gold,
Seven for a secret never to be told.

To kill or robin or wren, or even to take its eggs, is most unlucky because The robin and the wren Are God Almighty's cock and hen'. It is a particularly bad omen if a robin enters a house, and this should therefore be prevented at all costs. The most terrifying bird sign is the sound of the Seven Whistlers, which presages death and disaster. What makes matters worse is that no one is entirely sure which birds are involved. Some say the curlew, others the swift, which is also known as the devlin. There is a story that seven monks from Charnwood were led into sinful ways by the devil, and turned into devlins as a punishment. Their approach brought disease and death to crops, animals and people, until one man accidentally discovered that evil could be averted if he crossed his fingers. This is still recommended when the scream of the swifts is heard.

There are many predictive signs. A knife dropped indicates the arrival of a male visitor, and a spoon or fork, a female. Crossed knives foretell a quarrel. Dropped scissors mean a disappointment unless another person picks them up, in which case there will be a pleasant surprise. If no one else is available the scissors must be touched with the foot before being picked up. To stir tea in the pot is to stir up trouble, as is stirring up another person's tea. Leaves floating on the surface of a cup of tea signify a letter or a stranger. Another sign of a visitor is when a cockerel crows near to a door or window. A sooty film adhering to the bars of a grate also foretells the coming of a stranger. On seeing it, one should kneel on the hearth and clap hands while rehearsing the days of the week. The soot will fall as the day on which the visitor will arrive is mentioned. Incidentally, the fire will draw better if a poker is set up to form a cross with the bars of the grate, and an egg-shell should be crushed before being put in the fire, lest the devil ride in it. A long, licking flame in the fire is another sign of a stranger. A blue flame shows that a letter is to be received, as does a spark in a candle-flame. The person to whom the wick points must tap the candlestick and say the days of the week. The letter will come on the day indicated by the fall of the spark. Unfortunately, there is no equivalent with electric lights. A white spot on the finger-nail is called a 'gift' because it foretells the arrival of a present. A gift on the thumb is even better: 'A gift on the thumb is sure to come, A gift on the finger is sure to linger'.

Good luck is indicated by many other signs, such as treading on dog-muck or receiving a deposit from an over-flying bird. Good fortune can be assured for a whole year by wearing something new on Easter Sunday, or merely by happening to see the first lamb of the spring facing towards one. Turning money on seeing the first lamb will ensure that it will not lack for the rest of the year. Horseshoes bring good luck, but must be fixed to a door or lintel with the points upwards, otherwise the luck will fall out. Oddly enough, the horseshoes traditionally presented by all peers and members of the royal family visiting Oakham since 1600 are displayed with their points down. Worn-out shoes were once concealed in buildings to ward off evil. A man's shoe dating from the early seventeenth century was found to have been deliberately hidden in the roof of a shop in Loughborough when it was demblished in 1975. At least ten other examples are known in the county, one from the Augustinian Friary at Leicester, dating back to about 1400, the others of the eighteenth and nineteenth centuries.

The familiar black cat crossing one's path is lucky, as is finding and picking up a piece of coal. Finding a pin, perhaps partly because of the thriftiness involved, is also fortunate. Isobel Ellis, born in 1863, knew a verse which was still current a century later: 'See a pin and let it lie, You'll want a pin before you die'. A fuller version runs:

See a pin, pick it up,
And all the day you'll have good luck.
See a pin and let it lay,
You'll have bad luck all the day.

Various sightings bring good luck, such as two policemen together, a chimney-sweep (especially at a wedding) or a sailor, particularly if one could touch his collar. A cartload of hay is lucky, provided one spits three

Burying the dead, from one of the Wyggeston glass panels of the early sixteenth century

times. To see a cross-eyed person of the opposite sex is lucky; of the same sex, unlucky. To see a wooden-legged man from the front brings good luck; from the back, bad.

As might be expected, harbingers of death abound. A bird falling down the chimney, the prolonged nocturnal howling of a dog or the crowing of a cock, a swarm of mice in the house, a picture falling from the wall, thirteen people sitting down together to a meal: all these are lugubrious portents. Washing on New Year's Day is said to wash one in and one away, meaning a birth and a death in the family during the ensuing year. To dream of a wedding signifies death, as does, somewhat incongruously, to dream of riding in a cart and being greased with bacon fat. Other signs are a coffin-shaped hole in a loaf or fold in a table-cloth, and a clock striking

The church clock, Theddingworth

thirteen. At Theddingworth it was believed that if the church clock struck during the sermon there would be a death in the parish within the week.

A corpse was never kept behind a locked door at Caldecott, where it was also the custom that the youngest son would be the principal heir. The current system of primogeniture was introduced in 1255 on the intercession of Simon de Montfort, but the Caldecott people within living memory followed the even earlier custom that sons progressively left home to set up for themselves, leaving the youngest behind to inherit.

Bees were once informed when there was a death in the family, or any other important news, since it was thought that they would otherwise feel slighted and leave the hive. At Geeston, near Ketton, the widow of an old bee-keeper went down to the hive and was heard to say: 'He's gone, he's gone'. The bees hummed in reply. They could hardly have done otherwise, though I suppose they could have kept silent. Their humming was taken to mean that they would be staying. Some families even placed a mourning band over a hive.

A pewter plate containing salt was once placed on corpses awaiting burial. A matter-of-fact, if rather macabre explanation was that this prevented 'air from getting into the bowels and swelling up the body'. More likely is the belief that salt symbolised immortality at death, as it did at birth. The custom was thought to have died out in the eighteenth century, but it has come to light in the twentieth. In 1962 Miss M. Brown of Claybrooke Magna still had some pewter plates used by her mother for this very purpose at Sutton Cheney and Claybrooke. In both villages women had borrowed the plates, since for use in the ancient manner only pewter would do. The last instance of this practice was with the corpse of a suicide, in 1964 or '65.

It was believed at Leicester that a funeral cortege should never turn round in a street, to avoid turning another corpse out of it. In the case of a cul-de-sac all the vehicles would back out. At Knossington, as well as conventional mourning dress the women once wore large black hoods to a

64

funeral; white if it were a child's. At Macaulay's Claybrook a clergyman usually led the funeral procession of a farmer or yeoman, and the relatives followed the coffin 'two and two of each sex, in order of proximity, linked in each other's arms'. A young man being buried had six young women dressed in white as pall-bearers. A young woman had the same number of young men, wearing black, but with white gloves and hatbands. In the case of an unmarried woman it was the general practice to place a funeral coronet or garland in the church and leave it there indefinitely. Such a garland, which Shakespeare in *Hamlet* calls 'maiden's crants', could at one time be seen in the church at Waltham-on-the-Wolds.

The custom of not merely ringing but chiming the bells at funerals continued until the mid-nineteenth century in some villages, including Frisby, Oadby, Sapcote and Saxelby. Doles in the form of small loaves, sometimes specially baked, sometimes ordinary penny loaves, were dis-

Portrait of Robert Heyrick in the Guildhall, Leicester

tributed to everyone in the parish after a funeral at Kegworth, Stathern and Godeby (where a piece of plum cake was given in addition). Such largesse was originally intended to bring goodwill and prayers for the deceased. At least one man regretted not having been more generous in life, as his epitaph at Syston shows: 'What I gave I have, What I spent I had, What I left I lost by not giving it'. A more aggressive message to posterity was left by Robert Heyrick (1540–1618), three times mayor of Leicester and once its M.P. On his portrait in the Guildhall are painted these words:

His picture whom you see here
When he is dead and rotten
By this shall remembered be
When ye shall be forgotten.

5. Sickness and health

The threat of getting as fat as Danny Lambert was still issued when I was a child to those who ate too much. The warning had substance, since the person in question weighed over 52 stones. William Gardiner lived next door at Leicester when they were boys, and wrote: 'At the age of ten he was a tall, strong lad, of a very quiet disposition, not at all inclining to be jolly, yet possessing a fine open countenance'. At the age of fourteen, in 1784, Lambert started work in Birmingham as an engraver and die-sinker, but was obliged to return home when the factory was destroyed during the riots of 1791. Shortly afterwards he succeeded his father as keeper of the Bridewell Prison at Leicester. By this time he was beginning to put on weight, though he was still agile, and also strong. Armed only with a pole he put to flight in Blue Boar Lane a performing bear which had attacked a dog, but he was not aggressive. Indeed, he was rather shy, and 'highly sensitive upon the subject of his huge appearance; and when he ventured out, was aware that it drew upon him the general gaze'. He was very fond of swimming, and 'in the summer months he was never so happy as when wallowing for hours in the river, rolling over and over like a hippopotamus'. He could float in the water with two men standing on his back, and he also liked teaching children to swim.

By 1793 Lambert weighed 32 stones, and was obliged in 1805 to give up his post as prison-keeper. By this time he was famous, and supplemented his annuity of £50 a year by 'receiving' the curious. In 1806 he spent five months in London, where a steady stream of people paid a shilling a head to see him, from 12 till 5 daily. He went on tour to other towns, and it was in the Waggon and Horses at Stamford that he died, probably of fatty degeneration of the heart. He was five feet eleven inches tall, and measured 112 inches round the body and 37 round the leg. His coffin was made of 112 feet of elm board. When he was buried at Stamford on 23 June, 1809, it took twenty men half an hour, not to lower his coffin, but to manoeuvre it down a sloping ramp into the grave. Some of his effects have been preserved in museums at Stamford and Leicester. He ate a normal diet and drank only water, but was nevertheless used as a warning to others of the dangers of over-eating.

He is remembered with some affection, unlike another phenomenon, the so-called Elephant Man. Joseph Merrick was born at Lee Street, off Wharf Street, Leicester, in 1862. Three months beforehand, in May, his mother had fallen to the ground when the crowd surged back at Humberstone Gate Fair as one of the elephants in Wombwell's Menagerie was passing. The child was normal at birth, but abnormalities began to appear at twenty-one months. The worst was a mass of flesh which eventually protruded several inches from his mouth in a sort of snout which had some resemblance to an elephant's trunk. His mother began to talk of the ill-effects of having been frightened by the elephant during her pregnancy.

Merrick's difficulties were compounded by a fall which damaged his hip and left him permanently lame. His mother died, and his father remarried. He managed to work for some years, first in a cigar factory, then as a hawker of haberdashery, but his appearance attracted more and more attention and adverse comment. In 1879 he was driven to seek admittance to Leicester Workhouse, where he remained an inmate for over three years. During this time he underwent an operation in the Royal Infirmary to remove part of his facial growth, but in order to get out of the workhouse he was driven to seek opportunities to exhibit himself as a freak, along with living skeletons, fat women and dwarfs. Various impresarios were interested, and Merrick did some touring, during the course of which he came to the notice of Frederick Treves, a doctor at the London Hospital, who wrote this account: 'The showman – speaking as if to a dog – called out harshly: "Stand up". The thing arose slowly and let the blanket that covered its head and back fall to the ground. There stood revealed the most disgusting specimen of humanity that I have ever seen... From the intensified painting in the street I had imagined the Elephant Man to be of gigantic size. This, however, was a little man below the average height, and made to look shorter by the bowing of his back. The most striking feature about him was the enormous and misshapened head. From the brow there projected a bony mass like a loaf, while from the back of the head there hung a bag of spongy, fungous-looking skin, the surface of which was comparable to brown cauliflower... the osseous growth on the forehead almost occluded one eye... From the upper jaw projected another mass of bone. It protruded from the mouth like a pink stump, turning the upper lip inside out and making the mouth a mere slobbering aperture'.

Merrick was abandoned in Brussels by a showman who stole his entire savings of £50. He made his way back to England, and was admitted to the London Hospital as a patient of Treves. He spent most of the rest of his short life there (he died in 1890), partly supported by public subscription. He became something of a living medical specimen, and a minor celebrity. He was visited by socialites, including the Prince and Princess of Wales. There has recently been a revival of interest in his sad and extraordinary life, through a book entitled *The True History of the Elephant Man* (1980), by

M. Howell and P. Ford, and the fine film and stage play which it inspired.

If Leicestershire produced two men whose medical histories were used as cautionary tales, Rutland had one case which was held up as an example to others. The county's motto is *Multum in parvo*, much in little, and this could be applied to Jeffery Hudson, who was born at Oakham in 1619. He became the Duchess of Buckingham's page at Burley-on-the-Hill. When the duke entertained Charles I and Queen Henrietta Maria in 1630, Hudson was produced at the banquet from under a pie crust. He was eighteen inches high at the time, though 'without any deformity, wholly proportionable'. The queen was delighted by his antics, and invited him to court, where he became something of a favourite.

Despite his size, or perhaps because of it, he led a more eventful life than most ordinary men. He became known as 'Strenuous Jeffery' because of the efforts he made when fighting on the Dutch side at the Siege of Breda in 1637, and at the beginning of the Civil War in England was made a captain of horse. In 1644 he accompanied the queen on her flight to Pendennis Castle and thence to exile in Paris. There, in 1649, he killed Lord Croft in a duel. For this he was banished from France, having escaped worse punishment only through the intercession of Henrietta

Jeffery Hudson's house at Oakham

Maria. The ship on which he left was captured by pirates and he was taken to North Africa and sold as a slave. The hardships which he suffered made him begin to grow, and by the time he was ransomed and able to return to England his height had doubled to three feet six inches.

After the Restoration Hudson lived quietly for a time at Oakham with a pension from Buckingham. Then he ventured once more to London, where he was arrested in 1679 and imprisoned on a charge of complicity in the Popish Plot. He was quickly released, and given financial support by Charles II. He died at Oakham in 1682, having become a considerable celebrity. A number of poets and historians wrote about him, and many years later he figured in a novel by Sir Walter Scott, *Peveril of the Peak*. A painting by Van Dyck, still preserved at Petworth House in Sussex, shows him in the entourage of Queen Henrietta Maria. The house in which he is said to have been born can be seen at Oakham.

Before the advent of modern medicine health was a constant preoccupation, and people often had to seek their own remedies for illness. Indeed, the use of such remedies persisted to some extent throughout modern times and is currently enjoying a revival. It is unlikely that certain treatments will ever again be sought, however. Touching the neck of a hanged man was once thought to be good for the health. In 1817 seven people turned up for this purpose at Infirmary Square, Leicester, when William Bottomore was being hanged for a burglary committed at Loughborough. It is not known whether their request was granted, but hangmen, provided payment were offered, were usually amenable. Another touch, that of a king or queen, was once thought to cure scrofula, the king's evil. John Throsby, historian of Leicester and clerk of St Martin's Church, who died in 1803, remembered seeing in the vestry a royal proclamation of the time of Charles I which stated that all persons procuring a certificate from the churchwarden or minister might repair to London to receive the benefit of the royal touch. At least one person from Leicester, a 'poore widdowe' called Calladis, did approach Charles I, though whether she went to London or met him locally is not known. The corporation accounts say that she was paid ten shillings in 1627–8 'when she went to His Maiestie to seeke helpe for a child haveinge the Kings evill'. The last royal touch for this purpose was in 1712. The giver was Queen Anne and the recipient the future Dr Johnson.

By contrast, there were a great many homely cures for everyday hurts and illnesses. These fall into various categories. The placebo has no physical action but it succeeds, like faith healing, because the patient expects it to. Some popular remedies which appear at first sight nonsensical have been found to be medically beneficial for good chemical reasons. One example is the application of cobwebs to an open wound. Finally, psychological medicine was also widely used.

Certain things were thought to be good against disease in general, such as an adder's skin hung over the chimney-piece or a rabbit's paw or part of a sheep's skull kept in the pocket. A peeled onion was hung in some houses, and taken down every two or three weeks. If it were cut open and found to be black inside, it was adjudged to have taken away disease. The juice made by adding brown sugar to sliced onions was administered as a cough cure. A piece of onion was heated and held against the ear for earache, or inserted into a tooth for toothache. Toothache was also cured by putting a plaster on the wrist on the side opposite to the tooth.

Melted tallow from candles was applied externally to the ears, nose or throat for a severe cold. A simple but effective remedy for nettle stings, as I can personally testify, is to rub the affected skin with the leaf of a dock. Formerly the procedure was to whip the skin with the leaf, repeating in time with the blows these words: 'In, dock. Out, nettle'. I have not tried the churchyard mould treatment for rheumatism, which consists of stripping naked and then allowing oneself to be buried up to the neck in a churchyard for several hours at a time. Fortunately there are other treatments for the complaint, which include carrying a small potato or nutmeg and wearing a loop of cat-gut. Failing these measures, the part of the body affected can be whipped with nettles.

A poultice of fresh cow dung was applied by midwives to an abcess on the breast of a nursing mother. Mr O. D. Lucas of Wigston, who supplied this information, also relates how his aunt at the age of five was cured of diphtheria, after all other treatment had failed, by Mr Smith, the local blacksmith. He took a shovel of glowing coals, carried it into the sickroom, and then sprinkled on sulphur. The fumes made the little girl cough up a piece of membrane as hard as leather. She not only recovered, but lived for 69 years afterwards.

For the ague Robert Burton reported his mother's remedy in *The Anatomy of Melancholy*: 'a spider in a nutshell lapped up in silk'. As with much folk wisdom this is contradicted by another view, expressed in the adage: 'If you wish to live and thrive Let a spider run alive'. In Leicester it was even believed at one time that killing a spider caused the ghost of Cardinal Wolsey to issue from his tomb. To return to ague, William Gardiner noted that when it was common, 'Headley, a baker near St Nicholas Church, made a small revenue by selling charms for the complaint'.

A common ailment was whooping cough, which is again on the increase at present. Treatments included eating fried mouse, which is said to taste rather like chicken. This was also good for quinsy. Roast mouse could also be eaten, provided the eater was in ignorance of what was being consumed, and was sitting on a donkey facing the tail. Hedgehog oil was produced at Congerstone by a hermit and used for earache. At Knos-

71

sington it was used for whooping cough, another treatment for which consisted of creeping under and then stepping over a bramble while saying: 'Over the briar and under the briar, And may I leave my chincough here'. There was also a charm for whooping cough. The healer, usually an old woman, drew a circle nine times round the patient's face, pausing each time at the centre of the forehead and at the chin, while inaudibly repeating a formula. A Miss S. A. Squires wrote at the end of the last century of some friends whose younger sister had been charmed for whooping cough as a baby by an old woman who sat her on her knee and murmured some words. They could not be heard: 'probably they were transmitted from mother to daughter as a treasure to be secretly guarded, and may now be irrecoverably lost'.

To judge from the vast number of cures, by far the most common problem was warts. They could be rubbed with various things, such as wedding ring (which was also applied to styes), the cut halves of an apple, a piece of steak or a black snail. Afterwards the apple had to be buried, and as it decayed so did the warts. It was also possible merely to eat half an apple and give the other half to someone to hide. The steak, too, had to be buried, and the snail impaled on a thorn. A remedy from Hugglescote was to rub the wart with the rind of stolen slice of bacon, then to nail this up outside. As the bacon dried, so did the wart. Simply rubbing with a cut potato was used at Cropston. A widely-known practice was to rub with the inside of a broad-bean pod, then to throw it away over the shoulder without looking back. At Lutterworth the wart was rubbed with a piece of white chalk which was afterwards thrown into running water.

Most of these remedies involved a symbolic carrying away of the warts, but others relied on some form of chemical action. Washing soda could be applied, though this was very painful, or the liquid produced by filling a hollow cut in a swede with salt and water. This came from Anstey, where they also soaked a pearl button in lemon-juice, then anointed the wart. Alternatively they rubbed it with the head of a match or squeezed on the white sap from bindweed. Other plant remedies were the juice of the greater celandine or the application of a dandelion root cut through the middle. At Shepshed the milky juice of the sow-thistle was squeezed on, two or three times a day, for as long as necessary – and some of these cures took up to three months to work. The same plant was known as milkweed at Aylestone and milkwort at Billesdon, where after being rubbed with the juice the wart was tightly tied with a piece of wool, moistened with saliva. Saliva was also used at Loughbrough, provided it were applied immediately on waking: it was called 'fasting spittle'. The mere practice of milking cows by hand was thought to cure or prevent warts, presumably because of an immunity passed on by the cows. At Croft, rather more drastically, the practice was to stick a needle in the wart without making it bleed, then

The site of Leicester Abbey, the last resting place of Cardinal Wolsey

to hold a lighted match to the end of the needle until it was extremely hot.

Tying the wart figured in many remedies. Horsehair was widely used, including at Sileby. A Leicester woman remembered having a wart charmed in 1905 by an old woman who tied a knot for each wart in a piece of string, while muttering an incantation. Charms were widely used. The Wymeswold witch-stone, kept at Leicester Museum since 1852, was hung in a dairy to keep witches out, but it could also be used to charm warts away. A new pin could be stuck into the bark of an ash tree, then into a wart till it hurt, then back into the tree once more and left there. A separate pin was used for each wart, and this formula repeated: 'Ashen tree, ashen tree, Pray buy these warts of me'. A gipsy at Anstey is remembered as having bought a person's warts in 1930s for sixpence. They duly disappeared.

Some people became well known as wart charmers. At Aylestone a woman visited one in about 1900. The procedure was simply to hand over an envelope with the number of warts written in it, without saying the number or paying any money. It worked, after a number of other remedies had been tried without success. A Market Harborough woman remembered a diametrically opposite cure. She went to Tom Billingham in 1911 when she was sixteen, told him the number of warts and gave him a shilling. This also worked.

Until at least the 1960s there were wise women at Ibstock and Donington-le-Heath who could cure warts, and also a male charmer at the latter village, called George Ball. He was a miner who moved to Lough-borough after his retirement. His method seems to have been wishing the warts away. He was frequently consulted, as was Mrs Holehouse of High Street, Barwell, who died some time in the 1950s. She would draw a circle round the warts and say some words, but would not accept payment. Charmers usually found non-monetary rewards acceptable, however.

Another kind of healer was John Goodman of Barton-in-the Beans, who was born in 1765. He was a bee-keeper, odd-job man and Baptist preacher, who hired out leeches which people could apply to themselves for blood-letting. He obtained the leeches by visiting likely lakes in Cheshire and North Wales. He simply waded through the water with bare legs and the creatures attached themselves. A Markfield woman is said to have continued leech-hiring until within living memory.

Such healers, herbalists and charmers have a long ancestry. As early as 1523 John Thornton is recorded as having claimed for thirty years to have been curing animals with a 'moses rod'. Such practices were not without danger, as the Vicar of Fleckney found out in 1637 when he was charged before the Court of High Commission with making charms to cure toothache. Another clergyman, Thomas Daffy, was incumbent at Redmile from 1666. His elixir was famous for well over a century.

Anthony Draycott (1829–78) of Seagrave was famous as a herbalist at a time when the nearest doctor was many miles away. Amelia Woodcock was renowned as 'The Wise Woman of Wing'. She died in 1867 or alternatively, it is rumoured, killed herself because of accusations of witchcraft which were constantly levelled against her. People travelled miles to her little Rutland village, from as far away as Leicester, for her salves and ointments. She claimed to draw her powers from being the seventh daughter of a seventh daughter of a seventh daughter. Among her feats was the restoration of a withered arm to soundness, and some of her patients ascribed almost miraculous powers to her.

Some people used their abilities in other directions. Gardiner reports that 'a workman of ours, Thomas Rusk, who lived in Northgate Street, was constantly applied to for the discovery of things stolen or lost, and found conjuring more profitable than stocking making'. A spectacular instance of 'conjuring' took place in 1851. A gold watch was stolen from the house of a Rutland clergyman by a young lady who was attending a party there. When the theft was discovered suspicion fell on a poor woman and her daughter who had come in as helpers from the village. They were unhappy at the accusation, and also the visits and searches of the police, so they called in a wise woman from Leicester, who went into a sort of trance and said: 'I am going over hill and valley, and at length arrive at a village. I come to a gate, go through it into a yard, enter the house, and ascend the stairs.' She then gave an accurate description of the house and the room. 'I see a watch hanging on a nail. A short young lady in a pink dress, with dark hair, comes in, takes it, and puts it in her bosom. She goes two miles away. She is at this moment walking in a meadow with some children. The watch is in her bosom, and you will find it there; but you must be very quiet about it, for she is full of apprehension, and has been trying to get rid of the watch'. The information was brought to the attention of the police, who informed the people in the house where the young lady was staying. They were not disposed to believe the story. However, they searched her room and boxes, but without finding the watch: 'but on proceeding to a personal examination, the watch was found in the place specified'. The wise woman had stated that this was not the first instance of theft on the young lady's part, and this also was proved correct. The story was told by a member of the household from which the watch had been taken.

A vital factor in people's well-being was the weather, as indeed it still is. A tremendous amount of weather lore exists, to provide advice and warning. Good weather, and also good luck, is shown by the sight of the old moon in the arms of the new. Not surprisingly, the moon often figures in such beliefs. A clear moon shows good weather, but a moon with a ring round it, bad. If the crescent moon is on its back it holds on to the rain, but if it points down, the rain falls. All crops should be planted as the moon **waxes.**

Rain is forecast by cats frisking, or sitting with their backs to the fire, and by cows lying down. 'Hark I hear the asses bray. We shall have some rain today', says one rhyme. Swallows flying low are also harbingers of rain, but they show fine weather when they fly high. In the late autumn and early spring three frosts are followed by rain, and at any time a wet Friday brings a wet weekend, which in turn brings a wet week: 'Wet Friday, wet Sunday, wet week'. The shepherd's delight rhyme is universally known. It has this interesting variant:

Evening red and morning grey
Sure to be a fine day.
Evening grey and morning red
Sends the shepherd wet to bed.

The direction of the wind is highly significant:

When the wind's in the west
It's going to be wet;
When the wind's in the south
There's going to be a drought.

Or alternatively, and somewhat contradictorily:

When the wind's in the east
It's neither fit for man nor beast;
When the wind's in the west,
Then it's at its very best.

The appearance of certain landmarks also permits predictions. 'When Bardon Hill has a cap', says one rhyme, 'Hay and grass will suffer for that' Belvoir figures in two signs of bad weather:

If Belvoir hath a cap,
You churls of the vale beware of that.

When mist doth rise from Belvoir Hole
O then beware the weather's foul.

Every aspect of the weather, every season, every month had its saying or rhyme about the weather. Thus: 'if birds whistle in January, frost's to come'. The old half-way point of the winter, Candlemas Day (2 February) gives rise to several rhymes:

Candlemas Day bright and clear,
There will be two winters this year.

Snow at Candlemas
Stops to handle us.

Candlemas Day,
You should have half your coal and half your hay.

76

The last means that half one's stocks of coal and hay should be left for firing, and feeding the animals during the rest of the winter.

St Chad's Day is 2 March, and 'On the day of St Chad, Sow beans like mad, Whether the weather be good or bad'. Next, 'a quiet March borrows ten days of April', which means that March-like weather will continue into the following month. 'Frogs in March, frosts in May', says another adage with few words but many implications.

Good Friday is the traditional time for starting gardening. At Easter itself: 'If the wind's in the east of Easter Dee, You'll ha' plenty o' grass but little good hee'. In a number of rhymes and sayings the word 'May' refers to the month, in others to the blossom. 'When May is out, sow barley day and night' refers to the latter, as does this warning of cold snaps: 'May come early, May come late, May will make the old cow quake'. The month is meant in: 'Dry May, Good for corn But bad for hay', and: 'Those who bathe in May will soon be laid in clay'. Presumably this refers to open-air, rather than indoor bathing. Even washing blankets is unlucky: 'Wash blankets in May, Wash your life away'. The best-known rhyme connected with May is that of the bees:

A swarm of bees in May
Is worth a load of hay,
A swarm of bees in June
Is worth a silver spoon.
A swarm of bees in July
Is not worth a fly.

In some versions the fly is a butterfly.

'A dripping June Puts all things in tune', we are told, but the month is not good for cutting thistles:

If you mow them in June
You mow too soon.
If you mow them in September
You will have some to remember.

By September the thistles will have produced and shed their seed for the next crop.

'If the first of July be rainy weather, It will rain, more or less, for four weeks together', runs a gloomy prognostication; and if the first of the month is passed safely, a period of forty days' rain can follow if the fifteenth, St Swithin's Day, is wet. The consolation is that: 'All the tears St Swithin's can cry St Bartlemy's mantle wipes them dry'. St Bartholomew's Day is on 24 August, and 'If Bartlemy's Day be fair and clear, Then hope for a prosperous autumn that year'.

The month of September 'dries up ditches or breaks down bridges'. Either way, still conditions are hoped for: 'September blow soft Till the fruit's in the loft'. After that, 'If there's ice in October to bear a duck, The rest of the winter's as wet as a duck'. A similar prediction is made for the next month: 'If the ice in November will bear a duck The next three months will be all sludge and muck'; and this is varied to refer to St Martin's Day (11 November): 'When the ice before Martlemas bears a duck Then look for a winter of mire and muck', Later, on 25th November: 'If St Catherine's Day be fine and fair, So it will be in Februare'.

Christmas figures in many sayings, including 'Cold enough for Christmas', 'a green Christmas means a fat churchyard' (or, more cheerfully, 'brings a heavy harvest') and 'If the sun shines through the apple trees on Christmas Day, When autumn comes they will a load of fruit display'. Finally, 'If Groby Pool bear a duck before Christmas it will not bear a goose after'; and a hopeful look forward to the next year: 'Winter thunder Brings forth summer wonder'.

6. Work

'When I was a boy I started work . . . for three shillin's a week: twelve hours a day, 'a'p'ny an hour. If I 'ad 'alf a day off for the feast or to go to a cricket match the old farmer used to stop me threepence. Then I got up while I 'ad ten shillin's a week. I were there about seven year. I got so's I could carry sixteen stone o' corn into the waggon, so I says: "Master", I says, "I think it's time I 'ad two more shillin's a week". "What", 'e says, "all at a clash?" 'E'd only give me one'. Charlie Wilson of Empingham still wrily chuckled at the age of 75 as he recalled his thirty years' work as a waggoner, which meant not only driving waggons but ploughing too. He won seventeen prizes for ploughing, his chief success being the All-England Championship at Cottesmore in 1929. He retired in 1947, and died eight years later, at the age of 77, having been a cornet player for 55 years and a hand- and church-bell ringer for 59. He also knew some songs, including 'All Jolly Fellows', which was widely printed on street ballad sheets:

Charlie Wilson at the ploughing championships in 1929
(Photograph by permission of Miss E. Wilson and Mrs G. H. Hall)

When four o'clock comes then up we rise,
And into the stable, boys, so merrily flies;
When rubbing and scrubbing our horses I vow,
We are all jolly fellows that follow the plough.

When six o'clock comes at breakfast we meet,
And beef, pork and bread, boys, so merrily eat;
With a piece in our pocket I swear and I vow,
We are all jolly fellows that follow the plough.

Then we harness our horses and away we do go,
And trip o'er the plain, boys, as nimble as does,
And when we come there so jolly and bold
To see which of us the straight furrow could hold.

Our master come to us and thus he did say:
'What have you been doing, boys, all this long day?
You have not ploughed an acre, I swear and I vow,
And you are damned idle fellows that follow the plough'.

I stept up to him and made this reply:
'We have ploughed an acre so you tell a great lie.
We have ploughed an acre I swear and I vow,
And we are all jolly fellows that follow the plough'.

He turned himself round and laughed at the joke:
'It's half past two o'clock, boys, it's time to unyoke.
Unharness your horses and rub them down well,
And I'll give you a jug of my very best ale'.

So come all you brave fellows wherever you be,
Come take this advice and be ruled by me,
So never fear your masters I swear and I vow,
For we are all jolly fellows that follow the plough.

Charlie Wilson's version, which was recorded by Peter Kennedy in 1952, has a slightly different ending. After the offer of beer the spokesman replies: 'Not a jug of your old beer or your jolly old pin [barrel]; A glass of your whisky or a glass o' your old gin'. He learned it as a boy from a man called William Browett in the stable at night, after work, when songs and stories were often exchanged. Street ballads, purchased at markets or fairs, would also be sung. One of these, a light-hearted sexual odyssey entitled the 'Roving Ploughboy', has a verse which runs:

Then through the country he did start
Straight away to Crosen [Croxton] park;
And when he came to Melton town
He took his lodgings at the Crown.
A gipsy girl was drinking there,
She treated him with gin and beer.
He pleased her well you need not fear,
Then off went the roving ploughboy.

Chorus

With my ran tan tweedle hi ge wo,
We are the lads to reap and mow;
We are the lads to plough and sow,
Huzza for the roving ploughboy.

Unmarried farmworkers often lived on the premises. Discipline was strict, as instanced by the case of two young labourers from Ashby Magna. The appeared before Lutterworth magistrates in 1869 for going out for a short time after finishing work for the day, and were ordered to apologise to their master and pay costs of seven shillings each or face fourteen days' imprisonment. Until the Master and Servant Act of 1867 an annually hired labourer was liable to imprisonment if he broke his contract of employment, though the master faced only a fine for a breach. John Whittaker of Hose was sentenced to fourteen days' hard labour for running away in January, 1867, shortly before the act was passed.

The very term, 'master' – still used by Charlie Wilson, both in song and speech – shows a degree of deference now long since gone. However, the waggoner had a degree of dignity and independence, as the song shows. Following an ancient tradition he rose at four in the morning and baited and groomed his horses before having his own breakfast. At 6.30 a.m. he set off to the fields with his team. The names of the horses were restricted to a narrow range: Captain, Gilbert, Dobbin and Duke were the best-known. Mares were called Daisy, Betty or Duchess. A roan was nearly always Strawberry, a chestnut, Gilbert, and a dappled grey, Dumpling. By 2.30 in the afternoon the daily stint of one acre was ploughed. The waggoner would have walked thirteen miles behind his single-furrow plough, but his day was not finished until he had fed his horses and cleaned them and their tackle. Then he might look forward to a session of songs and stories after supper, in the stable or tack-room.

Despite their skill and dedication, farm workers were seldom well paid. In 1809 a farm servant would have received between six and twelve pounds a year and a lad, between three and five pounds, the same as a dairy maid. In the 1840s a labourer was paid from £18 to £29 a year and a shepherd about £28. It is interesting to compare these wages with the £26.12s per annum which Charlie Wilson was receiving in 1894. Only two years later the *Melton Mowbray Times*, reporting on the Royal Agricultural Society's Show at Leicester, proudly announced two local awards for long service. The prize for 'the carter, or team-man, above the age of 18, not possessed of property (except gained by his own servitude) who shall have lived the longest time, without intermission, with the same master or mistress, and who produced testimonials that he has never returned home intoxicated with his team' went to William Dolby, who had worked 15 years and seven months for Mr William Doubleday of Kirkby Bellars. It was the sum of £1. There were two others winners, in the section for 'the farm labourer, whether married or single, who had worked the longest time, without intermission, on the same farm, or with the same master or mistress, and who has never received parish relief except in sickness'. After 46 years with Mr E. Oldacres of Carlton Curlieu Thomas Tyers received £2, and Robert Burnham was awarded £1 as runner-up for 45 years and ten months with the Duke of Rutland at Belvoir Castle.

Until the 1880s the older labourers still wore the smock-frock and top-hat. James Hawker remembered that labourers' smocks were brown, farmers' white. The smock was worn for best in the first year and for work in the next. The thrifty kept it for a third year to wear when there was an especially dirty job such as muck-spreading or pond-clearing.

A good scytheman was expected to cut an acre of grass in a day, or three acres of corn. Sickles were in use until the 1870s, and were superseded first by scythes, then by machines. A picture of the late 1880s in *Charlie Hammond's Sketch Book* (ed. C.Fry, 1980) shows work done in 'The Old Way' on a Leicestershire farm. The artist comments: 'It was a revelation to see the neat work these Irish harvesters did with the sythe [sic], with a machine-like rhythm they follow each other across the field, leaving the crop in perfect rows, an even distance apart, ready for the horse-rake'. Another picture by the same man shows a machine-binder at work in a corn field with Peatling Covert in the background. Only a few square yards are left uncut, and men are shooting rabbits as they run out of the corn. At one time threepence each was paid for rats' tails. Ferrets would be taken to farms where the corn was being thrashed and sent into the stack when it was low. Netting would channel the rats when they emerged towards watchers standing with dogs twenty yards back. Up to forty tails would be bagged at a session.

The old ways of work on the land and much of their vocabulary are now gone, swept away by modern technology and agribusiness. In some ways they continued until well within living memory. I remember myself working on farms in both Leicestershire and Rutland during school holidays and university vacations in the late 1940s and early '50s. The scythe was still used for odd jobs like cutting thistles in meadows, and also clearing a way round the outside of a cornfield ready for the reaper-binder. This was not done in grass. The mowing machine, which went round clockwise, would cut the outer edge of the field by first making one turn in the opposite direction.

Although the horse no longer provided motive power for the major machines it was still used for pulling loads of hay and corn from field to farm. The art was practised of loading a cart in such a way that the

Thatching a stack in the 1930s. The author's maternal grandfather is on the ladder

83

contents would not ignominiously slide off in a great heap as soon as it moved. Great pride was taken in the workmanship of building stable and waterproof stacks. Mr O.D. Lucas of Wigston remembers the 'unspeakable crime' of losing hold of a pitchfork when working on top of a stack. The penalty was to be told: 'That's a shilling you owe me'. He also recalls being asked: 'Have you seen all these blind sparrows bumping into things?' The reference was to pieces of straw left sticking out of a stack.

Harvesting, c.1896. (By permission of Leicestershire Museums)

When men worked overtime at haysel (haytime), harvest or thrashing it was the custom for the farmer to provide a tea-time meal, which would be brought out by his wife or daughters. Beer was sometimes provided, too, in my recollection, but not the gallon-cask per man which was once the custom. A labourer would be sent down to the cellar to fill these casks from much larger ones, and as a precaution against temptation he was required to whistle the whole time he was so engaged.

As long as a farmer had a single stook (or 'shock', as we called it) in a field it was a signal that he had not finished carrying. As soon as it was removed, gleaning was permitted by customary right, during certain hours indicated by the gleaning bell rung at church (see Chapter 3). During the war of 1939–45 country people went gleaning, though what they collected was used to feed the pigs and poultry which many kept. There was no Queen of the Gleaners as once had appeared:

When elected, she is borne in a chair to the first field that is to be gleaned; a crown, composed of wild flowers and a few ears of corn, is placed upon her head, and she tells her laws to her subjects. They are informed that when there are fields to be gleaned, a horn or bell will summon them to the outskirts of the village, and that she will then conduct them to the field. . . . The rustic sovereign then declares 'her will and pleasure' to the effect that her people 'shall not stray from the field' to which 'she leads them'; and that any one who violates this law 'shall forfeit her gathering, and her corn shall be bestrewed'. Wishing for all a good harvest, and that they 'may glean it in peace', the queen is then borne from the field to the end of the village surrounded by her subjects, and conveyed home amidst mirth and song.

This was the ceremony at Rempstone, near Loughborough. Elsewhere it was less elaborate, though an acknowledged leader would precede the village women into the appointed field, ringing a handbell at the gate. The gleaners would go in two by two, and await a second peal before starting. Much of the corn made would be used for furmenty (see page 224).

Gathering in the harvest is a deeply satisfying experience. Bringing in the last load was once attended by ceremony. Rev. Edward Bradley of Stretton, who under the pen-name of Cuthbert Bede made many contributions to the periodical, *Notes and Queries*, saw the last load brought in at an unspecified Rutland farmhouse in September, 1875. His account is worth quoting at some length:

The load [of beans] was decorated with green boughs; and on the top of the load were several children, who were lustily cheering as the waggon came lumbering along the road. It was eight o'clock, and a resplendent harvest-moon was just rising over the trees that girdled the old church hard by the farmer's stackyard. A company of us stood at his gate to watch the scene. Near to us, but concealed by the hedge, were the female and other servants, ready prepared with buckets of water and pitchers, and also with baskets of apples. As the last load passed us, with its drivers and occupants shouting 'Harvest home!' and cheering, the liers-in-wait rose up to view and pelted the waggon-load with a shower of apples, and also dashed pitchers of water over men, horses, children and beans. This had to be done quickly, while the waggon was moving by; so they who ran the guntlet were not much damaged, and the children on top of the load got more apples than water, and were proportionately thankful and applausive. But the waggon had to go to the bean-stack in the well-filled stackyard, whither it was followed by those who had already received it with the salute of apples and water, and where also all the labourers on the farm were waiting for it. A liberal supply of buckets of water was there at hand for the reception of the last load and its attendants; and we followed to see the fun. As the wagon drew up at the appointed spot, and the ladder was reared against its side to assist the children from the top of the load, the signal was given for a species of free fight with buckets and pails of water. The children evidently did not relish their douche bath, and were helped down from the top of the bean-load, sobbing bitterly, and bewailing their socked condition. Friend and foe seemed to be treated with equal impartiality, and the water was scooped out of the buckets and dashed indiscriminately over male and female. A reverend gentleman, who was making off round the stack was not recognised (let us hope!) in the semi-darkness, and, falling between two fires, received a ducking. I had just left him, in order to follow the sobbing children and administer to them pecuniary comfort; so I escaped with dry clothes, being, I think, the only one on the spot who did so.

The village of Thistleton had a similar ceremony until at least the 1890s.

Harvest festivals are now celebrated in churches, and are rather solemn affairs. In my time a substantial supper was given by the farmer's wife to all the helpers on the last day of the harvest. The same tradition was relished by William Gardiner, born in 1770, when he was a child. 'At the head of the board', he writes in *Music and Friends*, 'sat the worthy host, by whose side I was placed. Then came Will, Ralph, Joe and Jim, and their wives and helpers. Presently a shoulder of mutton, scorching hot, as the day had been, a plum pudding and a roasted goose were put on the table'. After liberal draughts of gingered ale, Joe, who had a reputation as a singer, was called on, but, as the jokes grew coarser, young William was 'taken to bed from a scene not to be imitated'. The old harvest suppers with their feasting, their abundance of beer and rough-and-ready concert programmes were often held in a barn which had been swept and cleaned for the purpose. The music of fiddle, concertina and mouth organ added to the festivities. Such occasions are now few, though at least one harvest supper is still held at Laughton after evening service on Harvest Festival Sunday.

Harvest was the culmination of the yearly cycle of work on the land, which began with ploughing. Under the ancient open-field system a date had to be set for the beginning of ploughing. It was best to plough last and to reap first, said an old adage. The man who ploughed last could turn part of his neighbour's strip on to his own. The man who reaped first could take a generous view of his boundary. The day before which ploughing was not permitted was Plough Monday, the first Monday after Twelfth Day (6 January), and ploughmen held a festival on that day until

86

recently. The participants, who went from house to house making a collection of food, drink or money, had various names, depending on their locality: morris dancers, plough bullocks, plough bullockers, plough boys, molly guizers. They had some form of disguise, from simple blacking or reddening of the face to elaborate costume. At Glenfield they are remembered as having black faces and singing 'some quaint old songs'. Individual identity was submerged, and those taking part could appear as a collective, impersonal and even menacing body. 'We was terrified bacos we didn't know 'oo they was', said an old woman from Fleckney, and Mrs Dorothy Sutton remembers to this day her mother's tales of the fright she got from seeing the ploughboys at Arnesby as a child. Terror undoubtedly increased the likelihood of contributions; disguise ensured that the ploughboys would be immune from retaliation if they took reprisals against the stingy. Like many rites, this was considered a right, and those who rejected it were fair game for chastisement. At Ridlington the chant was: 'If you don't let us in We'll kick the doors in', which was paralleled by the Woodhouse Eaves song:

Tramp, tramp, tramp the boys are marching,
Cheer up, the boys are at your door.
If you do not let us in
We will kick the door in,
And you won't see your mother any more

'If yer didn' gie 'em owt' at Claybrooke they ploughed up 'the causey'; so, too, at Bagworth, and no doubt elsewhere. Another resort was emptying all the soft-water butts. In about 1850 an entire waggon belonging to a non-contributor at Willoughby Waterless was dismantled and re-assembled inside a stone-walled pound with a narrow entrance. The occasion was sometimes used merely to play high-spirited practical jokes. One person described it as a 'spasm of sheer, unadulterated devilment', a sentiment which would have been shared by the old woman living on the green at Grimston, who was regularly smoked out on Plough Monday by having a wet sack put over her chimney. 'Buffoonery and foolishness at best and 'hooliganism' at worst was how Plough Monday was described at Melton in 1860.

The ritual actions varied greatly. At Belgrave the ploughboys merely paraded through the main street 'dressed in long smocks and cracking their long whips'. In 1811 at Elmesthorpe 'Plough bullocks dressed in ribbons a gaudy show' were seen 'In a long procession, shouting as they go'. At Broughton Astley they 'paraded the neighbourhood from dawn till dark with a local band including tin whistles, combs and a drum'. In some cases, such as at Markfield, men harnessed themselves with ropes to a plough, which was then dragged through the streets, and used, if necessary, to plough up lawns. doorsteps or footpaths. Dancing went on at

Kings Norton, where the steps were probably those known as 'Nancy's Fancy'. In Leicester itself 'groups of bedizened yokels, with reddened faces, and grotesquely clothed, performed a rough dance in the streets and presented a money box with much uncouth urgency', said an observer whose attitude is very clear. At Market Bosworth 'it was the custom for some of the villagers to dress in grotesque masquerade and perform morris-dances before all the houses where they were likely to get money or drink'. The dance was 'a travesty of a quadrille, with ad lib. stamping and shuffling of feet', but it might indeed have been a form of morris. The men were sometimes 'accompanied by a gang of lads with raddled faces, half-hidden under paper masks', who dragged a plough. In addition:

Some of the performers, generally four, had on white women's dresses and tall hats. One of these was called Maid Marian. Of the other performers, one was the Fool, who always carried the money-box, and generally a bladder with peas in it on a string at the end of a stick, with which he lustily laid about him. Another was Beelzebub, in a dress made up narrow strips of flannel, cloth, &c., with the ends hanging loose, yellow, red, black and white being the dominant colours. The rest were simply grotesques.

The Greetham version of these costumes can be seen in a photograph taken between 1900 and 1920, and published in *Rutland Villages*.

The poet, John Clare, had strong associations with Rutland. He worked as a lime-burner at Ryhall, Pickworth and Great Casterton, wrote a poem about the ruins of Pickworth and married 'Sweet Patty of the Vale' from Great Casterton. He stated that his description of Plough Monday customs, written in 1825, applied not only to his native county of Northamptonshire but to Rutland . 'On this day', he wrote:

it is the custom for the plough boys (whose anxiety for the sport almost wakens them before the morning) to meet at the blacksmiths shop to dress themselves & get ready not with white shirts & ribons but to black their faces with a mixture of soot & greese & those that will not undergo this are reckoned unworthy of the sport & excluded the company they get an old skeleton of a plough with out share or coulter & attach it to a waggon rope in which sticks are crossed & on each side these sticks the boys take their station they are called plough bullocks the stoutest among them is selected for the holder of the plough & thus equipped they pull it round the village from door to door for what they can get . . . to those that will not give to them they let loose their mischief by pulling up shoes scrapers at the door or gate posts & winding up the person in the rope & as it is reckoned a lawless day the constable will rarely interfere if calld upon . . . the men grown servants 3 or 4 of them go round the Village dressed up in a grotesque manner they are called the 'plough witches' 2 of them has their faces blacd & a hunch back of straw stuck into their smock frocks their hats are tyd up into a three cockd form & figured with chalk in their hands they carry a beesom & a spoon filld with soot & greese to sweep the dirt or to black the faces of the servants maids they happen to meet with who generally take care to keep out of the way the 'she' witch as he is calld is dressed up in a laughable joanish manner in womens cloaths he has no hunch back & his face is ruddled they carry a box with half pence in it which they shake when they come to the door at night the bullocks & witches meet together in a sociable party & buying their supper of cake & ale this is the real custom of plough monday which is known to this day.

Another important activity was the performance of a play (for which, see Chapter 9), but the festivities always concluded, as indicated by Clare, with eating and drinking, usually in the local public house. On the surface, therefore, the dominant reason for the custom was the collection of money. As at Woodhouse Eaves:

I'll sing you a song
It won't be very long
But I'll sing it as pretty as any;
Put your hand in your pocket
And give a poor ploughboy a penny.

Or at Ab Kettleby, to the tune of 'Jim the Carter's Lad':

Beneath the surface there was the deep sense of satisfaction which the performance of customary rituals gives to both performers and spectators, coupled with a feeling that good luck and fertility were assured. In addition there was an assertion of the collective strength of the ploughboy.

Most villages seem to have kept up Plough Monday traditions until the first world war. Bisbrooke, Preston, Ryhall and Seaton continued them into the 1920s. Why did they decline? The *Leicester Chronicle* reported in 1889: 'The ancient customs . . . were partially observed on Monday, when the 'Plough Boys' accompanied by a brass band, paraded the village, But . . . even ploughboys appear to be influenced by the march of progress. On this occasion no complaints were heard of their rough demands for 'blackmail' and under these reformed circumstances, no one appears disposed to deprive the youngsters of an undoubted source of amusement to them'. The participants were losing conviction as the time-honoured *quête* became equated with cadging, even blackmail. There was opposition to the inversion of the social order and the ploughboys' right to take reprisals. The numbers of men employed in agriculture were steadily declining, and at the same time new, commercial entertainments were increasing. By the 1960s there were attempts at reviving at least the Plough Monday plays, but the other customs of the day seem to have gone for ever.

Blackened faces, disguise, often in women's clothing, defiance of authority, collective reprisal: these elements of the Plough Monday rituals seem to have been directly assimilated by the Luddites. Luddism is often taken to indicate blind prejudice and mindless opposition to innovation, but it was a principled movement by skilled workmen in defence of their living and craft standards. The word, 'Luddite', first appeared in print in 1811 (though the earliest reference is the *Oxford English Dictionary* is from 1812). It is said to have derived from the name of 'an ignorant youth, in Leicestershire, of the name of Ludlam, who, when ordered by his father, a framework-knitter, to square his needles, took a hammer and beat them into a heap'. Another version says that Edward Ludlam, hence Ned Lud, was 'a person of weak intellect who lived in a Leicestershire village about 1779, and who in a fit of insane rage rushed into a stockinger's house and destroyed two frames so completely that the saying "Lud must have been here" came to be used throughout the hosiery districts when a stocking-frame had undergone extraordinary damage'.

Oral tradition identifies the village as Anstey, whose inhabitants are still known as 'Neddoes'. After the death of his mother in 1763 Ned Lud is said to have been apprenticed by the parish to a stocking-weaver. (Stocking-weaver, stockinger and framework-knitter are interchangeable terms). He was thrashed for laziness, and retaliated by hammering a frame to

COUNTY of LEICESTER.

The Magistrates for the said County residing in the Hundred of West Goscote,

CAUTION

ALL PERSONS AGAINST THE CRIME OF

FRAME BREAKING.

EVERY Person forcibly entering a House in the Night time, **WITH INTENT TO BREAK A FRAME,** and every Person **IN ANY MANNER** aiding or assisting others in so doing, is guilty of **BURGLARY,** which is punishable by **DEATH.**

Persons being entrusted with the Frames of their **Employers,** who in any way connive at their destruction, are **ACCOMPLICES IN FELONY,** **CONCEALING THE NAMES OF FRAME BREAKERS,** in order to screen them from Justice, is punishable by **FINE AND IMPRISONMENT.**

Every Person **EXTORTING MONEY** for the support of **Frame Breakers, IS A FELON,** and punishable with **DEATH.**

Every Person **USING THREATENING LANGUAGE** respecting the Persons or Property of others, is liable to be imprisoned, untill he shall find **SUFFICIENT SURETIES** for his future good behaviour,

And the Magistrates hereby call upon all good and loyal Subjects **TO BE VIGILANT,** and to give the Constables of their respective Parishes **THE EARLIEST NOTICE** of all such Felonius **ACTS** or **THREATS** that the Offenders may be apprehended and dealt with, according to Law.

By order of the Magistrates,

CHARLES LACEY, their Clerk.

Loughborough, December 10, 1811.

W. RISTE, PRINTER, LOUGHBOROUGH.

Handbill of 1812 (By permission of the Public Record Office)

91

pieces. Alternatively, he smashed the frame to vent his anger at being mercilessly taunted with being stupid. A saying, once current, was: 'as daft as Ned Lud, who ran ten miles to see a dead donkey'. Whatever the truth of these stories, and some of they may have been put about through fear or in a deliberate attempt to discredit, Luddism was no laughing matter In 1812 frame-breaking was made a capital offence, despite Byron's impassioned opposition in the House of Lords. Men were hanged for it at Leicester in 1816 and '17. Three were executed at Derby, including one named Isaac Ludlam.

Stockings had originally been knitted by hand; one remembers Shakespeare's reference to 'the spinners and knitters in the sun'. The invention in Shakespeare's time, of an immensely complex frame, with over two thousand component parts, enabled the process to be done by a hand-operated machine. The first frame in the county was introduced at Hinckley by William Iliffe in 1640. Leicester followed suit thirty years later, with Nicholas Alsop being responsible. In 1705 Daniel Defoe remarked: 'one would scarce think it possible so small an article of trade could employ such multitudes of people as it does; for the whole county seems to be employed in it'. By about the middle of the eighteenth century there were about a thousand frames in Hinckley, another thousand in Leicester, and hundreds more in smaller towns and villages. William Gardiner paints an idyllic picture of this period, drawn from his father's reminiscences: 'Then every stocking-maker had his frame at home, and his wife and daughters had their spinning wheels. Scattered through the county, these artisans in the summer left their frames and wheels to assist in getting in the harvest, after which they returned to their usual employ . . . It was pretty sight in the villages to see a cluster of girls spinning under the shade of the walnut trees, combining with their love-songs the whizzing of their wheels'. John Nichols, who attended the free grammar school at Market Bosworth, and in 1778 married a great-grand-daughter of William Iliffe, underlines the point about music: 'Men, women, boys and girls all sat and worked at the frames, and they would be singing away as they worked, all over town'. Their stockings had to be finished by Friday, so that they could be taken by carrier's cart to Leicester on Saturday. Friday was therefore a busy day and Saturday lazy. There was often little work on Monday and Tuesday, since the carriers did not return with yarn for the new work until Tuesday evening. The period without work was called 'lay out' or 'shacking'. Other places in the county did not necessarily have the same arrangement with carriers' carts, but most kept 'Saint Monday' or 'stockingers' Monday' as a holiday. At Thringstone, for example, 'however much work was waiting to be done the stockingers regarded Monday as an 'off' day. They would toil till midnight, if necessary, on the other days of the week so as to make up for the lost time'. One of their favourite occupations on Saint Monday was to congregate on the green by an old stone barn, known simply as 'the Barn', for debates and discussions. The 'shoe hands' at Leicester celebrated the day by holding dog races in the abbey meadow, in the 1870s.

Life for the framework-knitters was often harsh. There is a tradition at Hinckley of apprentices having been chained to their looms, which might make the rage of Ned Lud seem more understandable. The expression, 'as poor as a stockinger', was once commonplace. The operatives were at times driven to violent action to protect even the precarious living which they enjoyed. Machinery was destroyed in 1757 at Loughbrough, Sileby and Mountsorrel; a frame capable of making twelve pairs of hose at the same time was smashed by workmen at Leicester Exchange in 1773; there was a riot in 1787 when Joseph Brookhouse's worsted-spinning machine was broken up, and on the same occasion the Mayor of Leicester received a fatal blow to the head from a stone.

The stocking-frames were usually the property of hosiers who let them out to middlemen or 'masters'. These in turn rented frames to the weavers, and also supplied raw material in the shape of yarn, to be made up into stockings and also gloves and various fancy items. The worker had to pay a weekly rent for the frame, however much or little he produced, and also a fee to the master for giving out the work. The yarn was available for collection on Monday mornings. There were suggestions that it was deliberately kept damp, so as to weigh as much as possible. When the finished goods were delivered on Saturday afternoon they would be drier, and therefore lighter; they would therefore earn less for the weaver, who was paid by weight.

He had to find the money for lighting, heating and needles, and he also had to pay someone for seaming the hose (stitching up the seam). He could be fined for any faulty work. The trade supported a host of specialist workers: woolcombers, dyers, framesmiths, comb-makers, winders, sizers, spinners, doublers, twisters, bobbiners, sinker- and needle-makers. At Hinckley in 1811, 1,500 frames kept over six thousand people in work, not counting the masters and hosiers.

It was precisely then that a marked decline in trade occurred, which was partly occasioned by a change in male fashion from knee-breeches, which needed long stockings, to trousers, which did not. The masters' answer was to reduce the prices paid to weavers, to employ a disproportionate number of apprentices (called 'colts') who were cheaper than tradesmen, and to introduce wide frames. Such frames produced a large rectangle of worsted fabric which was cut into lengths and sewn up into stockings. Since these had no proper selvedges they lasted only a short time, and brought the trade into disrepute, thus reducing demand. There were demonstrations at Hinckley, with black flags paraded and loaves dipped in blood. Warehouses were sacked, and their contents thrown into the streets. Anonymous threatening letters were sent to some Leicester hosiers, and at Shepshed in December, 1811, some twenty frames were smashed. The framework-knitters also petitioned Parliament about their grievances; a bill was later introduced in the Commons but rejected by the Lords.

The most serious outbreak of Luddism in Leicestershire was at Loughborough, and it concerned not knitting frames but lace-making machines In June, 1816, fifty-five 'Loughborough machines', as they were called were hacked to pieces by a Luddite commando at Heathcote and Boden's Factory, and the nightwatchman, John Asher, was wounded by a pistol shot. Although the attackers had their faces covered by handkerchieves their leader, John Towle, was recognised, and subsequently arrested. He was sentenced to death at Leicester Assizes and hanged in Infirmary Square in November, 1816. Twelve more men were tried later, and eight of them were hanged before a crowd of 15,000 people, again at Infirmary

A stocking weaver of the 1850s. (By permission of Leicestershire Museums)

Square, in April, 1817. Apart from one Chilwell man, they were all from Nottingham.

Such violence was born of desperation. Writing as late as 1940, Arthur Pickering of Hinckley observed: 'In these prosperous times such a state of things is hard to realise, but there are still a few old stockingers living whose memories are vivid with tales of the almost inhuman toil, the creak and boom of the old frames; the clink of the sinkers and the splutter of the "farthing dip" in its iron socket; then the disputes between master and man, and at times the necessary sting of charity'. At Hinckley there was a strike of framework-knitters in 1824. Disorders two years after were quelled only by the arrival of a detachment of lancers, which killed one man, and in 1829 a group called the 'Light Horse Men' went round forcibly taking food for distribution to the poor. There were strikes at Leicester in 1833–4. Three years later there were 7,000 unemployed in the town. When Thomas Cooper, later well-known as a Chartist, arrived in 1840 to start work as a reporter on *The Leicestershire Mercury* he saw stockingers lining the approaches of the town in order to try to beg sixpence from strangers. He conversed with one man who told him that he earned four shillings and sixpence. Cooper took this to be his daily rate, then found that it was his weekly wage.

In 1842 there were further strikes, and framework knitters at Mowmacre Hill, west of Birstall, were dispersed by the Yeomanry in what came to be called the Battle of Mowmacre Hill. In 1848 there were riots directed against the workhouse. The boot and shoe industry, introduced in the 1850s, allied to the manufacture of elastic webb which had begun in 1839, began to improve conditions. However, framework-knitting continued, and with it the problems of frame-rent and the middleman. A song of 1854 says:

The Middleman's a docking man,
A constant peace destroyer,
A warehouse rat that digs between
The employed and the employer.

The Middleman's a useless man,
He is not worth a tester;
And the sooner he becomes defunct
The better for old Leicester.

Fortunately, there were lighter sides to the framework-knitter's lot. Just as the ploughboy could appear in the guise of a light-hearted Lothario, so the knitter:

Framework knitters' coat of arms, from Pickering's *Hosiery Trade* (By permission of Ferry Pickering Group)

And when I came to Leicester, a stockinger by trade,
Then by the buxom girls I was counted a merry blade;
And oft times hose so fine I wove for many a pretty maid,
And for to garter up the same I never was afraid.

A ballad entitled 'The Love of Thomas and Mary' was published at Hinckley in 1859:
Thomas long had lov'd his Mary – gaz'd enraptured on her charms,
Took her oft to church and chapel – after service 'hung on arms';
And they walked in trembling silence, mingling thoughts like silent
skies,
Thomas sometimes interrupting with a 'bless them di'ment eyes'.

Till at last he'd made up his mind some important steps to take –Says
he, 'We have courted, Mary, two long years come Burbage wake;
I'm sick and tired of journey work, with drunken sprees and bother,
'Nough to make a parson swear or e'en to whop his mother.

'I'm promised a three-legger soon, a nice house I've found and shop,
But without you're willing, Mary, all this happy plan must stop;
For I want you, that is, Mary' – Thomas here began to stutter –
'If I get the legger working, will you come and be my footer?'

Need I tell you how she answer'd, though a word she could not speak,
Or how quickly Thomas read the mantling blush upon her cheek?
No, we'll leave them in their cottage, with its window filled with flowers,
And its little joys and sorrows making sweet e'en labour's hours.

96

Leave them to their work and loving – leave them to their sober life –
To their walks through shady footpaths, far away from crowds or
strife.
Where, though poor, they made be honest; without riches still not
mean –
So, contented with each other, he wouldn't change her for a queen.

Charming though the song is, it is escapist and retrospective, for the
coming age was not one of cottage workshops but of factories, one of
which at Fleckney, was nicknamed Rowley's Gaol. The new factories were
not without their customs. The 'sprees and bother' of the song may refer
to the practice by which a fresh workman paid his 'footing' to provide
drinks all round. It was called a 'shifting shilling' when a worker moved
from one place to another.

A raw hand was often subjected to practical jokes, such as having tools
or items of clothing hidden. He would be sent on fool's errands to ask for a
glass hammer or a tin of striped paint, or to fetch a load of post-holes.
When he asked for a 'long stand' he would be kept waiting for some time,
then told that he had received it. Young apprentices were sometimes
seized by women workers and had their private parts anointed with
grease. The women told lurid jokes and stories of married life to a
bride-to-be among their number, both at work and in a drinking session
on the wedding-eve. There was also the traditional presentation of a gift
or symbol of a phallic nature, such as a rolling pin, attended by much
horseplay and laughter. Man would be taken by their workmates, suitably
decorated, and tied to a lamppost outside the factory on the day before
their wedding. A photograph of Brian Deacon outside the Portland shoe
factory at the Newarke, Leicester, was taken as recently as 1982.

Humour provides welcome relief from drudgery, and jokes and anecdotes constantly circulate where people are at work. Some sewerage men
on their way to the sewer at Welford Road with a full cart for deposit
stopped to eat their 'snap'. They remained sitting on their cart. One man
said to his mate: 'Stop stirring that with your finger, I'm eating my dinner'.
'So am I', he replied, 'but I've lost my cheese'.

Since the thirteenth century there have been associations in Leicester
for craftsmen, the oldest being that of the fullers, dating from 1210. Most
had died out by the nineteenth century. The bricklayers, card-weavers
and no doubt others still had an organisation which supported members
who were out of work, and allowed them to go on tramp. They would
receive free accommodation and a small sum of money on presenting a
card at specified public houses as they travelled in search of work. One
bricklayers' rendez-vous was the Golden Fleece in the Cattle Market at
Loughbrough; many of the houses called The Bricklayer's Arms probably
had a similar function. The card-weavers had the Prince Regent at

Brian Deacon (Photograph by Theodore Sturge)

Leicester, where James Hawker received a free night's lodging and the sum of one shilling and sixpence in 1857 when he needed to make himself scarce after a poaching incident in his native Northamptonshire: 'I ran home as quick as I could and Drew my Travelling Card. For by this time I was a Trade unionist – almost before I knew what it Meant. But I knew even then Has I know now that in the Union is Strength. I belonged to the Card-weavers' Association'.

As late as the eighteenth century there were processions of some of the trades which recalled medieval traditions. The woolcombers would include a figure representing Bishop Blaize, the patron saint of textile workers, chosen because his flesh had been scored with iron combs before he was beheaded as a Christian martyr. In the celebrations at the end of the Seven Years' War in 1763 'The Bishop' rode through Leicester 'In an open landau, drawn by six horses, with three postillions and four pages, all habited. His lordship in a gown and cassock, a mitre of wool on his head; in one hand the Book of Common Prayer, in the other a woolcomb. A Shepherd and Shepherdess on horseback. Another Shepherd and Shepherdess. A stage, built on a waggon, with two combers at work, two doublers, two spinners, a framework-knitter at his calling, and a crown of wool on the stage. A procession of about twenty combers, all habited in wool wigs, sashes, ruffled shirts, and grey stockings, three and three'.

The Hinckley Whitsuntide Fair procession in 1792 also included 'Bishop Blaze, and his Chaplain the Rev. Mr LEE, the inventor of the Stocking frame', together with various tradesmen who were also celebrated in rhyme:

Observe the MILLERS in their floury dress
And pageantry, their honours to express;
While we extol, by soft enchantment draws,
The whole assembly well deserves applause.

Next in procession comes good BISHOP BLAZE;
To whom, we own, is due immortal praise;
And JASON too from Colchos who to Greece
With rapid steps did bring the Golden Fleece.

Likewise the reverend and ingenious LEE;
A great and worthy patron sure was he,
That hither into England ever came;
The sole inventor of the STOCKING FRAME.

. . .

Next unto this, to hail the Cavalcade,
The FRAME-WORK KNITTERS to display their trade,
In martial pride and grandeur now appear,
And join in splendid manner, front and rear.

With BUTCHERS, JOINERS, and CORDWAINERS too,
In fancy dresses, pleasing to the view;
And other different trades, as we descry,
Striving each other to outvie.

For good measure Lady Godiva was there too, 'characteristically habited',
or perhaps not habited. The figure of Bishop Blaise appeared until recent
years on inn signs at Barrow, Leicester, Loughborough and Melton.

Coal mining in Leicestershire goes back a long way; some say as far as
Roman times. There are documented records of pits in the thirteenth
century at Donington-le-Heath, Swannington and Worthington, and in
the fourteenth at Staunton Harold. Accounts of life in such pits are
extremely rare. Earl Cowper wrote this to his sister in 1726: 'I have
nothing very remarkable to tell you except that at Ashby de la Zouche in
Leicestershire I ventured down into a coal pit between 200 and 300 feet
deep. It was very safe going down. The way is a fellow gets upon a rope
and ties himself fast and then ye person yt goes down sets in his lap. When
I was down I could not stand upright so yt cou'd not go very far in it.
There are horses which have been down there for 8 or 10 years and never
once come up in all yt time. The cole mine yt I was in belongs to one Mrs
Wilkins who goes down herself very often and dines there and spends the
whole day there. It was so very wet that I came up like a drowned rat'.

The close-knit communities of miners produced their own way of
talking, with a large number of technical terms. 'To draw the wood' meant
to pull out the pit props, and the expression was used metaphorically for
tripping a player in football. The 'gob' was part of the mine which had
been abandoned after the coal had been extracted from it. The word gave
rise to 'gobby-hole', a cupboard full of odds and ends (sometimes also
called a 'bogey-hole'). A miner having difficulty in moving a tub along a
roadway would call for the 'roadman's hammer', a mythical tool capable
of overcoming all problems. At the end of a shift miners 'shirted it'
(stopped work), and met 'the Herefords' (incoming men, so called
because of their white faces). The traditional greeting among Leicestershire miners was 'old bud' (bird), which has now become 'me duck'.
'Sorry' or 'Surry' is also heard as a form of address, as it is in Nottinghamshire, where D. H. Lawrence claimed that it was a descendant of the
medieval 'Sirrah'.

Perhaps it is unsurprising that men engaged in such dangerous work
should be superstitious. Some would turn back if they saw a woman or a
parson on the way to the pit, since this was a bad omen. Many believed that
the Sound of the Seven Whistlers (see page 61) foretold calamity, and
under no circumstances would go underground after hearing it. One
explanation is that the birds were sent by providence to warn of impend-

ing danger, so men ignored the signal at their peril. Another story is that seven colliers were once drunk on a Sunday and whistled for a wager to pay for more drink. They were carried up into the clouds by a whirlwind and their spirits for ever perambulated the heavens to whistle a warning when fatal accidents were impending in the mines.

There was not always a warning, and accidents did happen, sometimes fatal ones. It has long been the custom on such occasions for the pit to stop work as a mark of respect. Fortunately, major disasters have been few in Leicestershire, but an underground fire in the main air intake at Whitwick led in 1898 to the deaths of 35 miners. Some of their bodies are still

A scene outside Whitwick Pit in April, 1898
(By permission of Leicestershire Museums)

entombed in the mine. A memorial tablet can be seen in Christ Church, Coalville. The inscription points out that 27 widows were left behind and 84 children under thirteen years of age. Whitwick Colliery ceased some years ago to exist as a separate entity. Only four pits are now left in the county and all will close during the next ten years. However, a new pit is to be sunk at Asfordby, so mining will continue.

The lore and customs of miners are very poorly documented, and those of the quarrymen of Leicestershire and Rutland await investigation. As a boy I knew an old Markfield quarryman, 'Uncle Pep.' (His name was Pepper). What tales he could have told in his broad Leicestershire if only I could have asked the right questions. Many of the old framework-knitters took jobs in quarries when their industry declined. Whittle Hill stone from Charnwood was once exported all over the world for use as whetstone. Breedon Hill has been quarried since the Iron Age for its limestone, which also comes from Could Hill nearby. Charnwood granite, Swithland or Collyweston slate, Ketton limestone: all these have a national

Workmen leaving Cliffe Hill Granite Quarries, 1900
(Unpublished photograph by Sir Benjamin Stone, reproduced by permission of Birmingham Reference Library)

reputation. At Mountsorrel the descendants of workmen of Roman times produced until the 1930s entirely by hand and hammer pavings, kerb stones and setts. Their great hammers had special names. The 'chopper' made a channel in a large block before this was broken by a 'burster', weighing thirty pounds. The 'knob hammer' was used to break off awkward lumps, and the 'squaring hammer' fashioned the setts. The 'spalling hammer' reduced odd pieces to manageable proportions before they were passed through a crushing mill ready for macadam. Quarrying remains an important industry, though much of the work is now mechanised.

The first brickmaker and the first bricklayer were recorded at Leicester in 1696, and the first brickyard, near what is now Welford Place, in 1715. Many years later, conditions of work for children employed in the industry were brought to public notice by George Smith of Coalville (as he came to be called). Smith, the son of a Staffordshire brickyard worker, was employed from 1857 until 1872 by the Whitwick Colliery Company as manager of a small yard at Coalville. He was appalled by the conditions which prevailed. Boys of nine carried lumps of clay weighing up to 43 pounds, and walked over twelve miles a day while doing so. At one Coalville yard Smith found a twelve year-old boy working an 84 hour week. He was able to insist on improvements in his own yard, but not elsewhere, so he published in 1871 a passionate book entitled *The Cry of the Children from the Brickyards of England*. Largely as a result Parliament passed a new factories' act to regulate the employment of women and children in brickyards. Smith received a purse of a hundred guineas from Lord Shaftesbury in recognition of his services, but he had antagonised local people, and was forced to relinquish his post and move with his wife and family to a small cottage. He nevertheless mounted another great campaign, this time on behalf of canal boat-people.

George Smith was well acquainted with canals. There were two, the Grand Union and the Ashby, within a few miles of Coalville, and he also had vivid memories of the boat-people from boyhood: 'Drunkenness, filthiness and cruelty, selfish idleness at the cost of children and animals; thieving, fighting and almost every other kind of abomination prevailed among them. I have often see the boat-women strip and fight like men (and if anything more savagely), pulling the hair out of each other's heads be handsful, after they had tired themselves by hard hitting, with sometimes a little biting into the bargain, to say nothing of kicking'. He put forward certain modest proposals: that schooling should be provided for children, that properly habitable accommodation should be provided on boats, and that health checks should be instituted. For this he was burnt in effigy in the streets of Coalville.

He was not the sort of man to be deterred. Another book, *Our Canal Population: A Cry from the Boat Cabins*, accompanied by tireless campaigning and lobbying, led once more to parliamentary action, this time in the shape of the Canal Boats' Act of 1878. Unfortunately, the act was a dead letter, since its enforcement was left entirely to the discretion of local authorities, and there were no penalties for non-compliance. Smith continued to struggle, helped by another book, *Canal Adventures by Moonlight* (1881), which partly consisted of an account of a journey from London to Leicester by canal. Three years later an amending act was on the statute book, requiring local authorities to insist on the registration of boats, to conduct an annual inspection, and to enforce school attendance for the children.

Despite his own poverty Smith went on to conduct yet another campaign, this time on behalf of gypsies, though by then he had moved to

Crick in Warwickshire. He died in 1895 at the age of 64, worn out. George Smith of Coalville was unusual in being a social reformer who came himself from the working class. He was a most remarkable man who deserved more from his Coalville fellow-citizens than burning in effigy.

Foxton Locks on the Grand Union Canal

7. Sports and pastimes

Children had many pastimes, usually involving minimal expenditure on equipment. Horse-chestnuts were used for the still-popular 'conkers', and five small stones for what we called 'snobs'. Specially-made stones could also be bought, as could marbles, for a few pence. Shove-halfpenny was a miniature form of soccer played on a flat surface such as a wide window-sill or a desk-top. Each of the two players had, say, a penny, which was flicked with a ruler in order to propel the ball, a smaller coin such as a half-penny, into the opponent's goal. There was also a miniature form of cricket, with near-normal rules, except that there were diminutive, home-made bats and a tiny ball, bowled underarm. Even whips and tops could be home-made, though they could also be bought from shops. 'There were some splendid tops', an Oadby woman remembered, 'grannies, corkers, carrots, flyers – and the boys could whip them the whole length of the pavement, even send them flying across the road, or occasionally, through a window-pane'. The technique for setting a top spinning was to wind the thong, preferably of thin leather but, failing that, of string, carefully round it then to pull the whip-handle sharply; but not too sharply, or the top would simply fly out of control. To keep it going one continued judiciously to apply the whip. The tops spun on the head of a nail inserted in the bottom, and their bright rings of paint made a blur of colour as they did so. One seldom sees them now, but once every child had his whip and top on Shrove Tuesday, and they were popular at least until the 1940s. The game of battledore and shuttlecock was also played on Pancake Day.

Bowling a hoop was another favourite pursuit, though it could be done at any time of the year. The more sophisticated variety was made of iron, with a handle permanently attached by a ring; but anything would do. An old tyre propelled by the hand or a stick was a favourite. We did not call it a hoop, but a 'bowler', rhyming with 'howler' – and the same pronunciation was used in cricket. It Rutland the hoop was called a 'trundle'. A motor tyre could be bowled along until it gathered too much momentum to be followed, when it was allowed to pursue its own course until it crashed spectacularly into a hedge or a fence.

Most of these games involved only one or two participants, but others needed a considerable number. Our Oadby woman's favourite was 'Tin Lurky', also reported from Ketton, which she thought 'grand for an autumn night in a warren of back alleys':

The author (right) and friends playing miniature cricket at Coalville Grammar School, 1948

A tin can was placed in a chosen spot to mark HOME and the person ON stood by it, covering his eyes (but of course peeping though his fingers) and counting up to fifty or one hundred, depending on the nearness of suitable cover, whilst the rest of the players hid themselves. The last part of the countdown was in full voice – 'Ninety-nine, 'UNDRED, and I'm COMING'. The game was to get back HOME and kick the tin without being caught.

A man from Oadby recalled playing 'at marbles, whip and top, hoops, can lid on a string, "mad hosses" along the village street, and one boys' static game in the school playground called "Jack Mop". Mr O. D. Lucas of Wigston knew this as 'Johnny Mop', and at Ketton it was called 'Bull Stag'. Those taking part would stand in a line, bending forward as for leap-frog. The boy going first would stand at the back of the line and shout:

Bull stag aroni,
My blue pony.
Those that I catch I'll put in a stable
And they shall not play.

He would then jump on the first back and make his way up the line, trying to break it with his weight. As he went along he would shout:

Bake cake, bumble bee,
One, two, three, four.

At 'four' if he had failed to break the line he was out, and the next boy would start from the back. If he broke the line the boy at that point would

)e out. The game was dangerous, and was banned by schools, along with
)ther boisterous, even violent activities like British Bulldog.

'Bull stag' was also played at Caldecott, where it was known as 'Little
lacky Aguwary'. The same village had 'Prison Bars', which has been
:nown under various names at least since the time of Edward III, when it
vas 'prohibited to be played in the avenues of the palace at Westminster
luring the Sessions of Parliament, because of the interruption it
)ccasioned to the members and others passing to and fro'. At Caldecott
here were two teams, one on each side of the street. At a given signal one
eam had to rush across to the other side with as many players as possible
ivoiding capture by the opposing team.

Another game from the same village, which was also widely known in
_eicestershire, was 'Duck Stone'. A small stone placed on top of a large
)ne had to be toppled by a third stone thrown by a player. If he succeeded
n doing this he had to run and pick up his own stone, without touching it,
n his cap. His opponent, meanwhile, would run to replace the small stone
ind tig the thrower before he could return to base. In an adult variant of

'ip Cat near the Castle Lodge, Leicester, in 1895
3y permission of Leicestershire Museums)

107

the game, played at Belton, four men would simultaneously try to dislodge the small stone, called a 'motty'. A 'mottyman' would have to replace it during play, which was a rather hazardous undertaking. One man in the village had his eye knocked out while doing so.

Tip Cat was also played both by children and adults; my father, born 1903, played it as a young man at Coalville. A version, simply called 'Cat' is remembered at Edith Weston. The 'cat' was a short piece of wood sharpened at both ends and resembling a shuttle. It was hit with a stick at one end to make it rise in the air, then a second time to make it fly as far as possible. The players stood in a ring, four feet across, marked out in chalk. After hitting the cat they would count the number of paces to it, and the one with the greatest distance would be the winner. 'Dick Trap', played at Edith Weston and also at Morcott, was similar, but had more complex rules.

'Up the needle and down the thread', from Greetham, was rather more sedate. It was played by a line of girls, each of whom held the one in front by the waist. The line would go round the playground until the leader reached a wall. She would put one hand on the wall, and the rest of the girls would process under the arch so formed. The leader would then go to the back of the line, and the second girl take over; and so on. In 'windows' there would be a ring of girls, holding hands. To the accompaniment of the song. 'In and out the windows', a girl would thread her way through all the windows or arches formed by the outstretched arms and then stand in the middle. Up to thirty girls would take part.

Songs and chants were also used to accompany set games such as 'Bingo', which involved not numbers but letters, 'Drop handkerchief', a form of hide-and-seek, and 'The Jolly Miller':

There was a jolly miller and he lived by himself,
As the wheel went round he made his pelf;
One hand in the hopper and the other in the bag,
As the wheel went round he made his grab.

Here, the couples stood arm-in-arm in a circle. One child, the miller, was outside. On the word, 'grab', the inner ring moved forward one place to take the arm of the next person standing in the outer ring. It was up to the miller to intervene at this point and capture an arm for himself or herself. Other chants accompanied less formal but still elaborate sessions of ball-bouncing or skipping. 'Green gravel' and 'The good ship sails' are still remembered, as is 'Pork pie':

Pork pie, mutton chops,
Tell me when the apple drops.
When they do, pick 'em up –
Out comes Johnny.
Oh, me Johnny, me bonny, bonny Johnny.

Of all the boys what I love,
I love Johnny.

Others had no actions, but were sung purely for enjoyment. They were thought to be daringly *risqué*, and derived considerable pleasure from avoiding a rude word while making it absolutely clear. One was an endless song, to the tune of 'Yankee Doodle':

Our [pronounced aar'] soldiers went to war,
Our soldiers fighting;
Our soldiers shot a bullet
Right up Hitler's – Our soldiers went to war . . .

and so on. Another was the mock-heroic story of 'The finest little Scotsman that Scotland ever knew'. The first verse were repeated after every other, as a chorus:

Aye dingle dangle a dingle dangle do,
The finest little Scotsman that Scotland ever knew.

When he was six he did a funny trick,
He slid down the banisters and landed on his – Aye dingle, etc.

When he was seven he went to Granby Halls,
He fell down the stairs and he landed on his – Aye dingle, etc.

When he was buried he was buried at St Paul's,
It took two thousand elephants to carry away his – Aye dingle, etc.

There was a good deal more in the same vein.

Adults also enjoyed their relaxation in sports and games. Like children, they used any available space. A form of bowls, probably similar to the modern French game, used to be played alongside the south wall of Teigh churchyard. Quoits, which involved throwing rings or horse-shoes at a peg, could be played almost anywhere, though set pitches or beds later developed. The game was already well established in 1467 when an ordinance of Leicester Corporation prescribed imprisonment for anyone playing for silver at 'dyce, cardyng, haserding, tenes [tennis], bowlys, pykking with arowes, coytyng with horsshon, penypryk, foteball ne cheker in the myre'. Some of these pursuits are unfamiliar, and certain explanations put forward by scholars merely compound confusion. 'Haserdyng' (hazarding) was probably a game of chance, played with 'a pool of balls'. 'Pykking' (pitching) arrows meant throwing them by hand at a mark, a forerunner of the game of darts, or possibly blowing them through a hole in a tree trunk at certain numbers, as a sort of lottery. 'Penypryk' (penny-prick) consisted either of throwing oblong pieces of metal at a mark or throwing to dislodge coins from sticks. 'Cheker in the myre' (chequer in the mire) might be an alternative name for nine men's morris; there is a Merel's Stone at Wyfordby, that is, a stone with holes drilled for the same game.

The Leicester ordinance of 1467 also prohibited all sorts of other things, including depositing rubbish in the streets, letting ducks wander, making 'ryottes and unlawful assembles' and setting up 'brodelles' (brothels). It cannot have been very effective, at least with regard to games, for a further measure was taken in 1488 to prohibit 'dyce, cardes, bowles, half bowle, hassardynge, tennys, pryckyng with arrowes, coytyng with horsshone, pennypryk, foteball, classhe, coyles [both forms of ninepins], checker in the myer, or shovegrote'.

Quoits remained popular until recent times. It may still not quite be dead in Rutland, where I have seen it myself. A club was formed at Oakham in 1852. Beds are remembered at several villages, including Ashwell, Ayston (in front of the rectory), Braunston (at the Plough), Edith Weston (in Tommy's Field), Greetham (behind the Crown and Anchor), and Preston. At Ketton the game was so popular that there were several beds. Mr A. Knox from the village was three times champion of England between 1928 and 1931.

Other ancient sports were a good deal more violent and bloodthirsty. Baiting animals was popular for a very long time. The beast involved was chained to a stake and mastiffs were unleashed to attack it, with bets taken on the outcome. As early as 1363 a Leicester butcher called Lambert was bound over for disregarding a law which forbade the sale of bull's flesh unless the animal had previously been baited, and the same ordinance was re-enacted in 1467. Lord George Grey, Dean of Newarke College, complained to the Bishop of Lincoln in 1525 that Sir Richard Sacheverell and his wife, the former Lady Hungerford, had permitted bear-baiting in his establishment, and had allowed their dogs, hawks and hounds to foul the church.

King John is said to have been greatly pleased with a bear-baiting which he saw on the green at Ashby-de-la-Zouch. At Leicester bears were regularly baited at a spot just outside the east gate, which became known as Bear Hill. (It was later called Coal Hill, then the Haymarket. The present Clock Tower stands more or less on the site). Bull-baiting also went on at Bear-Hill. Bear- and bull-baiting also took place at Uppingham, where heavy carts were drawn up round the market square to make a suitable enclosure. Shepshed had its bull-ring. The Bowling Green Inn at Hinckley and also the nearby Harrow Farm were used for bull-baiting. In his poem, *The Battle of Agincourt* (1627), Michael Drayton speaks of Leicestershire men marching under a banner showing 'A bull and mastive fighting for the game' and adds the note: 'A sport more used in that shiere from ancient time than in any other'.

Bull-baiting was made illegal in 1835, and cock-fighting fourteen year later. The latter, we are told, continued to be practised in 'secret cellars and mysterious yards'. It consisted either of a series of fights between specially trained cocks or a knock-out competition, with a single champion bird being left alive at the end. All fights were to the death, and a cock which showed cowardice would immediately have its neck wrung. Some of the terms used, such as 'coming up to scratch', 'bantam-weight' and 'feather-weight', were later used in boxing.

The sport, for such it was called, was originally the preserve of the gentry. On several occasions in Elizabethan times the Leicester records show details of expenditure on refreshments for those attending fights. In 1595, for example, the sum of 21 shillings and four pence was spent on sugared wine, cherries, cakes and bread for 'the Gentlemen att the Cockinge, and at the Cockepitt'. At that time the cockpit, as can be seen from Speed's map of 1610, was a small, six-sided building with a domed roof. It stood east of the present Granby Street, between Halford and Rutland Streets.

Newspapers frequently carried advertisements for cock-fights. The *Stamford Mercury* mentioned an event at the appropriately named Fighting Cocks Inn at Oakham in 1737 and another at the George two years

The Saracen's Head Inn at Leicester
(Photograph by courtesy of *Leicester Mercury*

Eighteenth century admission card for Leicester Cockpit, from Kelly's *Notices*

later: 'A main of cocks to be fought between the gentlemen of Oakham and the gentlemen of Exton . . . To show 15 cocks on a side and to fight for 2 guineas a battle and ten guineas the main'. The same paper announced in 1740 a main at John Stanger's House (now called Long Barn Farm), Ketton, and there was another at the Falcon, Uppingham, three years later. In 1768 the *Leicester and Nottingham Journal* published this notice:

> To all Gentlemen Cockers, that there will be a *Main of Cocks* Fought at the House of Mr. JOHN NEAL, at *Hathern Turn*, on the 28th and 29th of June 1768; between the Gentlemen of *Leicestershire*, and the Gentlemen of *Nottinghamshire*, to Shew and Weigh 21 Cocks for the Main and to Fight for Two Guineas a Battle, and Ten the odd Battle, and Ten Byes or One Guinea a Battle.

In 1774 the 'annual cocking' took place at the Saracen's Head (which still exists at Leicester) between 'the gentlemen of the town and the gentlemen of the county'. Another 'regular main' was held at the Uppingham Falcon in 1781 between the gentlemen of Rutland and the gentlemen of Northamptonshire, though of course the wretched cocks did the fighting.

Side bets could be anything from fifty to five hundred guineas, and there was passionately keen interest. William Gardiner wrote that in the late eighteenth century 'the grand amusement among the gentry was cockfighting', and added: 'The mains were advertised in every paper, and were as common as cricket matches at the time. Sometimes, one hundred cocks were slaughtered in a day. The theatre of this amusement, called the cock-pit, stood where now stand the Assembly Rooms [which were opened in 1750]. Even men of rank and fashion joined in this cruel sport, and, like our Saxon ancestors, hunted all day and drank all night'. Daniel

Lambert, like many other people of humbler status, was also a keen follower of cockfighting. Even the clergy joined in, and there is a story of a parson at Ashby called Jones who in the 1830s, would have a cloth laid on the drawing-room carpet on Sundays between services to exercise a couple of cocks, to 'give them wind'. On checking, I find that there was no such parson at Ashby at the time, but the substance of the story may well be true.

The old cockpit at Melton was behind Anne of Cleves' House in Burton Street, near to the Play Close wall. It literally was a pit, surrounded by tiered banking for spectators, and it remained in existence until the 1930s, when it was filled in. The most popular time for cockfighting at Melton was during Croxton Park Race Week, early in April, or at the end of the hunting season. So many people were attracted that a new pit, this time above ground, was built to replace the old at a cost of £800 in 1825. 'The New Pit', accommodating 500 spectators, stood in Goodricke Street. It was one of the last big pits to be built before the outlawing of cockfighting, and was often mentioned in newspaper announcements as in the *Stamford Mercury*, in 1826: 'A grand Main of Cocks betwen Lord Kennedy and Captain Ross for £1,000 and £50 a battle, to be fought in the New Pit'.

Contests were held in the yards of stables and taverns. Even natural hollows in fields were used, as at Knossington, just behind the rectory. Cockpit Field can still be found at Morcott, though not cock-fighting. Gardiner says that 'the lower orders' went in for 'all sorts of sports, as cock-throwing, football and singlestick'. In cock-throwing the bird was pelted to death with sticks, while tethered to a peg. Even schoolboys were encouraged to take part, until clay pipes were mercifully substituted for the cocks. These were fixed in the mouth of a wooden head, called Aunt Sally. Whipping the cock, according to Francis Grose's *Dictionary of the Vulgar Tongue* (1811) was:

A piece of sport practised at wakes, horse-races and fairs in Leicestershire: a cock being tied or fastened into a hat or basket, half a dozen carters blindfolded, and armed with ships, are placed round it, who, after being turned thrice about, begin to whip the cock, which if any one strikes so as to make it cry out, it becomes his property; the joke is that instead of whipping the cock they flog each other heartily.

After the suppression of cock-fighting, badgers were sometimes kept for baiting, and it is only within the last few years that this has become illegal. A rat pit at The Ship in Soar Lane existed until after the first world war. An open-topped cage was filled with rats and a dog was put in for one minute. The dead rats were counted and replaced by live ones. Then a second dog was put in. The process was repeated as many times as desired. The winner was the dog which killed the largest number of rats. Rats were taken clandestinely to the pit by women who carried them next

Soar Lane rat pit, from Read's *Modern Leicester*

to the skin under their blouses, through which they could be seen moving about. They relied on the knowledge that a rat kept in the dark and allowed relative freedom of movement will not bite. In the same public house one man used to nail a live rat to the counter and tear it to pieces with his teeth. Another man won bets at Braunston by biting live rats to death within living memory.

Catching rats with ferrets was a country pastime as well as a necessity. At least two things have to be remembered: if a ferret is bitten, pee on the wound to disinfect it; if a ferret will not let go, blow in its face and it will open its jaws. On one occasion a young lad's ferret was bitten. When he was applying the traditional treatment to the wound he got too close. The ferret seized the nearest part of his anatomy, and would not let go. The lad's companions laughed so much that it was some time before they could summon up the breath to blow on the ferret and make it release him.

Horse racing was first recorded at Leicester in 1603, when a gallon of sack with sugar was provided for 'the gentlemen at the horse-running'. A golden snaffle was mentioned as a prize in 1613, and, more conventionally, a gold cup the following year. The event was held annually in September on Abbey Meadow, though the horses were sometimes obliged to run up to their knee in flood-water from the Soar. In 1740 the course was moved to St Mary's Field, part of the vast South Fields, but this, too, suffered from proximity to the river, and the circuit crossed four turnpike roads. Gardiner tells us that when he was a boy the course went 'not far from the infirmary, round by Knighton windmill, passing the Aylestone toll-gate and Rawdikes, into the meadows below, at what was called the Flat, at the end of which the winning post was situated'. The race attracted a great deal of interest, and sideshows and attractions were provided for spectators, including fireworks and illuminations. Country dancing was available in Vauxhall Gardens on the evenings of the three days of the meeting.

In 1804 South Fields was enclosed. The racecourse moved to 'a large space of elevated ground, just beyond the Marquis of Granby turnpike, on the right hand side of the road to Harborough'. The area is now part of Victoria Park, but was locally known as 'the racecourse' until within living memory. Racing took place there round a mile-long circuit between 1806 and 1883, when the present course at Oadby was opened. Until the days of motor transport racehorses for Oadby were brought by train to Wigston and walked from there.

Loughborough, too, had its annual race meeting, which also had to be moved because of enclosure. At Bradgate Park there was a two-mile track from Rubbing House Gate to Sliding Stone Wood, down Old John's Watering to Hunts Hill Gate, and back again, which was used for exercise, speed trials and private wagers. Oakham had its races, as did Uppingham, both starting in 1737. The course at Uppingham was oval in shape and straddled the turnpike road to the south of the present village college. Three of the four gateways of that time are still in existence. The course was later moved to the west of the town. Even a village such as Empingham once had its races, as appears from an advertisement in the *Stamford Mercury* of 11 June, 1724, which pointed out that runners were to be entered at the White Horse:

> On Thursday, the 25th of this Instant June will be run for on Empingham Heath, in the county of Rutland, a Purse of Thirty Pound or upwards, by Galloways 14 Hands or under, Nine Stone the highest, to allow Inch and half-stone. Every Horse, Mare or Gelding belonging to a Contributor to pay Half a Guinea entrance, and such as do not belong to a Contributor to pay Two Guineas Entrance. The winning Horse, etc., to be sold for Forty Guineas.

Burrough Hill, near the village of Burrough-on-the-Hill, was used in the early nineteenth century for horse racing. White's *Directory* of 1846 records that 'these races were established some years ago by the gentlemen of the Melton Hunt and generally excite great interest in the neighbourhood'. The iron-age ramparts provided an ideal vantage point for spectators. The races later moved to Croxton Park, where they went on until the first world war, and Burton Lazars, where they continued at least until the 1930s.

The first man in England to have a pack of foxhounds is said to have been Thomas Boothby (1681–1752) of Tolley Park, near Desford, who was known as Old Tom o' Tooley. By the end of the eighteenth century Leicestershire was by far the most famous foxhunting county, with Melton Mowbray being the centre of the sport and also of the glittering social life which followed it. The season began in November, and up to six hundred horses (called hunters) would be stabled at Melton, and tended by three hundred grooms. The 'lovers of the chase' arrived too, bringing 'their ladies' (not all of them wives) and their French chefs. Mail coaches, and later the railways, conveyed 'every delicacy' to the town. No expense was spared: one nobleman thought nothing of spending £6,000, a fortune in those days, on his session. Largely as a result of hunting the permanent population of the town rose from 2,000 to 15,000 during the nineteenth century.

A huntsman needed twelve horses, which cost £1,000 a year to keep. Hunting was available six days a week, and two hunters a day were required. The huntsman and his second man rode to the meet, not on hunters, but on what were called cantering or covert hacks. These mounts were expected to cover twenty miles in an hour. At the hunt the second horseman, without tiring the second hunter, had to contrive to be in the right place to hand it over to his master when the first tired.

In the early nineteenth century there were four packs in Leicestershire and Rutland: the Duke of Rutland's (or Belvoir), the Earl of Lonsdale's (or Cottesmore), the Atherstone and the Quorn. Later these were supplemented by two more, the Fernie and the Pytchley. Each had its history and traditions, and even artists, such as George Morland, Francis Grant and John Ferneley. Ferneley was the son of the village wheel-wright of Thrussington, near Melton, and came to the attention of the Duke of Rutland though displaying some of his paintings in his father's workshop.

Between them the hunts covered not only Leicestershire and Rutland but also parts of Lincolnshire, Northamptonshire, Warwickshire and Nottinghamshire. Each had its own area, called its country, and the Quorn country was reputed to be the best in the world. It was liberally covered by formidable obstacles, including ox-fences and bull-finch fences. The first variety had a wide ditch, then sturdy blackthorn hedge, then, two yards further on, a strong rail of about four feet high. The second was a quickset hedge of perhaps 50 years' growth, with a ditch on one side or the other. Because of the height horses were unable to jump clear so they were obliged to jump through the hedge, which left no more trace of their passage than of that of a bull-finch.

The sport was very hard on horses, and many had to be destroyed each year because of injury. There was also a toll of casualties among riders, but it was thought very good for the character, always provided that the rider were 'not killed in the training'. Lord Wellington remarked of the Battle of Waterloo that: 'The best officers I had on the field were the Leicestershire fox-hunters'. However, one of the best-known riders in Leicestershire was not a soldier, but a clergyman, Rev. John Empson (1789–1861). He was a Yorkshireman who came to the county in 1814 after a spell at Lincoln. Only nine years later, grieving the recent death of his wife at the age of only 27, he gave up his curacy at Saxby and Stapleford, abandoned his beloved sport, and moved to London where he lived as a recluse. Yet he had made an indelible mark. 'The Flying Parson' or the 'Lincoln Crow', as he was called, was never forgotten. 'Nimrod' (Charles Apperley) said he was 'one of the best men who ever went over Leicestershire', and added: 'I never saw a quicker man over a country'. Even his horses were remembered for generations: the Mare, Grog, Spectre, Traveller, Shaven and Morven, the last of which appears, with his rider, in John Ferneley's picture, 'Hounds going up wind, best pace'. There is a story that after he had fallen while hunting with the Cottesmore his horse trod on his nose and almost severed it. He wrapped it with his handkerchief and went to Mr Orange, the Oakham doctor, who offered either to remove the nose completely, since it was hanging by only a thread of skin, or to stitch it up and hope for a cure. 'Do which you think Mrs Empson would like best', said the parson. The doctor sewed up the nose, and his work proved successful.

Empson wrote poems about hunting, and also prose, including the famous satire, 'Visibles, invisibles, and absentees, on a late celebrated day with the Quorn hounds, in a letter to a friend from one of the visibles'. It was written in February, 1817 (and, incidentally, made passing references to the Luddites), and was published by Guy Paget in 1934, together with a masterly commentary on the allusions to Quorn huntsmen of over a century earlier.

The same book deals with Dick Christian (1779–1862), another semi-legendary figure, though much lower down the social scale than the Flying Parson. He was born at Cottesmore, the son of a farmer, and spent most of his long life working with horses. He was also known for his three marriages, which included one elopement and produced twenty-two children. In his old age, at Melton, he was extensively interviewed by a writer called H. H. Dixon, who used the pen-name of 'The Druid'. Dixon published this remarkable material just as it came from the mouth of Christian, without alteration.

From the age of eight, Dick Christian rode to hounds, and later spent many years with the Quorn Hunt, during the masterships of Hugo Meynell and several of his successors. He was also Whipper-in for the

117

Cottesmore. Up to the age of 62 he was riding, and winning, steeplechases. These were cross-country races, with each rider choosing his own route, to a prominent landmark such as a steeple (hence the name), a windmill or a hill. One such was the race during the 1824–5 season from

Dick Christian

Great Dalby to Tilton between Christian, riding a horse called Clinker, owned by Captain Ross, and George Osbaldeston, riding his own mount, Clasher. The horses were worth a thousand pounds each. The owners had a wager of £1,500 on the outcome, and there was also heavy betting by spectators. After leading all the way, Clinker fell at the last fence, and Clasher won. The five miles across country were covered in sixteen minutes.

Christian was renowned for his courage, and once leapt 31 feet over Billesdon brook. He worked as a groom, and also for many years as a roughrider, responsible for training young horses and curing 'old uns' of bad habits: he is shown schooling a horse in a Ferneley picture. Although he was deeply religious, he had a fiery character, and he also believed in the power of the evil eye and the capacity of witches to turn themselves into hares or black foxes. He was remembered with great affection, which can by no means be said of all huntsmen.

George Osbaldeston (1786–1866), known as 'The Squire', was a friend of Empson's, and appeared in his *Letter*. He was successively master of several hunts, including the Atherstone, the Quorn and the Pytchley. He was a magnificent horseman and a fine shot, and also an excellent cricketer and billiards player. In 1831 he wagered 1,000 guineas that he could ride 200 miles in ten hours, given unlimited changes of horse. On a four-mile circuit at Newmarket Heath he achieved the distance in under nine hours, having travelled at an average speend of 26 miles per hour. He was quarrelsome and fiery tempered. He fought a duel, and horse-whipped a farmer for taking a fence too close to him.

In April, 1837, the Marquis of Waterford and his friends were terrorising Melton. Their pranks included breaking toll gates and painting the White Swan and other buildings with red paint, thus giving rise to the expression 'painting the town red'. Some of the noble gentlemen eventually appeared at Derby Assizes over the affair, but they were found not guilty of riot and fined (for them) the trivial sum of £100 each for assault. Dick Christian summed up the feelings of ordinary people: 'Lord Waterford was a rum un, the Mad Marquis they called him, he painted Melton red; they come here and got two o' my boys to carry their paint pots and brushes for 'em. I did not know what were up, or I'd not have let 'em go. I don't hold with them sort of goings on. It ain't fair to humble folk. They daren't retaliate; and if there's trouble, their position saves 'em, and their humble servants get the stick. A gentleman should ollers remember he is a gentleman and behave as sitch'.

Arrogance of such people as Osbaldeston and Waterford explains why huntsmen were not universally popular. Some farm lads would take cub-foxes and dock their tails, which made them very difficult to catch: a long, heavy brush greatly hampers a fox, especially when he is wet and tired. Mr O. D. Lucas remembers an elderly farmer and his three daughters at Highgate Farm, Wigston, who once refused the hunt access to their land, and barred the way with pitchforks. They were evicted at the next rent day.

The hunts continue to flourish, and they undoubtedly have colour, excitement and glamour, but there is an increasingly bitter debate between those who uphold the (relatively old) traditions and those who

Painting Melton Mowbray red

question whether the killing of any animal for sport should be permitted. At least in fox-hunting the humans involved risk their own necks, which was not the case in bull-baiting and cock-fighting. Many other sports consist entirely of one set of people pitting their skill and strength against others.

Even one of these, boxing, has its critics. Its earlier form was bare-knuckle pugilism, in which certain wrestling holds were also permitted. A round ended only with a knock-down, and a fight only when one of the combatants was incapable of coming up to the mark or scratch for the next round. Major contests drew great crowds, such as the 15,000 who assembled at Thistleton Gap in 1811. The precise spot, called No Man's Land, is in the parish of Wymondham where the counties of Rutland, Lincolnshire and Leicestershire meet. A similar place at the opposite end of Leicestershire is called No Man's Heath. Such sites were chosen so that in the event of trouble with the law the whole proceedings could move from one county to the next, thus leaving the jurisdiction of one set of constables and magistrates. Crowd violence often erupted, and in the end this led to the outlawing of prize-fighting.

Nothing untoward spoilt the fight at Thistleton Gap, at which Tom Cribb, the English champion, beat Tom Molyneux, the American challenger who claimed to be heavyweight champion of the world. Dick Christian was there: 'They fought on a stage. I was on horseback – not ten yards off them; I was crowded in, and I drawed my legs up and stood a top of the saddle all the time they were fighting. I thought at first go-off Molyneux would have killed him; he was a regular rusher. Cribb, he kept drawing away, and fought him all round the stage; he wanted to blow him. . . . In the third and forth round, Cribb had the best of it. I could hear the blows as plain as a drum; he did punish him then. They only fought eight rounds'.

In addition to being spread by word of mouth, news of the event was circulated in the form of printed ballads selling at a penny a copy:

You boxers all both far and near I pray you give attention.
For Crib he is the finest man of any we can mention;
A noted black from America call'd Molyneux by name, sir,
He thought to beat our champion, Cribb, and bear away the fame, sir.

September was the appointed time, and twenty-eight the day, sir,
When these two noble champions bold were to decide the fray, sir;
A stage was then erected at a place call'd No Man's land, sir,
When thousands both of horse & foot around the same did stand, sir.

At twelve o'clock & something more they mounted on the stage, sir,
They boldly stripp'd, each faced his man, and eager to engage, sir.
The bets ran three to one on Cribb before they struck a blow, sir,
But which was then to win the day perhaps they did not know, sir.

Hats off they cried all round the stage that they might all have sight,
Attentive ears with eager eyes were plac'd upon the fight;
After a minute's sparring then the black put in a blow, sir, sir,
Cribb played right and left again, Molyneux fell down I know, sir.

When both of them got up again the second round took place, sir,
A dreadful hit the black put in right upon Cribb's face, sir;
But quickly he returned it with force on the black's ribs, sir,
Likewise another left hand hit was put in by bold Cribb, sir.

With equal skill and courage bold they fought the next two rounds, sir,
The fifth the black advantage gain'd and threw Cribb on the ground,
                                                                    sir;
The odds of seven to four were laid on Molyneux by name, sir,
That he should beat our champion, Cribb, and bear away the fame, sir.

But anon Cribb did recover strength and boldly face his foe, sir,
And by a well directed hit he fractur'd the black's jaw, sir.
A serious rally then commenc'd and Molyneux was beat, sir,
Then three to one again on Cribb that he'll the black defeat, sir.

Then twenty minutes being expir'd the battle it was over,
Cribb danc'd a reel upon the ground when he did it discover;
Hard blows on both sides were receiv'd, I thought no favour shown, sir,
Now for the say which won the day, Cribb is the lad, I own, sir.

Cribb v. Molyneux at Thistleton Gap in 1811

The night before the fight Cribb stayed at the Black Bull Inn at North Witham in Lincolnshire, and Molyneux at the New Inn (now called the Greetham Inn), south of Stretton on the Great North Road. At the Ram Jam Inn, Stretton, which lies between the other two, there is still a Tom Cribb rooom, and the fight is depicted on a stone panel over the main door. Another sporting association at the same inn is with Lord Lonsdale, who finished a hundred-mile walk from London there in 1878.

Wrestling, too, was once a popular sport. An annual contest was held on Cross Bank at Kibworth. John Leland, who travelled through England between 1534 and 1542, described the games at Burrough Hill: 'To these Borowe Hills every yere on Monday after Whitsunday cum people of the country thereabout, and shote, renne [run], wrastel and dawnce, and use other feates of exercise'. Similar contests were held at the High Cross, where Watling Street crosses the Fosse Way, between the youth of Leicestershire and Warwickshire, but these fell into disuse about the middle of the eighteenth century. Athletic competitions of all kinds nevertheless remain popular now, as does the ancient game of cricket.

Originally cricket was a village game. Many of the local Feasts in Rutland included it. At Ridlington the players were given musical accompaniment on to the pitch by Adam and Eve Smith for their first match in which their traditional opponents were from the village of Wing. At Market Bosworth both cricket and football were played on 'the football piece', which was also the meeting place for settling local disputes.

At Melton Mowbray the cricket season went on until October each year. Contests were often less than sporting, partly because of the large sums of money – in one case £1,000 – wagered on games. One somewhat plaintive notice was inserted in the *Leicester Journal*: 'The gentlemen of Melton Mowbray are ready and have been ever since their first game, to meet the gentlemen of Cossington upon the new cricket ground in the town, to play the return match upon fair and honourable terms, but with this provision that the latter should abide with the decision of the Umpire without cavil; either for the same stake or double'. Melton Mowbray went on to field a side of twenty-two players against an All-England XII, in 1855 and in 1857. Having lost on both occasions, despite the advantage of numbers,

The Black Bull at Witham

The Ram Jam Inn at Stretton

they took the precaution of fielding W. G. Grace at a similar fixture in 1872, and won by 92 runs.

As might be expected, Leicester also had a side. The 'Gentlemen Cricket Players of the Society of Leicester' played against teams from Coventry and Nottingham. In 1789 a match with the latter was interrupted by a disagreement as to whether the visitors could be compelled to 'follow their innings' (follow on). The game was resumed several weeks later, and in a close finish Leicester won by a single run.

The enclosure of South Fields and the encroachment of building elsewhere caused severe problems for Leicester sportsmen. Some public spirited people clubbed together in 1825 and bought at the rather unlikely place of Wharf Street an eleven-acre site of which they made 'an excellent inclosed Cricket Ground and Bowling Green'. There was also provision for quoits. The ground remained in use for 35 years. Many games were played there, such as the one mentioned in Benjamin Chamberlain's diary for 14 July, 1831: 'To the Cricket Ground to see the match between Cossington and Leicester players – the former winning easy'.

Burley Park, at Burley-on-the-Hill, near Oakham, is now famous for its annual week of horse-trials. Up to the first world war the ground was used by the village cricket team. It was originally laid out by the Earl of

Winchilsea in the late eighteenth century. George Finch, 9th Earl of Winchilsea, was educated at Eton and Oxford. He had a keen interest in cricket, though he was also proficient at real tennis and billiards. He was a very strong man and used a bat weighting over four pounds, which compares with the two or three pounds normal today. He was the prime mover in founding the M.C.C. in 1787 and he played for the club for the next thirteen years. He also turned out for Hambledon, Hampshire, Middlesex, Surrey and England. It was in 1790 when he played for England against Hampshire at Burley. His last match was played in 1816 when he was 64, ten years before his death.

In Winchilsea's time there was no county championship as we know it, but there were county sides, which played against each other and against All England. Leicestershire began regular fixtures with Nottinghamshire in 1845, and with Derbyshire five years later. They played England at Wharf Street on several occasions, and in 1856 and 1860 were the winners. In the latter year their ground was sold for re-development, and for the next eighteen years matches were played on any ground available, including the racecourse (now Victoria Park). In 1878 the club acquired a ground at Grace Road, and entertained the Australians there the same year. They were the first county to meet a touring side. Ten years later they achieved the remarkable a feat of beating the Australians, but had to wait until 1894 to be given first-class status. There was another move of ground in 1901, to Aylestone Road, with a definitive return to Grace Road in 1946.

Under the banner of the running fox, many triumphs have been seen here since then, but perhaps the heart of cricket is still on the village green. There is a story from Burbage which illustrates the point. Some years ago the outstanding bowler in the local team was Mr Wilfred Hall, landlord of the Cross Keys. He boasted that in a set time he could bowl out a certain very good batsman. A wager was laid and a date fixed for the contest. The batsman went secretly to the carpenter and ordered a bat of vast proportions which would completely cover the wicket. Somehow or other the news reached the bowler, who quietly ordered a set of outsize stumps from the same discreet carpenter. When the day arrived, both bat and stumps were produced. The bowler was successful, and won the wager. The unusual equipment was displayed for many years afterwards at the Cross Keys.

The game of football originally had very few rules. It was played almost anywhere, including in the streets, where it was regarded as a considerable nuisance. It was forbidden by order of the corporation at Leicester in 1467 and again in 1488. Over a century later, in 1592, people playing at Oadby were referred to as 'abandoned persons'. For hundreds of years there was an annual game for all comers at the Newarke, but this was outlawed from 1847, along with the Whipping Toms (see page 223).

Later, the rugby and soccer codes separated, and the game was taken off the streets. Three rugby clubs combined in 1880 to form Leicester Football Club, which eight years later adopted the colours of green scarlet and white, and acquired the nickname of 'the Tigers'. In 1891 the club began its lease of the ground at Welford Road which is now one of the best-known in the whole country. The Boxing Day fixture with the Barbarians, now an accepted part of Leicester's Christmas, began in 1909 Another Tigers' tradition is the adherence to lettered instead of numbered jerseys for the players.

Soccer as a spectator sport followed hard on the heels of rugby. The Leicester Fosse Club was established in 1884 by old boys of Wyggeston School. All the players were amateur. The first professional, Harry Webb was signed from Stafford Rangers in 1889 at a salary of 2s. 6d. a week Wages and standards rose rapidly, and the club won a place in the First Division in 1908, since when it has enjoyed mixed fortunes. In 1919 it was re-named Leicester City. According to the present general secretary, Mr

Filling the sacks with hare pie, c. 1900, from *Sir Benjamin Stone's Pictures*

A. K. Bennett, 'Football is full of superstititions, including players wanting to be in a certain place as they go on the field, goalkeepers wanting a touch of the ball before kick-off, players wearing lucky charms, and mascots being carried on the coach'.

An example of the early form of free-for-all football can still be seen on Easter Monday at Hallaton, in the shape of the famous bottle-kicking and hare-pie scramble. Hares had ancient associations with Easter, and were traditionally held to be the favourite animal of the goddess, Eastre, who in turn represented the coming of spring and the renewal of fertility in men, beasts and crops. There was once a hare-hunting ceremony at Leicester (page 219), but at Hallaton the hares were in the form of pies, or should have been, but since they were out of season for eating, mutton, veal or bacon were substituted.

The custom, probably dating from medieval times, arose when a piece of land, originally called 'Hare-crop-leys' (though another field was substituted after the enclosure of 1771), was bequeathed to the rector on condition that he and his successors provided 'two hare pies, a quantity of ale, and two dozen penny loaves, to be scrambled for on each succeeding Easter Monday, at the rising ground, called *Hare Pie Bank*', about a quarter of a mile to the south of the village. There was no mention of bottle-kicking. In about 1790 the rector, Rev. T. C. Berricke, wanted to apply the funds to 'a better use', but was dissuaded by a slogan chalked on his doors and walls and on the church: 'No pie, no parson, and a job for the glazier'. A change was again discussed at parish meetings in 1878, but opinion was unfavourable.

The day began with a procession to the church of two benefit societies, one from the Fox and one from the Royal Oak, each led by a band. After hearing the 'club sermon' they went back to the inns for lunch. A deputation called at the rectory at 3 p.m. for the pies, bread and beer, which were taken to the Fox. A procession then set off for Hare Pie Bank, led by two men walking abreast, each carrying a sack with a cut-up pie inside. Then came three men abreast, each holding a bottle aloft. Two of these were the usual kind of small wooden keg used for taking workers' beer to the fields, the third was a dummy. Next, when it could be found, came a hare, mounted on a pole in sitting posture. Then, 'a band of music', followed by a man with the penny loaves in a basket. As he went along the loaves were broken and thrown to the crowds. At Hare Pie Bank the pies, too, were pitched out and scrambled for.

After this the first bottle of beer was thrown into a circular hole in the centre of the bank, and the real struggle began, between the Hallatonians and the men of neighbouring village of Medbourne. The object was to kick, propel, carry or manhandle the bottle over one of the boundaries. The successful party drank the beer. The second bottle dropped was the

A recent photograph of the bottle-kicking procession
(By permission of *Leicester Mercury*)

dummy, and its possession, even without beer, was contested fiercely:
'thereupon ensues a lively scene of disorder, which not infrequently ends
in a free fight'. After the third struggle the last bottle was taken to the
Market Cross and the contents shared between both sides, the winning
captain traditionally taking the first drink. Afterwards the empty bottles
were retrieved for use another year.

The ceremony remains substantially the same today, though the church
service is at 11.15 a.m. and the procession starts from the Fox at 2.15 p.m.
Since 1982 the penny loaves have been dispensed with, but the meat pies
are still provided. The Melbourne men are now reinforced by any
non-Hallatonian who wishes to risk limb if not life, but the contest is as
vigorous as ever. The tenaciously-held custom is unique to Hallaton
though it has affinites with the hood game at Haxey in Lincolnshire.

Some people favoured milder forms of recreation. William Hutton is
the author of a history of Birmingham and also a book on the Battle of
Bosworth. In 1750 when attempting to cross Charnwood Forest he
became completely lost: 'I was among hills, rocks and precipices, and so
bewildered I could not retreat'. Eventually he found shelter for the night

in 'a dismal abode', and escaped the next morning. Charnwood was not tamed until its enclosure in 1829, but long before this its more accessible places were much visited.

William Gardiner called it 'the Tyrol of Leicestershire', and singled out Bradgate, Breedon and Woodhouse for special praise. He wrote that in summer 'the romantic domain of Bradgate Park . . . is constantly visited by parties who "Spend the livelong day" in rural felicity; every one bringing his picnic basket well stored'. And again: 'Every vehicle and char-a-banc is loaded with youthful fair ones, and attentive beaux; not forgetting the well-stored baskets for the day's repast'. Later visitors were not always so peaceable, and the park was closed for six days a week in 1864 because of hooliganism.

James Bodell, a former soldier who had settled in New Zealand, returned to Leicester on a visit in 1883. 'On Bank Holiday', he wrote, 'I took 28 members of my Family including my Parents, accompanied by a Photographer to Bradgate Park. This is the ancient spot where Lady Jane Grey was born, to have a Photo taken of all in one Group'. He later reflected: 'What with attending Bicycling Racing for the Championship of England, Tea Parties, Theatres, Visits to Bradgate Park, Mountsorrel, Quorn, Cropston, Loughborough and other Places and not forgetting Leicester Races, I had enjoyed my time very much'. Since the 1920s Bradgate has been the property of the City of Leicester, and is more visited than ever.

The first ever excursion by train was organised in 1841, a day trip from Leicester to Loughborough and back. The name of the man responsible, Thomas Cook, is now known all over the world. A poster of his advertised another outing in 1850, this time to Ashby-de-la-Zouch. It included not only visits to Ivanhoe Baths, the Royal Hotel, the castle and Coleorton Hall, but 'a variety of Popular Amusements, including Cricket, Archery, Skittles, Quoits, & c., with one or more Quadrille Bands'. The return fares from Leicester were 2s. in covered carriages or 3s. 6d. for the first class seats. By the 1860s many employers were providing annual outings with, as the *Leicester Guardian* put it, 'master and man uniting once a year and going forth from the turmoils of business to enjoy the pure air of heaven'.

Victorian moralists were not keen on certain of the activities under the pure air of heaven, and in particular on 'disgraceful scenes on the river on the sabbath day'. The reference is to the practice of naked bathing, which men and boys indulged in by the North Bridge over the Soar and by Abbey Pastures until at least the 1870s. Pictorial evidence is available, in the shape of a sketch by John Flower. The scene shown is anything but disgraceful, and any ladies wishing to be embarrassed would have had to go a considerable distance out of their way to be so. However, public baths were later opened, in the appropriately-named Bath Lane, in 1879.

The Soar was used for skating in times of very hard frost, much as during the winter of 1793, when a pantomime was given on the ice opposite the Bath Gardens:

Harlequin and Columbine were represented by the fleetest skaiters. They were followed by Pantaloon and Justice Guttle. There had just been established a set of noisy watchmen in the town, with their great coats, rattles and lanthorns. These gentry formed part of the *dramatis personae*. Besides these there were sailors, milkmaids, gipsies and ballad singers who sang and sold droll songs, written for the occasion. Nuns and friars were not forgotten. The devil pursuing a baker caused much laughter, as his satanic majesty with his long tail rushed through the crowd. The characters were in masks and grotesquely dressed, and the harlequinade mightily pleased the spectators on the banks, who loudly applauded the scene.

In 1947 when the winter was perhaps once more as hard, games and skating went on day after day on Groby Pool and other stretches of water. Empingham Reservoir, now called Rutland Water, did not exist at that time, having been opened in 1976, but it is now the largest man-made lake in Britain. As well as supplying water it also provides amenity. In 1983 33,000 fishing permits were issued there, 7,500 people visited the nature reserves and 3,700 used the sailing centre, as new patterns of leisure began to emerge.

8. Fairs and markets

For ordinary people a fair was one of the highlights of the year. Statutes, known as 'statties', were for hiring workers. Wakes or feasts celebrated, originally on the day its patron saint, the founding of a church. Fairs proper provided opportunities for buying and selling. All were in addition social occasions, and had various sideshows and entertainments. Eventually the element of amusement became predominant, and it survives in the pleasure fairs of today. Markets, another ancient institution, are still with us.

Contracts for farm workers, men and women, indoor and out, were once on an annual basis. At the end of a year a servant could agree terms and remain for another year or seek employment elsewhere by going to a hiring fair. These were widely held, even in tiny villages such as Tixover (in Figsgreen Field) and in larger places like Kibworth (on Cross Bank). Leicester itself itself does not seem to have had one; instead there was a sort of primitive labour exchange at Coal Hill where men could wait almost any day to be hired. As at the statutes they would wear some emblem of their calling. A waggoner would sport a piece of whipcord in this buttonhole, a cowman, a wisp of hay, and a shepherd a tuft of wool. Indoor maids had a few strands from a mop.

Except for Leicester each place had its own set time for hiring, usually in the autumn during the lull after harvest. September was the month for Ashby, Hinckley and Melton. November was favoured by Ketton, Oakham and Loughborough.

The worker would be approached by potential employers and would discuss wages and conditions with them. If a bargain were struck the man or woman would receive a small advance of wages, usually a shilling, which was known as 'earnest money'. At Ketton, where hiring took place in front of the Midland Hotel, it was called 'hence money'. It could be spent there on gingerbread, coconuts, trinkets, ornaments, dancing to the fiddle of one Blind Billy, or simply on drink. Other places provided similar offerings, and the hiring fair was also an important time for meeting friends, who were also attending, in search of employment.

If a worker failed to find a place at one hiring he could go to another, and he was not confined to his own county. People in the east of Rutland often went to Stamford; those in south-west Leicestershire could choose

GRAND PIC-NIC DAY
AT ASHBY-DE-LA-ZOUCH.

MONDAY NEXT, JUNE 3, 1850,

A SPECIAL TRAIN

WILL LEAVE LEICESTER,

At 9 a.m.; RETURNING from ASHBY at 7-30. Passengers may be taken up and set down at
DESFORD and BAGWORTH.

FARES THERE AND BACK: FIRST CLASS, 3s. 6d.; COVERED CARRIAGES, 2s.

This being the first Pleasure Trip to Ashby since the opening of the Railway, the inhabitants are preparing to give the visitors a hearty welcome, and a Committee, consisting of some of the principal gentlemen of the town, is formed for the purpose of arranging and superintending the festive proceedings. It is expected that business will be generally suspended and the day devoted to mutual pleasureable intercourse.
Every facility will be given for viewing the various places and objects of interest in the town and its immediate locality.

THE
Ivanhoe Baths & Royal Hotel

With the extensive range of Pleasure Grounds adjoining, will be thrown open to the Visitors.

THE CASTLE AND PLEASURE GROUNDS

Surrounding, will also be opened for a free inspection and promenade. The arrangements will provide for a variety of

POPULAR AMUSEMENTS,

Including CRICKET, ARCHERY, SKITTLES, QUOITS, &c., and one or more

QUADRILLE BANDS

Will be engaged for the accommodation of DANCING PARTIES on the Grounds of the Baths and Castle.

TWO POWERFUL BRASS BANDS

Are also engaged, one of which, provided by Mr. H. NICHOLSON, of Leicester,—principal Cornet-à-Piston, Mr. J. SMITH,—will accompany the Train, and will perform at the Baths. The MELBOURN BAND is engaged by Mr. MILLS, of the Queen's Hotel, and will perform at the Castle.

THE BATHS will be at the service of those who choose to bathe at the reduced charge of 6d. to the warm fresh water bath, and the salt water baths at very reduced rates.

By the kindness and courtesy of SIR GEORGE BEAUMONT, Bart.,

THE GARDENS AND GROUNDS OF COLEORTON HALL,

Distant about two miles from Ashby, will be opened for the gratification of visitors by the Special Train, on shewing their Tickets; and the Hotel and Coach Proprietors of Ashby have liberally arranged for Omnibuses and other conveyances to ply to and fro at intervals during the day, by which parties will be conveyed at the nominal charge of 6d. each. The Winter and Italian Gardens are celebrated for their beauty and taste. Wordsworth, the late Poet Laureate, thus wrote in his dedication of "The Anniversary" for 1849, to the late Sir George Beaumont:—

" Several of my best poems were composed under the shade of your own groves—upon the classic ground of Coleorton—where I was animated by the recollection of those illustrious poets of your name and family, who were born in that neighbourhood: and we may be assured, did not wander with indifference by the dashing stream of Grace-dieu, and among the rocks that diversify the forest of Charnwood. Nor is there any one to whom such parts of this collection as have been inspired or coloured by the beautiful country from which I now address you, could be presented with more propriety than to yourself, who have composed so many admirable pictures from the suggestions of the same scenery"

Visitors will be conducted through the Gardens by Mr. Henderson, the head gardener, and it is confidently hoped that the great liberality of the noble proprietor will not in the slightest degree be abused by any act of damage or indecorum. Visitors are especially requested not to pluck flowers or handle the statues, &c.

THE PRINCIPAL HOTEL PROPRIETORS, vieing with the other respectable inhabitants in their desires to contribute to the comfort and pleasure of the visitors, have agreed to provide REFRESHMENTS on the following liberal terms:—COLD COLLATIONS, to be available from 12 :ill 2 o'clock, 1s. each person, (drinks excepted); TEA, from 5 to 7 o'clock, 1s. each. Mr. Bearington, of the Royal Hotel, will furnish tables in the Bath Rooms, and has engaged the Splendid Tea Apparatus of the Leicester Temperance Society, which will be fitted up under the collonade of the Ivanhoe Baths; Mr. Mills, of the Queen's Hotel, will fit up a booth for Tea and other Refreshments, on the castle grounds; and Mr. Usherwood, of the Saracen's Head, and Mr. Sutton, of the Lamb Hotel, will also erect booths on their respective grounds for the accommodation of visitors.
The feelings, views, and predjudices of all classes will be properly consulted, and it is the earnest desire of the Committee that all may blend in harmonious efforts to facilitate the pleasure of the whole.

TICKETS for the Special Train may be had at the Desford and Bagworth Stations, and of the Manager of the Trip,

T. COOK, 28, Granby-street, Leicester.

N. B.—As a matter of convenience to the Railway Company, it is earnestly requested that parties will secure their Tickets by Saturday night

T. COOK, PRINTER, 28, GRANBY-STREET, LEICESTER.

to attend the statutes at Polesworth, just over the Warwickshire border. This was 'probably the largest meeting of the kind in England', wrote William Marshall in 1784, adding: 'Servants come (particularly out of Leicestershire) five and twenty or thirty miles to it, on foot. The number of servants collected together in the "statute yard" has been estimated at two to three thousand'. Like other observers Marshall was concerned about what was regarded as turbulent or immoral behaviour:

> Formerly, it seems, much rioting and disturbance used generally to take place at this meeting; arising principally from gaming tables which were then allowed, and for want of civil officers to keep the peace. The principal nuisance, at present, arises from a parcel of balladsingers, disseminating sentiments of dissipation in minds which ought to be trained to industry and frugality.

Rev. Macaulay, writing seven years later, remarked that 'the practice of hiring servants at public statutes which prevails universally in Leicestershire is by many people strongly condemned in a moral point of view'. Another commentator, William Pitt, was equally concerned in 1809: 'Servants are mostly hired from Michaelmas to Michaelmas at public statutes, of which many are held in the county. ... I happened to be present at two of them by chance, the one at Melton, the other at some village in the vale of Belvoir; in the evening they turn into a kind of holiday romp, and have, I think, a tendency to dissipation'. These dark hints refer to the sexual promiscuity which was alleged to be a feature of all kinds of fairs. In fact there was usually a minor bulge in the number of births nine months afterwards.

As new methods of hiring came in, as the weekly payment of wages began to be preferred, as the numbers working on the land decreased, as the social climate changed, so did the hiring fair decline. Moral crusading may also have played a part. At Melton Statutes in 1842, 'the number of gingerbread stalls was very great, there were a large number of other shows there, a Victorian theatre, Batty's menagerie, and a host of minor ones', but 'all scantily attended'. At Oakham the 1857 hiring 'was pretty brisk and wages were slightly advanced on last year'. A dance was held in the evening and 'several disturbances commenced, but this was put a stop to by the police'. Thus the *Stamford Mercury*, which reported in 1865: 'The custom of hiring fairs seems to be dying out, although there was a fair attendance of servants. Holiday making seemed to be the principal attraction, very little hiring being done'. In 1871 there was a further comment that 'the statute of the hiring of servants at Oakham seems to be gradually passing away, very little hiring being done now on these occasions'.

Tixover's hirings had gone by the early nineteenth century. Kibworth's last was held in 1848, Ketton's in 1901. None survived the first world war.

Loughborough November Fair, c.1894
(By permission of Leicestershire Libraries)

Now there is only the occasional piece of family history such as the knowledge by Mr Lewis Eggington of Ibstock that his father was hired at Ashby Statutes in 1870 at the age of nine by a farmer from Congerstone. Where statutes still exist, as at Loughborough, they are now simply pleasure fairs.

Every parish once had an annual festival based on the feast-day of its patron saint. The preceding night was spent in hymn-singing and prayer in the church, after which more secular celebrations began. Later, this was generally modified into a church service on the Sunday immediately following the saint's day, with secular celebrations beginning on the Monday. At Hinckley, exceptionally, the wake was held on the Sunday after the fair. Macaulay, speaking of the area round Claybrooke, summed up the general practice: 'the cousins assemble from all quarters, fill the church on Sunday, and celebrate the Monday with feasting, with music, and with dancing'.

Writing at roughly the same time, the late eighteenth century, William Gardiner observed that every village had its wake, and on wake Sunday every artisan 'that had a voice and could lend a hand with hautboy, bassoon or flute, repaired to the singing-loft in the church, to swell with heart and voice the psalm or anthem'. At Ratby, he tells us, the wake was attended every year by a family from Derbyshire called Smedley. 'They were the last of the minstrels in this part of the country', and when they joined the choir they produced 'a grand *crash* that never failed to fill the church'.

Itinerant musicians also played at the secular part of the wakes. Gardiner mentions a nailer called Anthony Greatorex who played the hurdy-gurdy (not a barrel organ, but a genuine instrument) to accompany the dancing of his daughter. Another great favourite, Absalom Smith, the elected king of the gypsies, went to all 'local fairs, statutes and village wakes, where, in addition to the ordinary gypsy specialities he exercised the vocation of a fiddler, in which he greatly excelled, and late and merry was the dance when Absalom was in good form'. He was taken ill in February, 1826, during Twyford Wake, while playing at the Saddle Inn, and he died his camp soon afterwards, at the age of 60. He left a wife and thirteen children, to each of whom he bequeathed £100, and also 104 grandchildren. He was buried in Twyford churchyard without a headstone; instead a six-foot high oak palisade was raised round the grave.

By the 1830s Gardiner had come to the view that there was no longer 'leisure for music; and, in place of the viol and the flute at the wake, you have nothing but noise and vulgarity, attended with swearing and

A Stilton Cheese Fair in the Market Place, Melton Mowbray

drunkenness'. Be that as it may, some feasts in Leicestershire and many in Rutland continued to flourish for up to a hundred years more. In 1846 a list drawn up at Stamford for the benefit of itinerant tradesmen included 44 in Rutland and 4 in Leicestershire. These are:

Whit Sunday – Brook, Normanton, Sibson.
Trinity Sunday – Barrow, Teigh, Twyford.
Sunday after June 17 – Stockerston, Stoke, Wardley.
Sunday after June 24 – North Luffenham.
Sunday after June 29 – Barrowden, Bisbrooke, Casterton Magna, Exton, Empingham, Langham, Market Overton, Wing, Wymondham.
Sunday after July 6 – Uppingham.
Sunday after July 11 – Cottesmore.
Sunday after July 22 – Ridlington.
Sunday after July 25 – Seaton.
Sunday after August 15 – Greetham, South Luffenham, Ketton.
Sunday after September 19 – Ashwell, Belmesthorpe, Clipsham, Edith Weston, Manton, Morcott, Caldecott.
Sunday after September 26 – Burley-on-the-Hill.
Sunday after October 10 – Braunston, Lyddington, Thorpe-by-Water.
Second Sunday after October 10 – Thistleton.
Sunday after October 11 – Blaston, Whitwell.
Sunday after October 18 – Glaston, Ryhall, Pickworth, Tixover.
Sunday after November 1 – Casterton Parva, Tinwell.
Sunday after November 11 – Lyndon.
Sunday after November 30 – Hambleton.

About thirty of these were still in existence up to the early years of this century. Some, such as those at Bisbrooke and Caldecott, survived until the 1930s.

Although the feasts were spread over the period from Whit Sunday until 30 November, most were in late June or early July, during the lull between haymaking and harvest. In some cases the appropriate saint's day fell at the right time. St Peter's was on 29 June, and the Sunday following was the time of the feast not only for those listed but also for Preston in Rutland and Braunstone, Claybrooke, Knossington, Oadby, and no doubt others, in Leicestershire. If the day of their saint fell in the depths of winter, or clashed with that of a near neighbour, some parishes seem fairly arbitrarily to have adopted a feast day at a more convenient time. For example, Stretton chose the first Sunday after 6 July instead of its own St Nicholas' Day (6 December) and Whissendine the first Sunday after 13 July instead of St Andrew's Day (30 November). Neither of these appears in the list of 1846. In addition to the occasions of religious origin there were the purely secular club feasts, celebrations by the various sick clubs and friendly societies, and even the 'Co-op'. Barrowden had three of these annually, Exton one, on the first Thursday in May. Belton and Lyddington held theirs on Whit Monday. 'Club Monday' at Hinckley was in the week before Whitsun.

Music was an important element. Brass bands would accompany processions and hymn-singing. The tiny Barleythorpe had no church and no feast, so its villagers, led by a fiddler, walked to Langham, where the diversions included dancing. This was usual, too, at Braunston, Empingham and the Hambletons, where each couple taking part in the Finch's Arms had to contribute a penny to pay the fiddler. At Stretton they danced in the Manor Barn to the music of a concertina; at Bisbrooke in the Gate Inn's barn to the melodeon of Sam Dalby. Ayston's week of entertainment concluded with dancing on the green, to the fiddle and tambourine of Adam and Eve Smith, perhaps descendants of Absalom Smith. People danced behind the old Plough at Greetham, and at Ryhall one of the dances, called 'Cobbler's Knock', had steps resembling those of the Cossacks. The highspot at Clipsham was the fiddle playing in the barn of the Olive Branch of Charlie Alex from the village and Nobby Clark

St Wistan's Feast at the Durham Ox Inn, after a painting of 1794. The inn, at Long Street, Wigston Magna, was demolished in 1936.
(By courtesy of Mr O.D.Lucas)

137

from Pickworth. At South Luffenham 'great bouts of singing and dancing took place in the pubs'. It was 'the week to be drunk in' at Lyddington, and at Market Overton there would be so many people outside the Three Horseshoes that 'you couldn't put a penny between them'.

Various sports also had a part to play, such as catching a greasy pig at Cottesmore and other villages. At Ridlington a series of cricket fixtures held during feast week traditionally began with a match against Wing, before which the players processed to the wicket to the music of Adam and Eve. Langham's week included a match against Whissendine, and there were other games at Greetham and Bisbrooke. At Glaston, where the feast was held in the field opposite the old Three Horseshoes, there was both cricket and football.

Particular dishes were served, such as at Langham, where the traditional menu was roast duckling with new potatoes and garden peas, followed by curd tart. Pastries, plum cakes and curd cheese cakes were eaten at Cottesmore, and most villagers also contrived to have a home-cured ham available. The cheese cakes, incidentally, were made of grated cheese beaten up with eggs and sugar, coloured with saffron, and baked in pastry. At Whissendine, Grantham gingerbread was the favourite delicacy. This was also enjoyed at Cottesmore, along with brown and white rock. On the Sunday at Caldecott roast beef hash was served; on Monday, 'thrommery' (frumenty, made of boiled wheat and honey – for a recipe, see page 224); and during the rest of the week, metheglin, a kind of mead.

The food was sometimes eaten at home, sometimes as a banquet at the local inn, such as the Cuckoo at Wing or the Three Horseshoes at Glaston. Barns could also be brought into service, as at the Hall, Tinwell (now Manor Farm), or the Tythe Barn, Greetham (now demolished). Fairs, with their roundabouts, coconut shies, skittles, shooting galleries and other sideshows, were set up in any suitable spot. Langham used the Town Close Field (now a housing estate), Tinwell, ground at the rear of the Crown, Greetham, the Wheatsheaf paddock, Empingham, the White Horse paddock, Ketton, the Pied Bull paddock and later the back of the Northwick Arms, Barrow, Back Lane, North Luffenham, a field (now Pinfold Close), Barrowden, the green, Caldecott, the green and the Plough yard, and later the Pitts Meadows.

Feasts were an occasion when families gathered. Children had a holiday from school. Young people who had left the village to marry, to go into service or to find work elsewhere, did their best to return, as did any villagers who had moved away. At Exton those unable to go back sent presents. At Bisbrooke the dead were remembered, and flowers were placed on graves.

The High Cross, now in Cheapside, Leicester

139

The wakes and feasts of Leicestershire were broadly similar, though not so numerous, so long-lived or so well-documented as those of Rutland. Opposition seems to have been very fierce in Leicestershire. Just as Rev. Macaulay attacked hirings, so he opposed feasts: 'With the lower sort of people, especially in manufacturing villages, the return of the wake never fails to produce a week at least of idleness, intoxication and riot: these and other abuses by which these festivals are so greatly perverted from the original end of their institution render it highly desirable to all the friends of order, of decency and of religion that they were finally suppressed'. It is said that at Thringstone, a village of stocking-weavers, the wakes were discontinued on the grounds of a solitary complaint received from an Osgathorpe doctor that his horse shied as he was passing the large crowd of people assembled on the green.

Elsewhere, defence was more vigorous. At Melton, the feast coincided with the Whitsun fair. The sports associated with it were held in a field opposite the Cottage Inn, then transferred to Play Close. Attempted encroachments on the land threatened the feast, and were met with what is now called direct action. Buildings were pulled down, and trees uprooted by a party of men calling themselves 'Young Nationals'. In 1848 the law, in the shape of special constables, interviewed, and a general riot ensued. The matter was not settled until 1866, when the town bought the land for public use. By this time feasts and wakes were in decline, though in some villages they remained the highlight of the year until the first world war. People even used them for dating purposes, as is shown in such remarks as 'It'll be three months come Wake Sunday' or 'She must be seven now – she was born a fortnight after Wake Sunday in such a year'.

An anonymous writer in the *Leicester Trader* remembered in 1980 the simple pleasures of pillow fights on greasy poles, climbing a greasy pole to collect a watch from the top, and singing contests with a pig as prize: 'The winner was the man who could sing the best song with the pig tucked underneath his arm. ... When the singer started, the pig would sometimes gaze rather mournfully at him, showing that it was not quite devoid of musical appreciation, in its eyes a look of mild reproof, but if that was not enough to deter him, it would kick and squeal like blazes'. One year an Anstey man won by singing 'O the moon shines bright on pretty redwing'. The village lads quickly produced a parody, entitled 'O the moon shines bright on Tooley's pigsty'.

At Frisby-on-the-Wreake a church service on the second Sunday in July was followed by a modest festival which included three cricket matches, when 'most people had their only holiday of the year except Christmas'. Oadby, despite being a flourishing village, also had a quiet feast, on the first Sunday after 10 July. A field was specially mown for the fair, which consisted of roundabouts, swingboats and donkeys, accompanied by the music of a steam organ. At Ravenstone and Osgathorpe, before expiring altogether, the wakes were reduced to a couple of stalls, a coconut shy and the local band. However, at Wigston the event assumed much bigger proportions. There were two churches, St Wolstan's, which held its feast on 19 June by the Durham Ox Inn, and All Saints', whose feast took place early in November. The former changed its name to St Wistan's and its date to 1 June, but the latter came to predominate, and it attracted many visitors who came by special train from Leicester. In 1869 three village bands, Wignall's, Moore's and Glover's, marched round the streets to waken the villagers, then continued to play off and on throughout the day. There were stalls, shows, caravans, swing boats and roundabouts. Gilt gingerbread and 'paltry gewgaws' were on sale. The sum of one penny procured admittance to see a bison with six legs, a boa constrictor or Abyssinian pups which, as the showman put it, "ave not, nor will 'ave henny 'air on them'. Marionette theatres put on plays like 'The Blood-red Knight', 'The Great Men of Palestine', 'The Haunted Hen-roost' and 'The Mysterious Chaff-box'. At the same time, a writer in the *Leicester Chronicle* lamented the passing of older ways:

Every year the 'feast' grows small by degrees and beautifully less. Fewer shows, stalls and nondescript booths make Wigston their annual rendez-vous. True, the village green has been covered by these great requisites to a successful village fete, but there is about all a dejected air, as though they were conscious that in no remote time their occupation would be irretrievably gone. True, the inhabitants make the feast week a week in which to visit and be visited and a time in which to rejoice and make their hearts glad. True, the public houses are filled to repletion and the improvident dancing saloons are filled with a false joy. True is all this; but equally true it is that all this is but fitful and expiring, a struggle against an inevitable doom for feasts and wakes and fairs, and all their correlated customs are under the ban of an enlightenment before which they must pale their smouldering and ineffectual fire. But however we may rejoice at these signs of the times, a feeling of regret mingles with it when we consider that the customs that pleased our grandfathers and our grandfathers' grandfathers – the old Punch and Judy show, the wonderful ostrich, the serpents, the woolly men, and the uncommon monstrosities of nature, which now intinerate the kingdom – must soon stick fast in some sleepy hollow where, guarded by good Genii, they may form themselves into an antique museum.

Contrary to the writer's expectations, far from continuing to decline, Wigston feast, at least in the short term, grew in popularity. The demand for its attractions increased from Leicester people, who in the late 1880s and early '90s numbered up to a thousand a year except when bad weather 'put a damper on the feasters'. Thereafter came a gradual decline as other forms of commercial entertainment and organised spectator-sport catered for the urban working class.

The original purpose of fairs proper was for the sale of goods and livestock. This was also the case with markets, and has remained so. Fairs were held annually, and went on for up to ten days; markets, weekly, for one day. Both required a royal charter. In 1251 Henry III authorised weekly markets at Oakham on Mondays and Saturdays, and annual fairs on the Vigil, Day and Morrow of the Decollation of St John Baptist (29 August) and also on the Vigil, and Day of the Invention of the Holy Cross (3 May). Oakham Church is dedicated to All Saints, so the dates of the fairs must have been chosen for commercial reasons, though they depended on holy days. Narborough, which was also dedicated to All Saints, settled on the Eve and Day of the Nativity of St John Baptist (24 June). The patron saint at Hinckley is St Mary. The fair there was originally held on the Feast of St Mary, Assumption Day (15 August), but when the calendar was changed in 1752 the date was moved to 26 August. Practical considerations must have been paramount since, whatever the holy day, fairs could only be effectively held when the appropriate goods and livestock were available. Clashes of date with neighbouring towns also had to be avoided.

Even small villages once had their fairs and markets. Groby had both, by a charter of 1338. Hallaton enjoyed not only a Thursday market but three fairs for the sale of horses, horned cattle, pewter, brass and clothing (Holy Thursday, 23 May and 13 June). Some of these institutions were short-lived. Market Overton's market and fair, granted in 1315, were last recorded in 1338. Those at the Hambletons and Empingham do not seem to have survived the Middle Ages. Others proved more tenacious. Under a charter of Henry III horses are still sold each June at Belton, near Shepshed. It is said that the grant was obtained on the intercession of Lady Roesia de Verdun, the founder of Gracedieu Priory. Her monument can still be seen in Belton Church.

In 1285 the township of Bosworth, later to be known as Market Bosworth, was given a Wednesday market and two fairs (8 May and 12 June). The market, still flourishing, is approaching its seven hundredth birthday, though the fairs were less durable. Although its charter has not survived, Melton's Tuesday market is known to have been in existence by 1077, and tradition holds that it was granted by Edward the Confessor to Leofric, husband of Lady Godiva. By the nineteenth century Melton's markets had grown to five, of which four had their own market crosses. The Sheep Cross stood near the site of the present Baptist chapel in Nottingham Street, which was formerly called Spittle End. Some fifty to sixty thousand sheep were sold there annually until 1870. The Corn Cross at the top of High Street (previously called Merridine Street) showed where corn was sold. The Butter Cross, also called the High Cross, stood in the Market Place where dairy produce and eggs were on sale. During the Commonwealth banns were also given out here, and marriages celebrated. The cross was removed in 1808, but the market went on until 1918, when it moved to the Corn Exchange. The Beast Market, which had no cross, was held in Sherard Street until 1870, when a new Cattle Market was opened. The Sage Cross survived in the same street until the same year. It marked the place where herbs could be bought and sold.

By the early fourteenth century Melton had fairs at Whitsuntide and in August. The first was held on the Tuesday, Wednesday and Thursday of Whitsun Week, the second on the Vigil, Day (10 August) and Morrow of St Lawrence, continuing for a week. By the end of the nineteenth century the demand was such that there were eight additional fairs, together with a wool fair and three fairs for Stilton cheese. The locally-produced delicacy would be stacked on straw placed on the ground, and sell in its tens of thousands in April, September and December.

The oldest extant Leicestershire charter is Lutterworth's, issued in 1214, which provided for a Thursday market and ten fairs, also mainly on Thursdays, to be held at the High Cross which stood at the top of the High Street. The cross is no longer there, but the market can still be found on Thursdays on the same site. Ashby-de-la-Zouch had a Saturday market and five fairs, including one on Easter Monday specially for stallions. At Waltham-on-the-Wolds (19 September) it was horses, cattle, swine, 'Mr Frisby's rams' and goods of all sorts. Loughborough's five fairs, established in 1220, included three for horses and two for cheese. 'Its market is on Thursday', wrote John Throsby in 1777, 'and it is a plentiful one for corn; thither the bakers from Leicester go, to buy grain, most market days'. Market Harborough also had five fairs, including one for horses, cattle, sheep and hogs on 29 April and another, of ten days' duration, starting on 19 October, for beasts, fowls, cheese, pewter, brass, hats, clothes and leather (on the last day only). These fairs were not sufficient to meet the demand, and four more were added.

Hinckley's chief fair, established in 1550, was well enough known by the time of Shakespeare to be mentioned in one of his plays, *Henry IV, Part II*, where Mr Justice Shallow is asked by his man, Davy, whether he means 'to stop any William's wages, about the sack he lost the other day at Hinckley-fair'. The sack was probably full of wool, though the August Fair was best-known for horses, cattle, sheep and cheese. There were others at Hinckley on the third Monday after Epiphany (6 January), for horses and cattle; on Easter Monday, 'of little consequence'; on Club Monday (the Monday before Whitsun), for cattle; on the Monday after 28 October, for

143

cheese; and on Whit Monday. The last was once the most popular, then declined, but was revived in 1786. By this time it was less an occasion for buying and selling than for pleasure and pageantry, as can be seen from a notice issued a few years later.

Oakham and Uppingham were other important centres. Oakham had three fairs (15 March, 6 May and 9 September) to which twelve more were later added, such was the demand. Uppingham had two, dating from 1280, to which three more were added in 1860. Its two original fairs were called the Lent Fair (7 March) and the Cherry Fair (7 July). The former, although it was principally for horses, cattle and sheep, became known as Orange Fair from the large quantities of marmalade oranges sold from booths in the Market Place and along what is to this day called Orange Street. Other placenames in the town derive from the sale of cattle (Beast Hill) and pigs (Hogs Hill). Horses were tethered to rings set in the walls of the High Street before showing off their paces on the trial ground in School Lane. Sheep were sold from pens placed along both sides of the High Street for most of its length. Within living memory householders had to step through the pens to enter or leave their houses. Men circulated through the crowds with trays from which they sold hot pies, Nelson cakes and gingerbread horses. Entertainment was provided by the music, singing and dancing of the ubiquitous Adam and Eve Smith.

People would travel considerable distances to attend fairs and markets, both as vendors and as customers. Twelve or fifteen miles was considered a reasonable distance on horseback, and most English towns are about this far apart from each other. Farmers' wives rode pillion behind their husbands with kegs of butter and baskets of eggs slung on either side. Parson Ford of Melton would occupy the time while riding to Leicester by singing through the whole of the *Messiah*, and would reach the 'Amen' just as he was entering the town. A Knossington woman would walk with a basket on either arm to the markets at Leicester, Melton, Uppingham and Stamford.

The greatest attraction, inevitably, was Leicester, with its multiplicity of markets and fairs. The origin of the first fair at Leicester is lost, but it was certainly in existence by 1229, when Henry III authorised a change of date. In 1791 a local historian, John Throsby, listed six fairs, called May, Midsummer, Michaelmas, Palm and Low. Forty years later there were twelve. Wool, leather, cloth, sheep, horses, cattle and cheese were the main commodities sold. In addition there was a Shrove Tuesday Fair at the Newarke which was limited to the sale of oranges, gingerbread and other refreshments for the Whipping Toms (page 223).

Each fair was opened by a proclamation at the High Cross, to which the mayor and corporation solemnly processed, to the music of the town waits. The ancient cross was replaced in Elizabethan times by an eight-sided

HINCKLEY

WHITMONDAY

Shew Fair,

MONDAY, May 28, 1792.

THE PUBLIC are hereby informed, that the moft fpirited exertions are making by every Company of Tradesmen, &c. to vie with each other in appearance to celebrate their annual SHEW-FAIR, and that there will be added to the former exhibition feveral additional Companies ;----------there will be felect

BANDS of MUSIC

The Gentlemen of the CRICKET CLUB with bats and balls, preceded by an elegant FLAG, reprefenting the noble game of CRICKET ;------choice Companies of

MILLERS,	*BUTCHERS,*
WOOLCOMBERS,	*CORDWAINERS,*
FRAME-WORK-KNITTERS,	*BUILDERS,*

and the many different trades of the Town ;
with the addition of feveral new

FLAGS and STREAMERS,

ornamented with allusions and devices relative to the refpective trades, and each Company will be habited in fancied dreffes, decorations, &c.
The Officers of the TOWN in fancied and expreffive habits :
Several Children in different mafquerade dreffes and representations. And, in humble imitation of the celebrated

GODIVA,

a LADY will condefcend to grace the Cavalcade, by riding in the Proceffion characteristi-cally habited :-------Alfo, the

BARON HUGO de GRENTEMAISNEL

will be reprefented armed cap-a-pie, with pike and fhield :---the

BARONESS ADELIZA

in true antique ftile, with fteeple hat, ruff, points, mantle, &c.-----Alfo

BISHOP BLAZE,

and his Chaplain the Rev. M^r LEE, the inventor of the Stocking frame ;
And a young Gentleman will appear on Horseback, in the drefs and habit of a

NORWEGIAN.

* * The Public may be affured that the Shew is intended to be an elegant, entertaining,
* and GRAND PAGEANT EXHIBITION, far exceeding any former on the like occafion.

The Proceffion will begin to move exactly at 11 o'clock in the morning.

WARD, PRINTER, HINCKLEY.

Handbill from Pickering's *Hosiery Trade*
(By permission of Ferry Pickering Group)

market building, which in its turn was taken down in 1768 when the street was widened. A single pillar was left but this, too, was removed in 1836. It now stands in Cheapside, where it was re-erected in 1976. At Michaelmas, in what Susannah Watts described in 1804 as a 'grotesque ceremony', the old pauper men of Trinity Hospital joined in the procession, 'arrayed like ancient knights, having rusty helmets on their heads and breast-plates fastened over their black taberdes'.

The High Cross was also the site of one of Leicester's many markets, for butter and eggs were sold there, originally on Wednesday, and later on Friday also. In 1884 the two days of sale were transferred to the Market Place, to join the Saturday market held there since 1298. A detailed picture of this market is given in a sheet issued in the 1820s by the ballad printer, Cockshaw:

What a wonderful market is here,
And what wonderful people live in it;
Whose singular names shall appear
And I'll single them out in a minute;
There's Thacker for brandy and gin;
And Kirby sells Black and Bohea*, sir,
Then Mallet makes pots of block tin,

For Burgess's coffee and tea, sir.
There's Jackson's broad-cloth for a suit,
When tailorised up, sir, at May's;
With Gee's super-excellent boot,
And Tom Wilmot's tight lacing stays,
When Mellor has covered your crown,
West Weldale your fingers and toes;
You'll shine the first dandy in town,
With Parson's snuff at your nose!

Archer, weekly, his own coffee grinds,
With Coltman and Cooper's brown thread;
If Browne don't enlighten your minds,
Neighbour Webb will embellish your head.
At Bailey's then, make your next call,
By the Fountain, what mortal can pass?
At Cape's you may dress for a ball;
And from Lewis, get china and glass.

*Forms of tea.

And so on, for another seven verses. Some vendors preferred to cry or sing their wares. A wide range of food could be bought for a penny, as shown by the cries of 'Pies hot here, a penny each! Penny each, pies hot!' or 'Ham sandwiches a penny each, a penny each!' or, for sweet round cakes, 'Sold again! Four more a penny here, four a penny'. Others sang, such as the pinman described as a 'necessary element in the Saturday market':

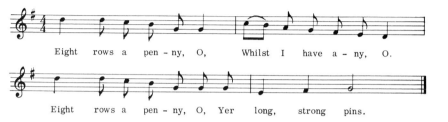

The last words were sometimes varied to: 'Yer fine London pins'.

Such cries were forbidden at Leicester Market in 1983 on pain of forfeiture of the vendor's stall. The decision aroused considerable resentment, even anger, among market traders, who launched a campaign for the restoration of their ancient tradition. Nevertheless, Leicester market continues to flourish, and it remains the largest of its kind in the midlands. Since 1872 other markets, for cattle, sheep and pigs, have been held on a purpose-built site off Aylestone Road.

Fairs, their role in selling having been taken over by markets and shops, have become merely entertainments. As such, as we have seen at Wigston, they were extremely popular in the second half of the nineteenth century. The May and October fairs held at Leicester in Humberstone Gate stretched almost a quarter of a mile from the Clock Tower to Rutland Street. In the 1860s the attractions included giants, contortionists, acrobats, a five-legged and a three-legged cow, a monstrous pig, Wombwell's menagerie, Croueste's circus, swingboats, roundabouts, shooting galleries, marionettes, freak-shows, pastries, patent medicines and fairings of all kinds. There was also a theatrical booth, and one of the most popular plays was *Richard III*, albeit reduced to ten minutes in length. Twenty years later the mixture was much as before, with the addition of 'blaring steam organs' and lessons in 'the noble art of self defence', given by 'famous lady boxers'.

There were also 'joyous rollicking larrikins of both sexes'. Young people used 'to parade the sidewalks in crowds, the lads pinching the arms of the lasses and the lasses paying the lads back in their own coin till the flesh of both was black and blue'. Practical jokes included a 'squirt' which shot a jet of dirty water, ticklers and confetti. Food available included oysters, freshly fried potato chips and savoury sausages. 'A glimpse of paradise' was how one woman summed up the experience of attending the fair, and her feelings were widely shared. Some 30,000 people patronised the October fair in 1888, and in the following year between twelve and thirteen thousand visitors were brought by special trains on the Saturday alone 'from virtually every town within a hundred mile radius' of Leicester.

Despite such success, or perhaps because of it, the city fathers were very unhappy. They considered fairs as 'useless relics of a bygone age'. Worse, they interfered with traffic and legitimate trade. Worse still, they were a danger to morals. The council tried unsuccessfully to suppress the Humberstone Gate fairs in 1889. Then after fifteen years of effort and negotiation they managed to buy out the fairground rights of all claimants for a total of £20,000. The last fair was held in May, 1904, after which Leicestershire people had to look elsewhere for their glimpse of paradise.

IN MEMORY OF

LEICESTER FAIR

WHO BREATHED HER LAST ON MAY 16TH, AFTER A GALLANT STRUGGLE FOR EXISTENCE.

At one time she had a very robust constitution, but old age and worry did its work, and although respected by many, and beloved by the young, (especially the feather ticklers) she was interred on Monday, May 16th, at the ratepayers' expense, the funeral costing them over £20,000, which many thought exhorbitant—no one, excepting some of her Humberstone Gate relations, being satisfied.

9. Drama and music

The earliest dramatic spectacles seen in Leicester were probably miracle plays, dramatised versions of stories from the Bible and apocrypha. Of these, nothing has survived, but some of the characters were represented in the pageant-like religious processions such as the one held on Whit Monday which took offerings for the Diocese of Lincoln (of which, until 1837, Leicestershire was a part) to the bishop's deputy at St Margaret's Church. Each parish was led by its clergy and the image of its patron saint. Women, dressed as the twelve apostles, each bore the name of the figure she represented on a piece of parchment. In addition there were, we are told, 'virgins, banner-bearers, musicians and members of the parochial guilds'.

There were six major guilds for the well-to-do, which were run largely with the object of raising funds to pay chantry priests to sing masses for the souls of the founders, members and well-wishers, and also to provide mutual support in adversity. All the leading men of the town and many of their wives belonged to the Guild of Corpus Christi, founded in 1343 and attached to St Martin's Church. Its annual feast and procession were held on the Thursday after Trinity Sunday (the fiftieth day after Easter). The Guild of St Margaret and St Catherine, dating from 1356, was based at St Margaret's Church. Among the benefits it conferred on members was the provision of a hearse, originally merely a framework in which tapers were placed, for their funerals. It also undertook to bring their bodies back for burial if they died within twelve leagues of Leicester. For the living it held a banquet on St Margaret's Day (20 July).

Perhaps the greatest civic function of the year was the Riding of the George, a spectacular procession in which the central figures were the saint and the dragon. It attracted large crowds of spectators in festive mood, and was organised jointly by the Guild of St George and the corporation, on St George's Day (23 April), or, presumably if Easter was late, on another day before Whitsuntide. The expense of four shillings for 'dryssyng the dragon' appears in the town accounts for 1536–41. The statue of St George, and presumably also that of the dragon, were kept at St Martin's Church, but cleared out in 1546–7 as a result of Edward VI's injunction against certain religious rites and ceremonies. The 'Horse that the George rode on' was sold by the church-wardens for twelve pence, and a banner for two shillings and eight pence. Apparently George's armour escaped, for it turned up during the reign of Queen Mary, when the processions were resumed. In the accounts of 1553–4 is listed the sum of 6. 8d. for dressing 'sent Georgs harnes'. There is no record of the procession after 1553, and no other religious pageant was held after 1559.

From the following year church plays were also stopped. There were presented by members of the 'occupations' or craft guilds, and included a passion play at Easter (also partly financed by the corporation) and at Christmas plays both of the nativity, at St Mary's, and the resurrection, at St Martin's. In addition, though it may seem strange, the churches put on performances of a Robin Hood play in May or at Whitsuntide. This was also known as 'The King's Game' or 'Lord and Lady', and the principal character, apart from Robin Hood, was Maid Marian, otherwise called 'the Lady' or 'the Queen of the May'. The performances, originally given in May, were so popular that they spread eventually over the whole period between Easter and Whitsuntide.

At St Mary's the churchwardens' accounts for 1520 show the receipt of £2. 6s. from the King's Game. A similar play raised £2 in aid of repairs at St. Leonard's in 1526, but the money seems to have been embezzled by the treasurer of the fund. In 1534 an ecclesiastical official at Leicester listed in his accounts the purchase of Kendal green cloth for the actors in the play of 'Robyn Hode', and also the hire of a coat and the loan of a sword. As late as 1559 St Martin's received four shillings from 'the mawrys daunce of Chyldren' and eleven pence the following year from a performance of 'the lord & the lady'. Similar items appear in the Churchwardens' accounts at Melton Mowbray. For example, 13s. 4d. was received in 1546 'in money yt ye Lorde gathered in Wytson Hollidays', and in 1556 29s. 8d. was donated by 'steven Schawyt he gethered & hys company at Robyn Hoods play ij yeres'. The revels were led by a Lord of Misrule, who, despite his title, was public-spirited enough to devote money raised to the repair of churches or, as in 1563, highways. Local people were so attached to Robin Hood's Day that when Bishop Latimer turned up to preach a sermon – he does not mention Melton in his account, but tradition places the incident there – he found the church door was 'fast locked'. He 'tarried there half an hour or more', after which the key was found, but 'one of the parish came to me and said, "Sir, this is a holiday with us, we cannot hear you, it is Robin Hood's day. The parish are gone abroad to gather for Robin Hood, I pray you, let [prevent] them not".' Latimer sensibly deferred to Robin.

The void created by the suppression of these spectacles was filled by professional, secular performers. The first payment to such a company, which had travelled from London, is recorded in the Leicester accounts of 1530–1, when a fee of a quarter of a mark, or 3s. 6d., was paid. In addition, spectators were charged a small sum for admission. By 1600, fifty such visits by companies of strolling players had taken place.

Performances were in the open air or, after its acquisition by the corporation in 1563, in the Guildhall, formerly the hall of the Corpus Christi Guild. Shakespeare's contemporary, Burbage, acted there, and tradition holds that Shakespeare did so himself, either in 1585 as a member of the Earl of Leicester's company, or eight or nine years later in the Earl of Derby's troupe. Other performances took place in the yards of inns, with some spectators (called the 'groundlings') on the same level as the performers, and others up in the galleries which ran round on three sides.

Drama must have been popular in Leicester, and performances became even more frequent in the early seventeenth century. In the single year of 1621–2 there were thirteen visits by royal companies alone, not counting others by noblemen's troupes. In 1642 players were rewarded by the town for the last time before the Civil War closed all the theatres. Performances resumed after the Restoration but the actors received only the takings at the door. The Guildhall was last used by them in 1739. In two centuries of the town's records of strolling players not a single play title appears. One can surmise that Shakespeare's plays, including *Richard III*, were performed in the town, but there is no evidence.

After 1750 plays were staged in the Assembly Rooms, newly-built at the top of Humberstone Gate, and only a stone's throw from the site of the present Haymarket Theatre. A new theatre was opened in 1800, but demolished in 1836 and replaced on the same site by the Theatre Royal. This, in its turn, was pulled down, by what has been called 'an act of vandalism', in 1956.

One of the first plays performed there, in December 1837, was entitled 'Black Anna's Bower, or the Maniac of the Dane Hills'. It was a melodrama written for his benefit night by one of the actors, a Mr Higgie. The *Leicester Journal* commented that it was 'so well continued in its plot, so judicious in its incident, and so respectable in its dialogue as to deserve a permanent place in the favour of all lovers of that species of dramatic entertainment'. Unfortunately, the text does not seem to have survived, though it appears that the plot turned on the murder of Mrs Clarke at the Blue Boar (for which, see page 195), with Black Anna's role being akin to that of the witches in *Macbeth*.

The formula must have been successful, for as part of a triple bill for the following Christmas, there was another play on a local theme which also brought in Black Anna. It was entitled *The Broken Heart, or The Rose of Newarke*, and seems to have been based on a chapter in Thomas Featherstone's book, *Legends of Leicester in the Olden Time*, which was published earlier in 1838. Like many melodramas the play, written by the theatre manager, featured murder and madness, seduction and destruction. The heroine, Mariana Clifton, loves Valentine Falkner, and marries him. His friend, Norland Wodefray, desires Mariana himself. When he and Valentine are called to their duties as parliamentary soldiers – it is 1645, and the Siege of Leicester is imminent – he murders his friend and then deserts. Norland goes back to Mariana, manages to ingratiate himself, and then to seduce her. Valentine appears to her in a dream – such scenes were played behind a transparent muslin curtain – to tell her that Norland has murdered him and buried his body on the Dane Hills. Mariana confronts Norland, who goes away. Valentine's baby, which Mariana has borne earlier, dies, and Mariana takes and buries it alongside its father's body. She then becomes demented, and during the course of her wanderings becomes known as Black Anna. She comes across Norland, who is hiding from the parliamentary soldiers in a hovel near the castle, and tries to kill him with a knife, but he escapes. In the meantime, Charles and his forces have entered the town and are sacking it. Later they set fire to the abbey. Mariana sees the flames from the Dane Hills and utters a terrible malediction on Norland. On cue, he appears, fleeing from the town. He claims that the murder of Valentine was her fault, because of the fatal power of her beauty, and plunges his sword into her heart. With her dying breath she calls on him to repent. He refuses, and is struck down by a sheet of flame from heaven.

Such 'judicious' incidents would no doubt have appealed to the audiences who flocked to the booths of travelling theatre companies which visited many towns and villages. Waites' Travelling Theatre went to Barrowden every year and performed in the clubroom or a tent in the Exeter Arms yard. Admission was two pence. This was later increased to three pence when visits from the travelling cinema started. At Oakham the theatre company was called Maggie Morton's, and the plays included *East Lynn* and *Miss Hook of Holland*. Holloways' Blood Tub regularly visited Wigston until 1914. A marquee, warmed in winter by coke stoves, was erected on Barrett Street Green (now a housing estate), and for a fee of twopence theatre-goers could see a performance of *Crippen, Maria Marten, Sweeney Todd* or *The Man They Could Not Hang*. Similar offerings were available in the theatre booths at Humberstone Gate Fair, where one could see a four-act tragedy, preceded by an overture and followed by a pantomime, all in ten minutes.

Much as had been the case in earlier times, with the miracle plays, pageants and Robin Hood plays, certain performances continued to be put on by local people. These were happenings rather than plays, rituals rather than entertainments. William Kelly, writing in 1865, complained that 'the "more work and less play" system which prevails at the present time in our manufacturing towns has long since driven the Christmas mummers from Leicester, with other old customs'. He vividly remembered, thirty-five years previously, 'seeing parties of Mummers going about the town from house to house, some of them wearing high conical hats of pasteboard, decorated with ribbons and gilt paper, and carrying wooden swords, a club, frying pans, &c.'

In fact, such plays survived at many places in Leicestershire and Rutland, and Kelly himself obtained the text of one performed round about Lutterworth at Christmas in 1863. P. F. Woodward wrote that during his childhood at Kibworth in the 1860s on Christmas Eve 'in would walk the Mummers, a troupe of boys, who annually performed ... Harry or David Knapp, I believe, took the part of St George; Harry Brown the Dragon; William and Alfred Lee, David Atkinson, Joe or William Green, and Joe Buckby were the Men-at-arms'.

Several people remembered the mummers of Belgrave (then a village but now a suburb of Leicester) in the 1870s or '80s. They were seen at Belgrave Hall by Isobel Ellis, and the characters included St George and the Dragon, the Turkish Knight, the Princess Sabra 'and the doctor who restored the dead to life'. The same team was seen on Boxing Day in the taproom of the Bull's Head: 'They wore their waistcoats with the flowered linings inside out, donned paper hats, presumably from crackers, and fought with wooden swords'. Similar Christmas players were recalled at Bosworth, Burbage, Caldecott, Edith Weston, Gilmorton, Glaston, Ibstock, Knossington and North Kilworth. The 'Mummiers' Play', as it was called, was performed up to the turn of the century at Caldecott by men who toured the public houses at Christmas. In about 1905 youths of between fourteen and sixteen years of age took over, and extended the performances to neighbouring villages. The characters all had blackened faces except Guier (pronounced to rhyme with 'wire'), who had to reddle his face and hands. They wore old clothes, roughly appropriate to each character. Beelzebub was dressed in rags and tatters and carried a club. The doctor had an old frock-coat and a black bag. The miser was dressed in rags. In all there were seven characters: Open your Door, Guier, King George, Slasher, Beelzebub and the Miser.

THE CALDECOTT MUMMIERS' PLAY

OPEN YOUR DOOR
Open your door and let me in,
I beg your favour for to win.
Whether I rise, stand or fall,
I'll do my duty to please you all.
Room, room, it's room I require,
So step in Guier and show your face like fire.

GUIER
I am Guier, Guier is my name,
Of English nation bred and claim.
I've searched this country round and round,
To find King George ten thousand pounds.

KING GEORGE
I am King George, a noble champion bold,
'Twas 'e who fought and won three crowns in gold,
'Twas 'e who fought the fiery dragon and brought it to its slaughter,
And by this means I won the Queen of Egypt's daughter.
If you don't believe what I 'ave to say,
Step in my little soldier and clear the way.

SLASHER
I am a soldier, Slasher is my name,
Sword and buckle by my side I'm bound to win the game.

GUIER
Oh Slasher, oh Slasher, don't talk so 'ot,
There's a man in this room you little think you've got.
He can 'ash you, smash you, as small as a fly,
And send you to Jamaica to make a mince pie.

SLASHER
Oh 'e can neither 'ash me, smash me small as a fly,
Nor send me to Jamaica to make a mince pie.

GUIER
Draw forth your sword and fight,
Draw forth your purse and pay.
Satisfaction we will 'ave
Before you go away.
Slasher and Guier have a sword duel.

GUIER
Stand off, stand off, for your time draws nigh.
After a time of clashing swords.
Stand off, you dog, for now you die.
Slasher falls, mortally wounded.

OPEN YOUR DOOR
Oh cruel, cruel Christian, what 'ast thou done?

Thou 'ast killed and wounded mine only son.
Doctor! Doctor! (*very loud*) Ten pounds for a doctor!

DOCTOR
I am a doctor and a doctor rare,
I've travelled all this country far and near.

OPEN YOUR DOOR
What countries 'ave you travelled, most noble doctor?

DOCTOR
Italy, Scotland, France and Spain.
I can cure that man that lays there slain.

OPEN YOUR DOOR
What pains can you cure, most noble doctor?

DOCTOR
Hipsie, pixie, palsy and the gout,
If the Old Man's in I'll fetch 'im out.
I 'ave a little bottle in my left and sleeve waistcoat pocket called okum
                              pokum.
'Ere, Jack, take a little of my nip-nap,
Put it up your snip-snap.
Rise, Jack, and fight again.
Ladies and gentlemen standing round,
See I've cured this man safe and sound.
I've 'ealed 'is wound and cleansed 'is blood
And gave 'im something that done 'im good.
Ain't I, Jack?

SLASHER
Yes, and I liked it, too.

BELZEBUB
In comes I, old Belzebub.
On my shoulder I carry a club,
In my 'and a dripping pan.
Don't you think I'm a funny old man?

THE MISER
In comes I, the old miser, with all me old brown rags.
For the wants of money I'm forced to cadge.

My pockets are lined with cat's skin
And they're getting very thin,
So I would like a little of your Christmas money
To line them well within.
If you please, ladies and gentlemen.
He goes round the company with a tin.

The performance sometimes finished with this song, usually if it was in a
public-house. The verses were taken in turn by the various characters
holding out the appropriate piece of clothing.

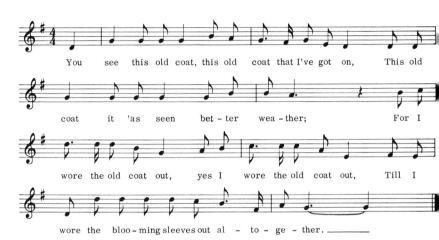

You see this old 'at, this old 'at that I've got on?
This old 'at it 'as seen better weather,
For I wore the old 'at out, yes, I wore the old 'at out,
Till I wore the blooming crown out altogether.

You see this old weskit, this old weskit I've got on?
This old weskit it 'as seen better weather,
For I wore the old thing out, yes, I wore the old thing out,

You see these old trousers, these old trousers I've got on?
These old trousers 'as seen better weather,
And I wore the old things out, yes, I wore the old things out,
Till I've worn the blooming legs off altogether.

You see these old socks, these old socks that I've got on?
These old socks, they 'ave seen better weather,
For I've wore the old socks out, yes, I've wore the old socks out,
Till I've wore the blooming feet off altogether.

You see these old boots, these old boots that I've got on?
These old boots they 'ave seen better weather.
I've wore the old boots out, yes, I've wore the old boots out,
Till I've wore the blooming soles off altogether.

A similar play, though usually with the addition of a 'wooing' or courtship sequence, was performed in some areas on Plough Monday (for which, see page 86). At Oakham the actors practised in a stable for about a month before performing from Plough Monday until the following Saturday, in the evenings. Their takings for the week would be between five and ten shillings each. By tradition the head man was the waggoner of the chief farmer in the district. Other performances took place at the same time at Clipsham, Market Bosworth and Ratby. The play was performed at Sproxton (pronounced 'Sprowston') on Ploughboy Night until the 1890s. In the early years of this century it was taken over by children, then fell into disuse. A very successful revival was staged by the Leicester Morris Men in the 1960s.

There are six characters: Tom Fool, Recruiting Sergeant, Farmer's Man, Lady, Beelzebub and Doctor, together with an assistant who passes round a collecting box during the last song. Tom Fool is dressed as a clown and the Recruiting Sergeant as a red-coated soldier. The Farmer's Man wears a smock frock or corduroys. The Lady, who is played by a man, has a blouse, shawl, skirt and an extravagant hat. Beelzebub dresses as far as possible in black, and wears a black skull-cap. His club, about eighteen inches long, is made of a black stocking stuffed with straw, with a stick inside for stiffening. The doctor has a top-hat, black swallow-tail coat and riding breeches and boots. He carries a doctor's bag.

FOOL

In comes I who's never bin yet,
With my big head and little wit.
My head is large and my wit is small,
I can act the fool's part as well as you all.
Okum, pokum, France and Spain,
Walk in, Sergeant, all the same.

SERGEANT

In comes I, the Recruiting Sergeant,
I've arrived here just now.
I've had orders from the king
To enlist all jolly fellows that follow the carthorse at plough.
Likewise tinkers, tailors, pedlars, nailers, all that take to my advance.
The more I hear the fiddle play, the better I can dance.

FOOL

Faith, lad, think I've come here to see a fool like you dance?

SERGEANT

Yes, Tommy, I can dance, sing or say.

FARMER'S MAN

In comes I, the Farmer's Man.
Don't you see my whip in hand?
When I go to plough the land I turn it upside down.
Straight I go from end to end,
I scarcely make a balk or bend,
And to my horses I attend.
As they go marching round the end
I shout 'Come here, gee whoa back'.

LADY

Be - hold a la - dy bright and gay, good for - tunes and sweet
charms, How scorn - ful I've been thrown a - way right

out of my true love's arms, He swears if I don't

wed with him as we some day p'raps may, He'll

'list for— a sol - dier and from me run a - way.

SERGEANT

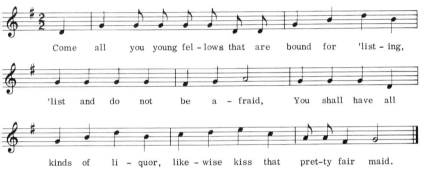

Come all you young fel - lows that are bound for 'list - ing,

'list and do not be a - fraid, You shall have all

kinds of li - quor, like - wise kiss that pret-ty fair maid.

FARMER'S MAN

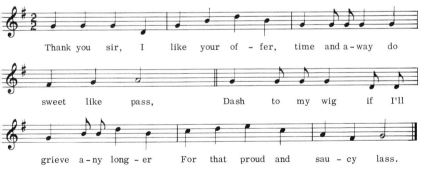

Thank you sir, I like your of - fer, time and a - way do

sweet like pass, Dash to my wig if I'll

grieve a - ny long - er For that proud and sau - cy lass.

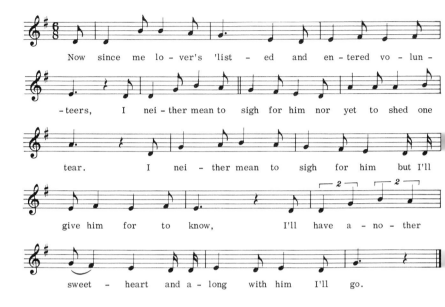

Now since me lo - ver's 'list - ed and en - tered vo - lun -
- teers, I nei - ther mean to sigh for him nor yet to shed one
tear. I nei - ther mean to sigh for him but I'll
give him for to know, I'll have a - no - ther
sweet - heart and a - long with him I'll go.

FOOL
Dost thou love me, my pretty maid?

LADY
Yes, Tommy, and to me sorrow.

FOOL
When shall be our wedding day?

LADY

Tom - my love, to - mor - row.

ALL

We'll shake hands and we'll make bands and we'll get wed to - mor-row.

FOOL

Stop, stop, stop to me old flip-flaps. I want to ask some of you old riff-raff to me and my old girl's wedding. What you like best you'd better bring with you. I don't know what you like best. Some like fish, some like flesh, some like fruit and frummity. What me and my old gel likes best we're going to have.

ONE OF THE OTHERS

What's that, Tommy?

FOOL

A barley chaff dumpling buttered with wool, cut up in slices fit to choke an old bull. If your saucy old flats ain't satisfied with that, you'd better go without. So right away, lads, we'll get married tomorrow.

ALL

Sing, as before:

We'll shake hands, and we'll make bands, and we'll get wed tomorrow.

BEELZEBUB

In comes I, Beelzebub.
On my shoulder I carry my club,
In me and a drip leather pan.
Don't you think I'm a funny old man?
Any man or woman in this room dare stand before me?

FOOL

Yes, I darest, cos me 'ead is made of iron,
Me body's made of steel,
Me hands are made of knuckle-bone,
No man can make me feel.

BEELZEBUB

What? I don't care if your 'ead is made of iron,
Your body made of steel,
Hands are made of knuckle-bone,

161

I can make you feel.
I'll smish you, smash you, small as flies,
Send you to Jamaica to make mince pies.
Hits him with club, on shoulder. Fool falls to the ground, as if helpless.

FARMER'S MAN
Oh Bellzie, oh Bellzie, what has thou done?
Thou's killed the finest man under the sun.
Here he lays bleeding on this cold floor,
Faith, never to rise no more.
Five pound for a doctor.

BEELZEBUB
Ten pound for him to stop away.
What's the good of having a doctor to a dead man?

FARMER'S MAN
Sxteen pound for him to come in.
Step in, doctor.

DOCTOR (*at the door*)
Whoa, boys, hold my horse's head by the tail and mind he don't kick you.
He's only a donkey. I'll show you the bright side of a shilling when I come
out again.
Enters
In comes I, the doctor.

SERGEANT
Are you a doctor?

DOCTOR
Yes, I am a doctor.

SERGEANT
How became you to be a doctor?

DOCTOR
I travelled for it.

SERGEANT
Where did you travel?

DOCTOR
England, France, Ireland and Spain,
And I come back to old England again.
Just below York there I cured an old woman from Cork.
She fell upstairs, downstairs, over a half-empty tea-pot full of flour, and
grazed her shin-bone above her right elbow, and made her stocking-leg
bleed. I set that and made it straight again.

SERGEANT
What else can you cure?

DOCTOR
Ipsy, pipsy, palsy and gout,
Pains within or aches without;
Set a tooth or draw a leg,
And almost raise the dead to life again.

SERGEANT
You must be a very clever doctor. You'd better try your experience on this
young man.

DOCTOR
Just wait while I take off my big top-hat, kid gloves and corduroy
walking-stick, and I'll feel this man's pulse.
He bends down and feels round him.
This man's pulse beats nineteen times to the tick of my watch,
He's in a very low way indeed – couldn't be much lower without digging a
hole. He's been living on green tater tops for three weeks all but a
fortnight. This morning he tried to swallow a young wheelbarrow for his
breakfast. Tried to cut his throat with a rolling pin. I'll stop him from
doing all them tricks. Give his some of my old riff-raff down his chiff-
chaff, that'll make him rise and fight. Also I'll give him some of my epsy
doansum pills. Take on tonight, two in the morning, and the box
tomorrow dinner-time. If the pills don't digest the box will. If he can't
dance we can sing, so let's rise him up and we'll all begin.

ALL

Good mis - ter and good mis - ter - ess as you sit round your

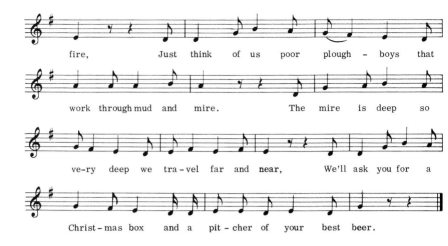

fire, | Just think of us poor plough - boys that

work through mud and mire. | The mire is deep so

ve-ry deep we tra - vel far and **near,** | We'll ask you for a

Christ - mas box and a pit - cher of your best beer.

Second verse to same tune:
We're not the London actors that act upon the stage,
We are just country ploughboys that work for little wage.
We're not the London actors, I've told you so before,
We'll wish you all goodnight, friends, and another happy New Year.

Music played a considerable part in the mummers' performances, as it did in the medieval plays and processions. There were minstrels at Leicester Castle for most of the fourteenth century, but their function was to make music for the nobility, not the townsfolk. The corporation had a group of salaried musicians, called waits, from at least as early as 1499. These were in effect musical watchmen, operating between Ascension Eve (the day before Easter Thursday) and Michaelmas Day (29 September). They also played on civic occasions and were available for private hire. They were equipped from 1504 with silver badges of office, and in 1577 their uniform was 'cotes or orringe color, and the sinckle file of [cinque foil on] there sleves'. By this time their duties were 'to kepe the towne, and to play euerye night and morning orderlye, boethe wynter and somer, and not to go forthe of the towne to playe except to fayres or weddings then by the licence of Mr Mayor'. In return they had a closed shop agreement which provided that 'no estraungers, viz. waytes, mynstrells or other muzicions whatsoeuer, be suffered to playe within this towne, neyther att weddings, or fayres tymes, or any other tyme whatsoeuer'. Even musicians from within the town were forbidden to play at any time 'att or in a mans howse, dore, wyndowe, or att anye weddings (or bryde howsses)'. The only exception was during the assizes, and even then the musicians involved were allowed 'to playe butt onlye to straungers'.

Despite these favourable conditions there were often difficulties. In 1602 the waits were all dismissed over a quarrel as to whose son should play the bass viol. They were reinstated a year later, but had their wages stopped in 1627 and their badges called in because of 'negligent service'. From time to time they received special gratuities, such as for playing on the occasion of the restoration of Charles II in 1660 or the coronation of William and Mary in 1688. By 1780 their wages had risen to fifteen shillings a quarter, but in 1797 there were again complaints of 'Neglect of Duty'. In 1819 the traditional viols were exchanged for newly-purchased wind instruments: horns, clarinets, piccolos and a bassoon. All these were sold, together with the silver badges, when the waits were abolished in 1836, along with the old Leicester Corporation. One badge has been preserved in Leicester Museum.

In 1842 the waits were revived 'to play round the town' in the weeks before Christmas. By the late nineteenth century they were popular enough to be photographed for a picture postcard, and they did not finally disappear until the 1950s. They are still recalled with affection. Mrs M. Robinson, born in 1903, wrote, eighty years later: 'I can clearly remember when I was a little girl and my mother paid half a crown just before Christmas. This was for what we called the Town Waits to play carols during the night about a week before Christmas. We were a large and poor family and my mother could ill afford this. She then would tell us

Leicester Waits (By permission of Leicestershire Museums)

165

when they were coming. We would all jump out of bed, our faces to the window, to listen to this band of men under the lamplight with their lanterns, playing "The Mistletoe Bough" and other carols under our window'. Mr G. Matthews, born in 1907, lived in Catherine Street. His recollection of the waits was that 'We went to bed early but on Christmas Eve always heard them – "Happy Christmas, Mr So and So. Past twelve o'clock" or "two o'clock".'

Christmas was a good time for music, as it still is. Mr Woodford of Kibworth, who remembered the nummers' visits on Christmas Eve, also recalled the arrival of 'the blind fiddler, Billy Parsons, dressed in his old-fashioned cord breeches, buttoned at the knees with brightly polished brass buttons, blue worsted stockings, and heavy nailed shoes; his coat of black cloth with very high-cut collar; his waistcoat of scarlet cloth, with bright brass buttons which also adorned his coat. An old-fashioned beaver hat completed his attire'. He not only played tunes but accompanied himself in songs. 'The chorus of one only which I remember was –

When a poor man comes home at night
And sits him down to supper
Barley pudden he must eat
Wi' ne'er a bit o' butter'.

Billy Parsons would take his leave after a large glass of hot elderberry wine and a piece of cake, not forgetting 'the usual gift from father'. There were many local musicians like him. Some would play at church, before the days of organs; some at secular events like fairs and wedding parties; some at both.

William Gardiner, who was born in 1770, mentions several church musicians, including a Sapcote farmer called Smith, a 'tall stout man, with an extraordinarily powerful voice', who accompanied himself on the 'cello. A stockinger at Shepshed, Harry Lester, wrote a carol every Christmas which was performed round the town. Gardiner himself took part as a boy in one of the Shepshed performances, this time of the *Messiah*, in 1782, and was particularly impressed by the violin playing of a man called Young. He says that the 'musicians of the forest' took part not only in church music but in glee singing. He was a member himself of the Glee Club which met at the Three Crowns in Leicester.

At fairs and wakes people played for dancing and singing. Instruments such as the hurdy-gurdy, concertina, fiddle and melodeon were played by local musicians (see page 135). In addition there were itinerant professional performers such as Absalom Smith (fiddle) and Adam and Eve Smith (fiddle and tambourine). Unfortunately, the tunes and songs were hardly ever noted, even by title, but at least one of Adam and Eve's songs has been remembered. It is 'the Quart Pot', better known as 'the Jolly Shilling'.

Village band at Waltham-on-the-Wolds, c.1860
(By permission of Leicestershire Museums)

Songs were not sung merely on high days and holidays, but were also part of the fabric of everyday life. Charlie Wilson of Empingham (page 79) sang about his daily work. The reapers once sang in the fields as they wielded scythes or sickles. Irish labourers, over for the harvest, sang in unison as they worked, and could be heard up to half a mile away. At a village near Coalville, after working until darkness had fallen, harvesters would sit down in the fields and sing Moody and Sankey hymns. Stockingers, too, were a by-word for singing, and whenever a few of them were working together there would be songs.

Some of these songs, like Harry Lester's carols, would be home-made. A complete ballad opera, *The Charnwood Opera*, was written in 1753, to back up a campaign against encroachment on the common land. One song, previously unpublished, begins:

When Popish Jemmy rul'd this Land he rul'd it like a King,
And Bloody Jeffreys went about hanging & Jibbeting.
The Warreners prick'd up their Ears, that was a Time of Grace,
Some Laws & Justices were made and Rabbets bred apace.
But now, whilst George the Second reigns we'll pull the Vermin out.
If little Squires should spoil our sport we'll make the Marplots fly,
The Warrener and all his Gang, Rabbets and Popery!

James Harrold was a gifted song-writer who appeared at the popular tripe suppers held in the late eighteenth century at the Globe Inn, Hinckley. He 'celebrated every local and national event in song of his own composing', but none of his work seems to have survived, any more than that of a tramp called Yates who 'was often to be seen in Bosworth in the earlier 1840s, an old man with a pack, hooting "'Ere you 'as 'em! A new spoiretail song by Jonathan Francis Yates – that's may".'

Other ballads, printed for sale at a penny a time, were hawked in the streets and markets. Some have been preserved. One example, printed in London in the late seventeenth century, is entitled 'The Leicestershire Tragedy: or the Fatal Overthrow of two Unfortunate Lovers Caus'd by Susanna's Breach of Promise'. It is the story of Susanna Lynard who promises to marry one man but forsakes him for another. The first kills himself on her wedding day and his 'bleeding ghost' haunts her. She falls into a 'feaver' and dies, thus serving as a warning to false lovers. 'The Leicester Chambermaid', widely printed in the early nineteenth century, through not apparently in Leicester itself, has an altogether lighter touch, while still giving a warning:

It's of a brisk young butcher as I have heard 'em say.
He started out of London town upon a certain day.
Says he, 'A frolic I will have, my fortune for to try;
I will go into Leicestershire some cattle for to buy'.

When he arrived at Leicester town he went to an inn;
He called for an ostler and boldly walked in.
He called for liquors of the best, he being a roving blade,
And presently fixed his eye upon the chambermaid.

The day it being over and the night it being come,
The butcher came to the inn his business being done.
He called for a supper and his reckoning left unpaid,
Says he, 'This night I'll put a trick upon the chambermaid'.

O then she took a candle to light him up to bed,
And when they came into the room these words to her he said:
'One sovereign I will give to you all to enjoy your charms'.
This fair maid all the night slept within the butcher's arms.

He rose up in the morning and prepared to go away.
The landlord said, 'Your reckoning, sir, you did forget to pay'.
'O no,' the butcher did reply, 'pray do not think it strange.
I gave a sovereign to your maid but did not get the change'.

He straightway called the chambermaid and charged her with the
same,
The sovereign she did lay down, fearing to get the blame.
The butcher he returned home well pleased with what was past,
But soon this pretty chambermaid grew thick about the waist.

'Twas in a twelve-month after he came to town again,
When then as he had done before he stopped at an inn.
'Twas then the buxom chambermaid she chanced him to see,
She brought the babe just three months old and placed it on his knee.

The butcher sat like one amazed & at the child did stare,
And when the joke he did find out how he did stamp and swear.
She said, 'Kind sir, this is your own so do not think it strange;
One sovereign you gave to me and I have brought the change'.

The company they laughed again, the joke went freely round,
And soon the tidings of the same was spread through Leicester town.
The butcher was to justice brought, who happened to live near;
One hundred pounds he did pay down before he could get clear.

So all you brisk and lively blades I pray be ruled by me,
And look well to your bargain before you money pay;

Or soon perhaps your folly will give you cause to range,
For if you sport with the pretty maids you're sure to have your change.

Leicester had its own ballad printers in the nineteenth century. Often they merely reproduced material first printed elsewhere. One such ballad, issued by T. Warwick of Loseby Lane, was written in the 1830s by T. H. Bayley and set to music by Sir Henry Bishop. It is entitled 'The Mistletoe Bough', and tells the story of a young bride suffocated in a chest during a game of hide-and-seek. It is said to have been inspired by the death of Catherine Noel, the eighteen year old daughter of the owner of Exton Old Hall in Rutland, who died in a similar way during an amateur performance of *Romeo and Juliet* at Christmas, 1700.

Contenders at elections often used ballads to appeal to the voters. 'The Leicestershire Freeholders' Song,' for example, appeared in 1714–5. Thomas Babington Macaulay, the future historian of England, wrote a ballad in 1826 in support of the radical candidate in a Leicester parliamentary election, William Evans, a Derbyshire cotton-manufacturer. It was entitled simply 'A New Song', went to the tune of 'derry down', and began:

So you doubt whom to choose of our Candidates three;
Come hither, good Weavers, and listen to me;
And tho' not an Aesop, yet if I am able,
I will tell you my mind in the guise of a fable.

This was only one item in what has been described as 'a veritable snowstorm of squibs, lampoons, broadsides and cartoons' produced during the campaign. Similar materials appeared at other elections.

Other ballads reflected social changes in Leicester, such as the coming of the railways. The Leicester and Swannington line opened as early as 1832, and the following year a railway whistle was heard for the first time anywhere. Previously a horn had been used, as on the stage coaches, but a Leicester organ builder designed and made the first steam-whistle. Leicester was linked to the developing national rail network in 1840 with the arrival of the Midland Counties Railway, and the event was celebrated by the issue of 'A Most Curious and Interesting Dialogue on the New Railroads, Or, the delight and pleasure of Travelling by Hot Water'.

Such ballads and their singers were themselves subject to the influence of social change. An anguished correspondent wrote to the *Leicester Chronicle* in 1875 to lament their passing:

Old Ballads and Ballad Singers. What has become of them? The man and woman standing toe to toe, with their mouths all awry, frequently a broken nose – and a black eye – and a nasal twang as to make their voices distinguishable above the din. Where are the lines upon lines

170

Farmer's Warning.

Cockshaw, Printer, Leicester.

COME, gentlemen farmers, I pray now attend,
Listen awhile too these few lines I have penn'd,
The blessing of God on the poor now will smile,
While half of your farmers will quickly run wild.

The hops they have mist, and the corn it is come,
Half of you will break, and away you will run,
Therefore, dear farmers, let down your pride,
Never mount such gallant steeds when to market
  you ride.

Your slow team of horses with dainty corn is fed;
They are nothing but dog's meat when once they are
  dead;
But keep a team of oxen to plough up your land,
When their work is done they are meat for a man.

Here is silver buckles and fine silver spurs,
And nothing goes down but Madam and Sirs,
A good old master and dame is kick'd out of door,
As a man does a wife, when he takes in a w——e.

There is your wife, with her ruffles, caps, and fine
  troloppes,
With their fine white petticoats, as fine as you please
Their heads are dressed up like a roll,
With their fly away caps makes them look like an owl

For these several years you have had your own way
And on the poor you do craftily play:
Think of these words when I am out of sight,
And lower down your pride before you're ruin'd
  quite.

At Michaelmas your Landlord calls for his rent,
Having no money breeds discontent,
Immediately he calls for his lawyer to seize,
And tears down your pride, you may like it as you
  please.

So now to conclude and to finish my song,
I hope that you here will not take me wrong,
You that have got money, and I have none,
Come buy up my ballads, that I may have some.

171

that used to be propped up against 'a dead wall' – for the gratification of the 'Johns and Molls' at the Statutes and Fairs? I often wonder, for I remember as a youngster possessing quite a choice of 'songs', which I always carried in my jacket pocket; but, alas, for my peace of mind! a pious old lady, who took more interest in my spiritual welfare than I cared about, by some means (I think it must have been underhand) obtained the whole lot and consigned them to the flames. I hope all the old ballads haven't gone that way; although some of the singers might have been a trifle better for a little purifying.

Street singers lingered at Oakham until at least the end of the century. They could be heard 'drawling out doleful ditties' such as 'Sweet Belle Mahone', 'Just after the battle' and 'Where is my wandering boy tonight?' They also sang about topical events. 'I remember', wrote an eye-witness, 'a man and woman carrying a board on a pole, with a page from the *Police News*, depicting a horrible crime, and singing "Kate Webster you must meet your maker to answer for the deeds you've done", to the tune of "Just before the battle, mother". They sold copies of the song at a penny apiece'. There were also musicians playing in the streets of Oakham, on tin-whistle, flute, cornet, trombone, clarinet, fiddle, harp, dulcimer, and even hand-bells and musical glasses.

Music and ballads of this kind did suffer a long eclipse, but they have been revived in recent years, not so much in the streets and markets (though some young people do choose to make a living by singing and playing there) as in the upper rooms of public houses where folk song clubs meet as the glee clubs did two centuries before.

10. Crime and punishment

Tangible reminders of bygone punishments can still be seen at Market Overton and Bottesford in the shape of stocks and whipping posts. Under the buttercross in the Market Place the stocks still exist at Oakham. They have five holes, for which there are two possible explanations. One is that a frequent offender had a wooden leg, and therefore needed only one hole to secure his sound limb. Another that five drunkards were confined by one leg apiece. There is a story that some clowns from a visiting circus put themselves in the stocks to try them out, but found themselves obliged to pay a fee of half-a-crown each to the keeper to be released.

Stocks were set up in many towns and villages. In most cases the memory of such things has now gone, but in one village at least, Manton, it is preserved in a name: Stocks Hill. At Uppingham they were on Beast Hill, near the pinfold. Until the nineteenth century they stood in King Street at Melton and in the market place at Market Bosworth. Leicester

The stocks at Oakham, c.1900

173

had no less than nine sets, spread through the town, and they are often mentioned in the records. In 1524–5 the 'mendyng of the stocks twyse at the Berehyll [Bear Hill, or Barrell] Crosse' occurs, and in 1547–8 'mendyng of the cage and stokes', which cost two shillings, and also the 'stoks at the north gate'. A pair at 'thold hawle', the Old Hall in Blue Boar Lane, is mentioned in 1557–8. 'Reparacions' at a cost of two pence were made in 1566–7 to the 'stockes at Senvye Crosse'. Repairs and replacements seem to have been needed often. In 1610–11 fifteen shillings was spent on 'a newe paire of Stocks to stand in the Saturdaie Markitt', and in 1627–8 one shilling and sixpence was paid to 'John Kirke and others for fyndinge and takinge up the Stoks at the West gate they beinge throwen into the Soare'.

Those confined to the stocks lost their liberty for a time, and also suffered public humiliation. Someone who was unpopular could find himself taunted or even pelted. People were put in the stocks for failing to pay small fines, for begging without a licence, for drunkenness, or just to cool off, like Henry Jervis who was taken up by the watchmen in 1665 'for abuseing severall persons by traduceing terms and swearing many oathes'. Stocks are last mentioned in the Leicester accounts in 1744, but as late as 1832 an Oakham boatman called Austin Chamberlain was kept in Loughborough stocks for six hours for assaulting a constable. Market Overton stocks were last used in 1838. In 1855 a man was confined at Melton for six hours in the 'stiff stockings' for a drunken assault. In about the middle of the nineteenth century two vagrants were confined for the night in the stocks at Knossington. Next morning, both prisoners and stocks had disappeared. According to local tradition the vagrants managed to release themselves, then uprooted the stocks and threw them into the village pond, which is reputed to be bottomless.

The pillory was similar to the stocks, except that the prisoner was required to remain standing with his hands and neck fastened, whence the alternative name of stretch-neck. The pillory stood in the High Street at Oakham, where it is shown on Speed's map of 1610. At Leicester it stood in the Market Place, near the Pigeon Tree, an elm beneath which the country women sat to sell pigeons, and seems to have been used mainly for dishonest tradesmen such as those who sold beer under measure or strength or bread under weight. The offence would be placarded, as is shown by an entry in the accounts of 1575–6 'for pentinge [painting] 2 papers for the cosoners [cheats] that were sett on the pillorye, 8d.' The last references occur in the seventeenth century, though the punishment did not become illegal until the nineteenth.

Another way of immobilising an offender was to put him in a cage. Like the stocks and pillory, this frequently appears in the accounts because it needed repairs. In 1575–6 an unspecified sum was received for 'the old wood of the broken cage', then in 1600 it was agreed 'that theire shalbe a cage presently made, and to be sett vppe in the place called the Barrell Crosse, or theire abowtes'. The cage was later moved to stand by the pillory in the Market Place, but its subsequent history is not known.

Whipping was a common punishment, the offender, whether man or woman, being first stripped to the waist, then secured to the back of a cart or a post: '*Item* pd to Wm Sheene for A poste for correction of Roagues ij *s*.', 1605–6. Several whippings are mentioned in the constable's accounts at Melton for the years 1595–7:

Payde for meat for a rogue wch. was whypte iijd.

Payde for whyping Bess Knowles iijd.

Payde to a poore man and his wyff that was whypte and went to Buckminister iiijd.

At Leicester 'a cart to whype vaccabonds' was hired for fourpence in 1557–8, and three years later, after the expenditure of seven pence on 'waxe and small corde and 2 whyppes to whippe vagaboundes', one Richardson was paid a shilling and three pence 'for his carte fyve tymes abowte the towne with vagabonds'. In 1592–3 there is the grim record of payment for 'the whippinge of a lame crippell & of his hore & her husbond theire bawde & for a carte twice abowte the towne'. Theft could also be publicised in this way, as appears from an entry of 1611–2: '*Item* paide for a horse and carte to leade one Nicholas Okeley and William Cooke aboute the Towne xij *d*., and for cord to tye them to the carte i jd. and for whippinge of them for steyling wood 4*s*. xviii *d*.'

At Oakham whippings are recorded until the late eighteenth century. In 1765 Mary Smith was 'publickly whipt' at the Market Cross for a felony and John Smith was imprisoned for ten days in the House of Correction as 'a rogue and vagabond', and 'severely whipt two Saturdays in the open market'. Elizabeth also received the latter punishment for the same reason. As late as June, 1790, Edward Hodgkins and William Lewis of Braunston were whipped for stealing wood, the property of Sir Gilbert Heathcote. A woman 'Being an old offender', was similarly punished at Uppingham in 1785, also for stealing wood.

Sometimes, parading offenders round the town seems to have been sufficient punishment in itself, providing the offence was published. At Leicester in 1556–7 there is a record of one penny spent (and it is interesting that such a sum should be recorded in the accounts) 'for a paper to sett upon a woman's head'. This would have carried the information that she was a 'harlott'. 'A carte to carry a woman throughe the markett place' is mentioned in 1568–9 and again in 1574–5. The 'cartinge of a bad woman' occurs in 1599–1600, together with a 'carte to carte a man and a woman aboute the towne'. To attract the fullest attention a bell was rung, as appears from an entry of 1613–4: '*Item* paide for a horse and cart three holberde [halberd] men and one other man to ringe the bell when John Cambden and his wentch and allso Robert Webster were by order of the sessions carted aboute the towne iij*s.* vi*d.*'

Although both sexes could be stocked, pilloried, whipped or carted, certain punishments came to be reserved for women only. A 'refractory or loose-tongued' woman could be forced for a stated time to wear the branks, a sort of iron gag, padlocked to the head by a frame, and otherwise

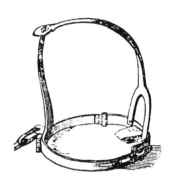

Scold's bridle, from Kelly's *Notices*

called a gossip's or scold's bridle. Alternatively she could be paraded round the town on a chair known as a cucking-stool or cuckstool. This appears in the records of Melton for 1631 ('Itm. for a chere to the cucke stoole and for a locke and stapell') and often in those of Leicester, where in 1467 it was ordered 'That alle maner scholdys that are dwellyng withinne this town, man or woman, that are founde defectyf by sworne men before the Maire presented, that then hit shall be lefull to the same Mayre for to ponyssh them on a cukstool afore there dore as long as hym lyketh and thanne so to be caried forth to the iiii gates of the town'. References in the accounts include an unspecified payment in 1547–8 for 'makyng the cookstoole' and the sum of twopence authorised in 1557–8 for 'carrying the cockystole twyse to the halle'. A total of 24s. 8d. was paid in 1602–3 for 'the charge of the Cucke Stoole, the Carte and the Stocks, and for the mendinge of the windows at the olde hall'. In the same year 'the carriage of the Cucke Stoole to the West bridge' cost threepence. The entry has an ominous ring, for if a woman were not silenced merely by an appearance in the chair she might be sentenced to be ducked in it, in which case she would be taken to the West Bridge and lowered into the river, once or several times. Ropes were attached to the chair for the purpose, as is seen from an entry of 1605–6 'for mendinge the Cuckstoole and for A corde for it xvj*d*.' The last mention in the accounts of the subject is £2 for a new cuckstool in 1768–9. Some ten years later John Throsby remarked that 'to the credit of the nimble-tongued fair it is now a long time since it was used'. The chair in question, once wrongly known as Alderman Newton's Chair, is still in existence in Leicester Museum.

Apparently there was another type, 'a kind of chair without legs, fixed at the end of a long pole', which was described to William Kelly in about 1850 'by an aged inhabitant of the town'. The same man remembered, when a boy, 'to have heard his mother say that a few years before she had seen the Cucking-Stool placed at the door of a house in Shambles Lane [which was in the area now covered by St Nicholas Circle], but that the woman, having managed to leave the house previously, escaped the ducking intended for her'. Another man, aged 80, recollected seeing the stool placed 'as a mark of disgrace in front of a house in Bond Street', and added that the woman living there had 'twice done penance in St Margaret's church, for slander'.

Penance, which did apply to both sexes, was usually for ecclesiastical offences. The ancient turf maze at Wing may have been connected with pagan ritual but there is a tradition that people guilty of various religious misdemeanours were obliged to tread round it as a penance. Similar

Turf maze at Wing

mazes once existed at Medbourne and at Priestley Hill, near Lyddington. Macaulay mentions the more normal penance of 'standing in the middle aisle during the time of divine service invested with white sheets', which was undertaken in about 1785 at Claybrooke by a man and a woman who had been presented by the churchwardens to the spiritual court for fornication. The last public penance in Leicestershire was in the 1840s at St Margaret's Church, Stoke Golding, which Nikolaus Pevsner, incidentally, describes as being one of the most beautiful churches in the country. The offender was a Mrs Frith, 'the landlady of the principal inn'. After a change of seating arrangements in the church she found a man sitting in what she still regarded as her pew, whereupon she 'lugged and gowged him'. She was charged with brawling in church, and sentenced by the ecclesiastical court at Leicester to stand wrapped in a sheet and holding a candle at the church door for three successive Sundays while the congregation entered. She complied, and 'multitudes assembled' to see the sight.

Finger pillory at St Helen's Church, Ashby-de-la-Zouch, from Kelly's *Notices*

In St Helen's Church at Ashby-de-la-Zouch is another form of penitential punishment, a finger pillory. It has thirteen grooves to take fingers of various sizes. One from each hand, perhaps, would have been inserted in a bent position, then secured in place by a hinged beam. There is no record of when it was last used.

Secular miscreants were sometimes kept in tiny village lock-ups such as the one still in existence at Breedon-on-the-Hill. There were similar structures at Snarestone, Packington and probably elsewhere. People would be put in for trivial offences, much as in the stocks, or perhaps to await escort for trial on more serious charges, and it should be borne in

The lock-up, Breedon-on-the-Hill

mind that at one time almost any crime affecting property was potentially serious. Almost at random one can turn up newspaper accounts such as this, from the *Stamford Mercury* in January, 1828: 'William Starsmore of Oakham, chimneysweeper, was found guilty of stealing some soot from the Hon. Henry Lowther of Barleythorpe Hall and was sentenced to seven years' transportation'. Broadsheets were issued with details of sentences, and one of these summarises the cases of 73 men, women and children who were tried at Leicester on a single day in March, 1833. Seven were sentenced to death, including Robert Francis Hall, aged 17, for breaking and entering and theft, and Henry Botterill (29) and Levi Burdett (21) for the highway robbery of two shillings and a watch. All terms of imprisonment of any length were served at penal settlements in Australia such as Botany Bay, and twelve of the 73 were sentenced to such transportation, for life. They included Thomas Coats (39) who stole four geese and four ducks at Bardon Park, and Carr Evans (50) for stealing a spade at Wilson, near Breedon. Fourteen years was the punishment for five prisoners, and ten years for one, David Bland (18) for 'intent to destroy seven stocking-frames belonging to B. Noon, at the parish of All Saints,' Leicester. The five receiving seven-year terms included William Mackew (20) for stealing a fowl, and Joseph Standell (18) for 'entering a wood at Staunton Harold belonging to Earl Ferrers'. There were four sentences of one year and eleven of sixth months or less. Four children, aged 11, 12 and 13 were sentenced to the 'whipt' for small thefts. Twenty-one cases were dismissed, or the defendants found not guilty. Of the three remaining sentences no details are given.

Similarly dismal catalogues of human misery go on for month after month, year after year, but the severity of punishment did not stem the tide of crime. In the recollection of James Hawker, the celebrated Oadby poacher, the 1840s were wretched times:

> Sheep Stealing, Highway Robbery and Burglary were common. It was not Safe to go out after Dark. If a Man Stole a Sheep he Had 14 years Transportation. If hunger made a man go into the woods to get a pheasant, he too would get fourteen years. Two men in Oadby Had 14 years – Jack Baurn, Bill Devonport – for attempting to take Pheasants in Tugley Wood, in 1847, so this is No Dream.

John Shipley Ellis (1828–1905) recalled a time during the 'hungry 'forties' when farmers at Glenfield, Kirby Muxloe and Anstey often found their flocks one short in the morning, but could not catch the thief. Then one day at dawn a man from Glenfield who was walking along the Groby Road to Leicester noticed a man in front of him at Gilroes. The second man had a sack on his back, and as the first man overtook him he surreptitiously felt the heavy sack and discerned what seemed like pieces of flesh in it. He walked on into the town and warned a constable, who stopped the man with the sack, and found parts of a sheep in it. The poacher was duly arrested.

Executions for sheep-stealing were not uncommon. William Dunn, a Yorkshire engineer working on the construction of the Oakham to Melton Canal saw one at Oakham in August 1801: 'Three persons were condemned but one was reprieved for transportation – and the other two, a man and a woman, were executed about 9 o'clock amidst a great concourse of spectators. The man met his fate which apparent fortitude: the Woman was much dejected and unhappy'.

At Barwell in the mid-nineteenth century a man called Bottewell was sentenced to death for robbery, despite his protestations of innocence. He sat up in his coffin meditating the whole night before he was due to be executed, but thanks to the efforts of the local rector, a Mr Metam, he was reprieved, and the sentence commuted to transportation to Botany Bay for life. Shortly after arriving in Australia Bottewell was pardoned, after another man had confessed to the crime. He returned to Barwell and lived the rest of his long life there.

Highway robbery and poaching attracted a good deal of attention, and also sympathy. One seventeenth century highwayman and his wife are commemorated to this day by two coverts close to the A50 road, just past the Saddington-Bruntingthorpe crossroads on the way to Husbands Bosworth, which are called John Ball and Jane Ball. This couple would fall on carriages and coaches as they toiled up the steep hill by the crossroads. They would rob and kill the passengers and run off the horses until, eventually, they were caught, and later hanged at the scene of their crimes. Twin coverts, planted some forty years later, were called after them, though there is an alternative story that the woods commemorate two millers who died on the hill when their cart overturned.

Dick Turpin is said to have hidden in Pear Tree Lane, Thistleton, and to have spent a night at the Ram Jam Inn at Stretton. This inn, formerly the Winchilsea Arms, takes its name from a potent drink concocted by an eighteenth century landlord, Charles Blake, and sold to coach passengers. The recipe is now lost. There is a story that a highwayman (sometimes a mere traveller) was unable to pay his bill for board and lodging, so devised a way of leaving without doing so. He told the landlady that he could show her how to draw both mild and bitter beer from the same cask. She was incredulous, but agreed to follow him into the cellar for a demonstration. He took up an augur and drilled a hole in the side of a barrel and told the landlady to stop it with her finger to prevent the ale from running to waste. Then he removed the spigot tap and invited her to stop the flow from there with her other hand. Then, ignoring her no doubt pertinent comments, he made his escape. This shows the quickness of wit associated with highwaymen, if not the chivalry.

On the other hand, Jack Ovet, a Nottinghamshire shoemaker turned highwayman, who often operated in Leicestershire, was furious when a squire from whom he had taken a purse with twenty pounds publicly complained that he had been attacked from behind. Ovet returned the purse and challenged the squire to a duel. It was fought with swords, and Ovet killed his man. He was hanged at Leicester at the age of 32, in 1708, for killing another man in a brawl.

William Nevison was given the nickname, 'Swift Nick', by Charles II on hearing of his riding from London to York in a day, a feat later attributed to Dick Turpin. Nevison committed many murders and robberies but was well-liked for his generosity; he indeed robbed the rich and gave to the poor. He was captured at Leicester in 1676 and imprisoned in the Highcross Street Gaol. He feigned sickness with the aid of painted spots which the doctor diagnosed as plague. Then he took a sleeping draught, and was pronounced dead. His relatives were allowed to take him out in a coffin, and he resumed his career. He was eventually re-captured at York and was sentenced to death, thanks to the evidence of an ex-confederate who accepted a reward offered by the governor of Leicester Gaol. Nevison was hanged in 1684, at the age of 45.

Throsby records that a clergyman, Rev. Hubbard, was sentenced to death at Leicester Assizes in August, 1753, for highway robbery. Apparently, after dining with a Mrs Burbage at Oakham he followed her 'at a distance for some miles' as she went towards her home at Melton, then, 'disguising himself, with a cloak, and visor, rode up to her, and ordered her to deliver her money, which she complying with he rode off; but he was detected by Mrs Burbage having a knowledge of his horse'. The outcome was his death sentence, but 'in consideration of his function he was transported'.

Leicestershire's best-known highwayman, George Davenport, was born at Wigston in 1758. In fact he operated more on foot than on horseback, and therefore was a footpad rather than a highwayman. One of his main sources of income was derived from enlisting as a soldier and deserting after receiving the bounty, then repeating the procedure with different regiments. He became something of a hero, renowned for open-handedness, though in fact he was callous, disloyal to his associates, and by no means averse to robbing the poor. He frequently held up stage coaches on the Oadby to Wigston road at a point where they slowed to ford a brook near a copse. Davenport's downfall came in 1797 through a comparatively trivial offence. He was fined five pounds for poaching fish, but gave the name of George Freer, and was not recognised. Since he was unable to raise the money the magistrates ordered that he should be kept in gaol. On the way there his escort allowed him to go into the Saracen's Head for a drink, and there he was recognised and identified by a former associate. Davenport was quickly put on trial on a charge of robbery, and after only ten minutes' deliberation the jury found him guilty. He was sentenced to be hanged. One account says that he was executed on a gallows close to where Mayfield Road now joins London Road, opposite Victoria Park; another, at Red Hill, Birstall. One story says that he rode in a cart, another that he drove stylishly in a carriage and pair. Whichever the case, he is remembered to this day.One man recalls his father's telling him, while on a walk from Oadby to Wistow Park, that one dark night two travellers once kept company on the same road. The talk turned to the infamous Devenport, and one said to the other: 'He'll never find my money. I keep it in my boots'. At the next crossroads the second traveller said: 'I'm Davenport. Now take your boots off and give me the money'. Davenport's descendants still live in Leicester but they now earn their living in a much less eventful way than their ancestor: by reconditioning domestic gas cookers.

Despite their dashing image, highwaymen were much feared, at least by people who had something worth stealing. William Dunn was alarmed by the news of robberies in December, 1800. In one case two highwaymen held up a man on the Great North Road and stole £50, and in another the Whissendine parson was attacked 'between there and Stapleford; two fellows with short [smock] frocks had tied the gait but he being an excellent rider and upon a hunter he leaped over the rails that is on the side of the gait and escaped'. Sometimes the outcome was less happy. In April of the same year 'a dreadful robbery happened':

about twelve miles from Cold Overton in the Parish of Thurnby two footpads robbed a man of the name of Wm. Popple about dusk in the evening – They broke both his arms and laid him on his back, and then one of them stood about a yard Distance and jumped upon his breast and broke it in . . . he lay till twelve at night when a stage coach passing by the Horses started from their road which the Coachmen knew was something extraordinary, he stopt them, got off the Box and found the poor man in a helpless condition, unable to speak, but alive, and as as there was no blood to be seen the Coachman etc. thought he was dead drunk. However they found very soon he was but just alive; they put him into the Coach and took him to a Public house in Leicester and sent for Dr Bishop who has almost made a cure.

'It has been much talked of', wrote Dunn to his family in Sheffield; 'they have apprehended one man on suspicion he is in the County jail where he will remain till the next Assizes'. It is possible that the man in question was the William Robins who was hanged at Leicester in 1801 for attempted murder.

Like highwaymen, poachers aroused a good deal of public sympathy, especially when they were considered to be striking a blow for the have-nots against the haves. The lady at Exton who delivered stolen partridges to Stamford for sale by tying them round her waist under her dress was no doubt secretly admired. Jack Thompson who lived in the Thatched Cottage on the green at Barrow was said to be so skilful as to be able to take a hare with his bare hands. His enemy was Black, the local gamekeeper, who became the subject of rhymes, along with Kitty, his horse, and Bolton, landlord of the Sun at Cottesmore:

Kitty in Bolton's stable was put,
Saddle and bridle they were cut.
The man as cut 'em cut 'em well;
Black was drunk and off he fell.

Once a hare was caught and left nailed to a signpost with this notice:

This little hare was caught in a snare,
And the man as caught it didn't care
For old Black, nor yet the young 'un.

Thompson, perhaps finding things too hot for him, emigrated to America in 1871.

In the first half of the nineteenth century three poachers lived in a little house in the High Street at Uppingham. They were all big men, and so fleet of foot that they could run down a deer or a hare. Their terrain was the wooded triangle with Uppingham, Wardley and Stoke Dry at its points. They kept themselves very much to themselves, and when one of their number died he was unceremoniously dragged downstairs by the feet, then propped upright in a parlour chair until a coffin could be made for him. Each in turn was treated in the same way.

A gang of poachers at Caldecott stole deer from Rockingham Forest. The venison would be hidden in the roof of their house or in a hidey-hole behind the chimney which was ventilated by a tiny window completely hidden by the overhang of the eaves. One of the men, Richard Vicars, was so agile that even at the age of 70 he could do a standing jump of three yards, either backwards or forwards.

Near Oakham lay the royal forest of Leighfield, the pronunciation of which is indicated by a variant spelling, Lyfield. It was partly in Rutland and partly in Leicestershire. Disafforestation began in 1235, and has continued ever since. There are stories that Robin Hood once took refuge there and that, centuries later, a band of army deserters made their home in the forest during the first world war, living rough and poaching for the pot.

The most celebrated Leicestershire poacher was James Hawker, who claimed to have poached 'more for Revenge than Gain'. He was born at Daventry in Northamptonshire in 1836, and started work at the age of eight at a bird-scarer for fourpence a week. He started poaching as a young man, and left Daventry when he was wanted by the police. He travelled to Leicester and took work in a shoe factory under the name of

James Collis. After enlisting in the army, then deserting, he moved to Oadby, in 1858, and spent the rest of his life there. Despite taking over 300 hares and also other game, he boasted that he had been in prison only once, and that unjustly, 'for getting a Poor old widow woman a Bundle of Sticks'. A witness swore that he had a gun, and was in search of game. Hawker was fined, refused to pay, and spent seven days in Leicester Gaol. 'Since then', he wrote, 'I have Poached with more Bitterness against the Class. If I am able, I Will Poach Till I Die'. And he did so, but avoided land on which he had permission to shoot, since he considered that took away all the fun. His autobiography, published in 1961 under the title of *A Victorian Poacher*, has become a minor classic.

Many other poachers fared less well. As late as 1884 a keeper called Collier struck a poacher at Burley on the head with a cudgel, and killed him. He was tried at Oakham Castle, but acquitted on a plea of self-defence. 'The Oakham Poachers', according to a ballad sheet of the 1840s or early '50s with this title, were the brothers John, Robert and George Perkins. They were confronted by keepers in 'Epping old wood' (probably Empingham Wood), and in the ensuing melee one of their opponents was killed. The brothers tood trial, and were found guilty of murder:

Young men in every station
That live within this nation,
Pray hear my lamentation,
A solemn awful tale.
Concerning three young men
That now do lie condemned,
And heavy bound in irons
In Oakham county gaol.

On the ninth of January,
Against the law contrary,
Five young men unwary,
A poaching went we here.
Epping old wood did ramble
And fired at pheasants random
Among the bushes and brambles,
Which brought the keepers near.

The keepers did not venture,
Nor care the woods to enter,
But outside near the centre
In ambush there they stood.
The poachers being tired,
As to fly away required,

At length young Perkins fired,
He spilt the keeper's blood.

He on the ground lay crying,
But no assistance nigh him,
Like one that was a dying,
His blood in streams did flow.
Our way for home were making
With nine pheasants we had taken,
Another keeper faced us,
We fired at him also.

Then we were taken with speed,
For this inhuman deed,
Which caused our hearts to bleed
When we were to prison sent.
The assizes they were near,
And one [of] our comrades swore
That we three brothers fired,
For it we do not repent.

Their names I now will mention,
John, Robert, and George Perkins,
Three brothers tried for poaching,
Found guilty as we hear.
Unto the judge they cried,
Pray mercy don't deny us,
Oh! do my lord have mercy,
Upon our tender years.

May he who feeds the raven
Grant them peace from heaven,
May their sins be forgiven,
Ere they resign their breath.
There ne'er were three brothers
Before condemned together
Within a dreary prison
And sentenced unto death.

So all young men take warning,
And don't the law be scorning,
For in our days just dawning
We are cut off in our prime.

So don't the laws be scorning,
Two of them are transported,
The other hung at Oakham,
My God forgive their crime.
The sheet was printed in Birmingham. Another version appeared later
at Preston, with the scene changed to 'Uppingham woods' and the new
sub-title of 'The Lamentation of Young Perkins'. As late as 1921 the
ballad, now called 'The Bold Poachers', was still being sung in Norfolk.
Although it seems to have been based on a real story I have not been
able to trace any other report or record of the Perkins' trial and
sentence.

Murders always aroused tremendous interest. News of them often
circulated on printed sheets, called broadsides. These could be in prose
or verse, which was sometimes intended to be sung. One example has a
comprehensive title: 'An Account of a Brutal Murder, At Hinkley [sic],
in the County of Leicester, on Saturday, Oct.22, 1836. Discovered by
means of a DREAM, by a person having Dreamed that his Sister was
Murdered by her Husband; when, on search being made, the bodies of
the Wife and CHILD was found murdered and thrown into a well,
underneath a heap of stones. The apprehension of the Murderer, and
his being conveyed to prison'. Another sheet, published in 1826, is
headed 'A Copy of Verses of the Unfortunate J. Akril, Who now lies
under sentence of death at Leicester, for Mare-stealing at Berwick, in
the Isle of Ely. To be hanged on 16th April'. It begins:

O, JOHN AKRIL, it is my name,
I've brought myself to grief and shame,
For Mare stealing I am doom'd to die,
On the fatal gallows tree so high.

Akril was hanged at Infirmary Square, one of the traditional places for
executions. Until the infirmary buildings had occupied the site in 1771
a space outside the south gate, known as 'The Gallows Field', had been
used. Leading to it was Hangman's Lane, later called Newarke Street.
In earlier times beheadings had taken place on the Castle Green, and
some executions were carried out at the High Cross. A Leicester men
called Kettell was hanged, drawn and quartered there for high treason
in 1554. Afterwards his severed head was fixed on top of the cross and
one of his quarters placed at each of the town's four gates.

Malefactors were sometimes hanged at or near the scene of their
crimes; sometimes the bodies were taken to the scene after hanging
elsewhere, to be displayed in chains or gibbeted, as it was called. Empingham's gibbet was still standing in 1900 at a spot appropriately called
Bloody Oaks. The last body exposed there was that of a sheepstealer.
Another sheepstealer was more fortunate. He was hanged on a hill near

Tilton but escaped death by standing on tiptoe – he cannot have been hanged very high – until the coast was clear and his friends could cut him down. Robin-a-tiptoe Hill bears his name to this day.

Two brothers, William and Richard Weldon, were hanged in 1789 at Gibbets Goss [Gorse] in their own village of Nether Hambledon. They had killed a baker with a pitchfork and robbed him of a £10 Stamford banknote and eight guineas in gold before throwing his body into the River Gwash. They were soon caught, and imprisoned at Oakham, where Richard also killed the prison keeper. Their mother was compelled to watch the hanging from her cottage, and then to endure the sight of her sons' dead bodies left for the crows. If this were not suffering enough she was sent to Coventry by the other villagers until she died. Afterwards her house was left untenanted, and allowed to fall down.

An eye-witness account of the affair comes from Dick Christian (for whom, see page 117):

I saw those two brothers hanging on the gibbet, with white caps on; they murdered a baker called Freeman. I was only seven when they were hung [which would make the year 1786]; I stood on my father's pony, and looked over his shoulder; I wasn't ten yards off them. The youngest of them, Bill, father had hired him to be a shepherd; he had

Hambleton viewed from Gibbets Gorse across Rutland Water

been at our place only a week before he was took, to settle about coming. Poor fellow, he cried sadly; his brother Dick, he was a regular hardened one – you know what he said about not dying in his shoes: I heard him say it distinct. He could see Appleton [Hambledon], the village he lived at, from the gallows, and he turns his face right towards it, and he says, 'Now I'll prove my mother a liar; she always said I'd die in my shoes'. They were his very words; and away he kicks them among the crowd. I think I see him a-doing it. Father went quite white, and fairly trembled in his saddle. They had chains from the waist down between their legs, and they hung on the gibbet that way. That was a great plum year, but there was no sale for them round Oakham; people wouldn't buy them if a fly had been at them; they had a notion they'd been at the gibbet, and sucked the flesh. I took no notice of it: I always ate plums when I could get them. They hung till they fell down; the good one lasted the longest; people watched for that. . . . That green field . . . just on this side the windmill is where they were hung; that house is where the doctress lady lives – her that makes the wind pills. I've heard she's got as many as one hundred and fifty patients; she takes two or three days to get once through 'em.

The intersection south of Lutterworth of the A426 with the A5 (Watling Street) is called Gibbet Crossroads. The body of a robber and murderer was gibbeted there in 1676. The slate headstone of his victim, William Banbury, can be seen in Lutterworth churchyard. One of the few remaining gibbet posts stands between Twycross and Bilstone, near the spot where John Massey, who was known as Topsy Turvy because of his skill in wrestling, fatally injured his wife in 1800 by kicking her into the mill-stream. He was convicted on the evidence of his ten year-old step-daughter, who had been treated in the same way as her mother, but had survived. Massey was hanged at Red Hill, Birstall, after which his body was taken to be exposed at the scene of his crime. His skeleton survived for nearly twenty years as a warning to others.

An even more spectacular case was that of John Cook, a twenty-eight year-old bookbinder whose workshop was at the back of the Flying Horse public house in Wellington Street, Leicester. One evening the attention of passers-by was attracted by what they thought was a chimney on fire because of dense smoke pouring out of it. Flesh was found burning in the grate. Cook explained that it had been intended for his dog, but surgeons identified it as human. Cook fled, but was caught at Liverpool as he was rowed out to a ship bound for America. He was brought back to Leicester for trial. It emerged that a Londoner called John Pass had called on Cook to ask for a payment of twelve shillings and had been battered to death, cut up and burned. Cook pleaded guilty, and was sentenced to be hanged outside Welford Road Gaol. Interest was enormous, and 30,000 people

The Gibbet at Twycross

urned up for 'Swingham Fair' on 10 August, 1832. One man noted aconically in his diary: 'Went to the Infirmary to see Cook hanged – who lied very firmly'. Possibly the hospital patients were among the spectators. Certainly, in the late 1850s and early '60s, according to a house urgeon, all the patients who were well enough were allowed to watch when there was an execution. A further 20,000 people assembled on the lay after the hanging to see Cook's body hoisted in an iron cage to the top of a 33 feet-high pole set up on a piece of waste ground by the junction of Aylestone Road and Saffron Lane. The body was taken down after three lays and buried on the spot. Workman digging a ditch there in 1930 ound the coffin. The cage can still be seen in the Guildhall.

Public executions did not end till 1868. At Oakham they took place just outside the town at the end of Hangman's Lane and Gibbet Gate (now called Uppingham Road) on a rise with the grimly ironic name of Mount Pleasant. On their last journey felons caught sight of the gallows as the road crossed a small stream, the water of which was convenient for reviving them when they fainted with shock. The place is still called Swooning Bridge.

The scene at an Oakham execution was described in the *Stamford Mercury* in April, 1813. On this occasion it took place in front of the gaol.

John Holes and William Almond who were convicted at the Assizes of a burglary in the dwelling house of the Rev. Richard Lucas of Casterton Magna were executed ... in the presence of a great concourse of people. The chaplain of the gaol, the Rev. Williams administered the sacrament before the men were brought out. They appeared on the platform over the front of the gaol and joined in singing hymns for hearly half an hour. At twelve the prisoners mounted the fatal drop, and the executioner immediately proceeded to adjust the ropes. Extreme agitation worked on their frames and features, but they repeatedly declared that they were comfortable and at peace with all men. A few minutes after twelve, the supporters of the platform were knocked away and they had soon passed the ordeal of human suffering. Almond appeared to be insensible of pain after the lapse of a few seconds, but Holmes struggled on the brink of eternity for a minute or two. After the bodies had hung the usual time, they were taken down.

On one occasion in the 1830s Rev. Doncaster, who was both Gaol Chaplain and Headmaster of the Grammar School, gave the boys a holiday so they could witness just such a spectacle.

Not all murderers were brought to justice. One case came to light only through a death-bed confession made by an old woman at Braunston to Rev. C. Collier. When she was young, in 1801, she had worked as housekeeper for a man called Smith, who farmed by Owston Wood,

Knossington. She had been forced to help Smith murder a cattle dealer called Samuel Johnson, to whom he owed money; she had helped to hold down Johnson while Smith beat him to death with a coal hammer. The body was buried and the place concealed by having a haystack built on top. Smith did not prosper, and died a pauper. A human skeleton was found on the farm by a later tenant, and reinterred at Knossington. The woman was the last survivor of those involved in the murder.

Even more macabre tales are still told. At Baggrave Hall, near South Croxton, a maidservant gave refuge to a woman while her employers were away. To her horror, she then noticed that the person was wearing heavy boots, and she reached the conclusion that it was a man in disguise, come to rob. She therefore plied him with wine until he was insensible, then cut off his head. On their return she presented it to her employers in a bag for burial, which is how Baggrave Hall got its name. Another story concerning thieves and a mansion is told of Bumble Bee Hall, Sharnford. A lad tending sheep on the thorn hills near Glebe Farm overheard thieves plotting to rob the house. He informed his master, and the plan was foiled. The thieves found out that the lad had given warning and in revenge they waylaid him and skinned him alive. In a refinement of cruelty they also killed and skinned a sheep, and put the boy in its skin; his own skin they hung on a thorn bush. The boy was still alive when found, but died within a few minutes, after saying that 'it didn't hurt very much, except when they pulled the skin over my finger and toe-nails'. At one time local people could point out the very thorn bush on which his skin had hung.

All that is left of the village of Wistow, between Arnesby and Great Glen, is the Old Hall and St Wistan's Church. Wistow is the traditional scene of the death of Wistan, who was murdered in 850, and later canonised. He was a prince of the royal house of Mercia, and should have succeeded to the throne on the death of his father, King Wigmund, but asked his mother, Queen Elfleda, to rule as regent. Berhtric, Wistan's cousin, wanted to marry her, and thus take power, but Wistan refused to agree to a match which he considered incestuous. Berhtric murdered him at Wistanstowe, which has been identified with Wistow. The crime was discovered because a column of light appeared over the spot where Wistan had been buried, and hair sprouted from the ground where the blood had run. Berhtric went mad. Wistan's remains were taken to Repton, and later moved to Evesham Abbey, where they were visited by pilgrims until the Reformation. There is still a belief that hair sprouts

Cook's irons in the Guildhall, Leicester

Staunton Harold

from the ground at a particular spot at Wistow on 1 June, the anniversary of the murder.

There was no miraculous element in the Blue Boar murder, of 1605. King Richard's bedstead, unreclaimed at the inn after the Battle of Bosworth, for obvious reasons, passed from tenant to tenant until Agnes Clarke, the wife of an Elizabethan landlord, discovered a secret drawer containing gold coins dating from the time of Richard III and earlier. The hoard was worth £300, an enormous sum for the time. It caused the landlord, Thomas Clarke, to prosper, and he became Mayor of Leicester in 1583, and again in 1598. Some years after his death his widow, Agnes, was murdered during the course of the theft of the residue of the money. A number of men were let into the house by a servant, Alice Grumbolde; 'as for Mrs Clark herself, who was very fat, she endeavoured to cry out for help, upon which, her maid thrust her fingers down her throat, and choaked her, for which fact she was burnt, and the seven men, who were her accomplices, were hanged at Leicester'. Thus Throsby. The money was never recovered.

One of the few peers ever to have been hanged was Laurence, Earl Ferrers, of Staunton Harold. His persistent cruelty caused his young wife to seek a divorce, and a steward was appointed to receive rents and pay any sums due to her. The earl took a violent dislike to the man, John Johnson, and one day summoned him to the hall. 'Down on your knees', he said, and when the terrified steward complied, shot him. Dr Thomas Kirkland was sent for, from Ashby, but Johnson died of his wound. Despite threats, Kirkland refused to keep silent, and his evidence led to the earl's arrest. Ferrers was lodged in the Tower of London to await trial by his peers. He appeared before the House of Lords, and was found guilty of murder and sentenced to death. On the appointed day, wearing his wedding suit of white silk, he drove from the Tower to Tyburn in his own landau, drawn by six horses. The press of people was so great that the journey of a few miles took three hours. Ferrers ascended the scaffold, and was hanged by a cord of silk. Eventually his body was returned to Staunton Harold.

I was told as a boy that the room in which the murder was committed was locked up immediately afterwards, and had remained untouched ever since. No doubt it is open today, since the hall is now one of the Cheshire Homes. Thomas Kirkland died in 1798, aged 77, and is commemorated by a plaque at St Helen's Church, Ashby. It is said that he was riding to Ashby with a companion on 18 January, 1760, when at about 4 p.m. he stopped to let his horse drink from a stream. He fell into a sort of trance, and saw a magnificent funeral pass, including a coach decorated with the Ferrers arms, drawn by six horses. Kirkland was atonished that his companion had seen nothing. On arriving home he was immediately

195

called to Staunton Hall, where he found that Johnson had been shot at 4 p.m. Ferrers' funeral, which Kirkland had seen in his vision, took place four months later.

Dr Kirkland's plaque at St Helen's Church, Ashby-de-la-Zouch

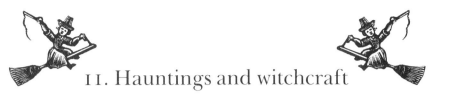

11. Hauntings and witchcraft

Ominous signs and portents , such as Garendon Pool's turning blood-red in 1645, caused deep concern. Fourteen years later, meteors were seen at Markfield, the sound of armies with their muskets and cannon were heard in the sky, and there was a fall of halberds, swords and daggers of ice which quickly melted on the ground. No conclusions were drawn, but the clergyman at Shepshed judged that the end of the world was at hand when unusual lights were seen in the sky over a period of eight years from 1715. Another sign of impending disaster was a black dog with blazing eyes. Such a creature lived in a pit and haunted Back Lane at Birstall until at least the 1930s, and similar apparitions were reported from Leicester Forest and Narborough St John's.

Fear and consternation are still aroused by the mischievous, even malign activities which are now attributed to poltergeists. Before the term came into use people asserted that the ghost of a dead person was responsible for the phenomena. At an Earl Shilton house in 1778 tables and chairs danced, pewter dishes jumped off shelves and hats and wigs flew of the heads of their wearers. The local explanation was that these were the doings of a dead person who could not rest because he had been defrauded in life. Violent knockings were heard in an old farmhouse at Edith Weston in 1896 which were so loud they could be heard fifty yards away. People were stationed on both sides of a door to find out what was happening but the thunderous knocks continued unabated. Another time, the cellar door was loudly knocked from the inside, but when it was opened the cellar proved to be empty.

In 1933 the *Daily Mirror* reported that gouts of water were issuing from time to time from the inner walls of a house (now demolished) in Bell Lane, Leicester, without apparent explanation. No dampness was caused, the wallpaper was not wetted, and investigations by the Water Department failed to find any cause. The vicarage at St Margaret's, Leicester, was affected by poltergeist activity and also haunted by the hooded figure of an old lady that glided through walls. When the building was demolished in the early 1960s strange phenomena started to occur in the church. A teenager was inexplicably terrified during a visit, violent movement appeared to take place inside an empty chest, a lampshade shattered in daylight, even though the bulb remained intact, and the church bell rang although the belfry was locked and the key secured. In an attempt to stop the activities of another poltergeist a ceremony of exorcism was carried at a house in Factory Road, Hinckley, as recently as 1973.

A classic ghost is the spirit of a dead person who revisits the scenes of its earthly existence. Sometimes it appears merely as a vague white shape flitting through a churchyard, as at Greetham, or down a road, as in the High Street of Fleckney. Three wraiths have been seen at Stocken Hall, near Clipsham, of which one is in the shape of a little white pup which does no harm but produces 'a sense of intense chill as it slinks past'. At Teigh there is an apparition at the rectory. A shapeless white mist appears at a pub in Churchgate, Leicester, which might be connected with the death of a former landlord, Harry Staines, caused by his falling down the cellar stairs, in 1896. Sometimes nothing at all is seen, but people hear strange noises and feel a sudden fall in temperature. At a house in Friar Lane, Leicester, in the 1820s heavy footsteps were heard going up and down stairs, into the cellar and into the bedroom. A constable was called and the house searched, but nothing was found. Similar sounds were heard over a century later by a young typist working in the same house. More heavy footsteps, said to be connected with the ghost of a cellarman, were heard as recently as 1984 in a house at Barrow-on-Soar which was formerly the Bishop Blaise Inn. Workmen who were in the house rushed upstairs, thinking to find an intruder, but no one was there.   The Belper Arms at Newton Burgoland, near Ibstock, is said to date from the twelfth century. It has a ghost familiarly known as 'Five to four Fred', from the usual time of its appearance. It has been given masculine gender because of its predilection for feeling women's faces or slapping or pinching their bottoms. Men feel a choking hand over their mouths and have to go outside to breathe. Both sexes feel an intense coldness. A similar choking sensation was felt by a woman in a Humberstone house. She told the *Leicester Murcury* in 1980: 'I was roughly awakened, feeling that my life was being choked out of my body. Although I couldn't see anyone in the darkness I . . . could actually feel someone – something – exerting a vice-like grip round my throat, so much so that I was forced back into the pillow. It was not a nightmare. I was fully awake, but unable to scream. In addition the temperature dropped considerably'. Her husband, who was present at the time, advised her always to wear a crucifix when she was in the house.

A music shop in Belvoir Street, Leicester, was once owned by Sir Herbert Marshall, who was Mayor of Leicester in 1869. After his death certain chords were repeatedly heard coming from the piano when no one was in the room. In addition books fell from shelves to the floor, a locked door flew open and an icy coldness was felt. A person spending the night there in 1977 to raise money for charity was awakened in the early hours of the morning by the sound of approaching footsteps. He then felt

The haunted inn at Newton Burgoland

a weight on his campbed, as though someone were sitting on it, but was powerless to turn his head and look. When the shop was unlocked the next morning he described his experiences to two radio reporters, who recorded the interview on separate tape recorders. On replay, each found an inexplicable thirty-second gap at the same point on his tape.

Another invisible presence was felt by Mrs Jennifer Morrison of Newbold Verdon in January, 1967, when she used for the first time a cotton nightgown which had belonged to a great-aunt of hers who had died three years previously. She had asked to be buried in the gown, but the request had not been met. When Mrs Morrison wore it she felt a tremendous force dragging on the sleeve. She promptly took off the nightgown and threw it outside her bedroom door. Then she heard a long drawn-out sigh. She never wore it again.

Many ghosts are clearly recognisable as human shapes, though their precise identity is not necessarily known. Between Kilby and Fleckney the spectre of a stark-naked man is reported to pursue village girls at night. A hooded figure has been seen in the churchyard of St Martin's, Leicester. A nanny in a long white uniform appears upstairs in a house at Tinwell called The Limes, especially when a child is ill. A mysterious man was seen at a bakery in Abbey Lane, Leicester, in the 1970s. Once only the shadow of his head was visible, then it disappeared into a wall. Other places of work have been visited by apparitions. Until the closure of Ibstock Pit Tumby's ghost was said to haunt the workings. This may have been a corruption of Thirlby, an old miner whose ghost wished to help or warn the living, or possibly the spectre of a miner who had been killed underground. In 1978 a strange woman was seen several times at Fisons Pharmaceutical Division in Derby Road, Loughborough, by a new cleaner called Lilian Dakin. These were secure premises, and careful checks were made when she reported the various sightings of the intruder. No one was found. Mrs Dakin lost her job. In the same year a ghostly girl was seen in the head offices of Golden Wonder crisps at Market Harborough. People felt uneasy ('the hairs on the back of your neck start to rise') and voices were heard, doors opened and closed, taps were turned on, apparently without human assistance. Most of the happenings were in the old Manor House, which had been incorporated into the office building. They remain unexplained.

The old Palace Theatre (now demolished) in Belgrave Gate, Leicester, was formerly checked by the manager every evening after the performance. Once he saw the stooping figure of an old man shuffling towards the exit. Next day he rebuked the usherette for not clearing the gallery. She asked: 'Was this a bent-up old man in a tatty coat?' When he confirmed it she said that she had seen the man twice before. Once she had cornered him but as she went to speak to him he disappeared. He resembled a tramp previously found dead in the entrance to the Floral Hall Cinema, which adjoined the Palace. Just down the road at the modern Haymarket Theatre a boy in an old-fashioned sailor suit was seen backstage and told to clear off. He did so, by vanishing. However, he was seen on other occasions, the last time being in 1981.

Still more ghosts wandered the roads and streets. Barkby Lane (now called Bedford Street) in Leicester was once avoided by children after dark because they were afraid of 'Squeaking Jenny', the figure of a woman dressed in white which uttered squeaking sounds. This was perhaps the ghost of a rag-and-bone woman of the same name. A fearsome female spectre was that of Poll Peg, which could be sometimes seen sitting on a stile by the roadside between Cossington and Sileby, close to the Coss Brook. For some unknown reason the woman's body had been buried by the roadside. An unidentified presence haunted Scholar's Bridge, between Sapcote and Stoney Stanton, and was 'a nightly terror to many of the inhabitants of both villages'. On the road between Seagrave and Sileby, near Quebec House, a ghost used to appear at midnight. Later, glass bottles containing hearts transfixed by pins were found buried in the garden of the house. Perhaps the ghost was that of a person killed by witchcraft. In addition, fairies were seen nearby, dancing in a ring, at least according to a report of 1875. Galley Hill on the road from Caldecott to Uppingham is said to be haunted by the ghostly sound of trotting hooves and Gipsy Hollow, close by, is rumoured to have been the place where murders were committed.

In the twentieth century people travelling in cars have encountered ghosts. In 1948 a car was travelling towards Wymondham at about half past seven on a bright moonlight night. Having gone up Saxby Hill it had reached a point were the road makes a sharp left-hand bend, when the driver's wife suddenly said: 'Look out, don't run into that man with a bike'. The husband said that no one was there, but his wife was so agitated that he turned round at the next junction and went slowly back to the point in question. No one was to be seen, either on the road or in the fields, yet the wife's mental picture of the man remained vivid. He was exceptionally tall, and was wearing a long grey cloak which came nearly to his ankles and had three lippet-type layers of cloth round the shoulders. He was hatless. The bike he was pushing towards Wymondham was not modern. It had rather large wheels with a few thick spokes, and narrow handle-bars which seemed to be made of wood.

In Evington Road at Leicester motorists sometimes narrowly miss a figure seen at the last split-second, or even think they have run it down, but find no trace when they stop to look. Near Brooksby Hall, close to the Leicester-Melton Mowbray road, a driver once saw a figure which seemed to be walking on its knees. On reflection, she realised that the level of the road had been raised at that point. At the same place another driver saw a figure in front of his car at the last moment. He braked violently to a stop, expecting to find a badly injured person, but no one was there.

Brooksby Hall itself, which dates back to Tudor times, seems to be the focal point for a number of strange happenings. A few days before Christmas a spectral coach and horses in regularly seen dashing towards the house at midnight. It stops, appears to unload a heavy object, then thunders off. The ghost of a former mistress of the house, Lady Caroline, appears from time to time, and the phenomenon may be linked with the discovery in 1891 by workmen engaged on alterations of a woman's skeleton. The hall at Husbands Bosworth also has a ghost, believed to be the unquiet spirit of a protestant lady enduring torment for refusing to allow a priest into the house to administer the last rites of the church to a dying Catholic servant. In an effort to expiate the guilt a Catholic chapel was built at the hall in 1873, but the lady's spirit still walks to this day, or her footsteps are heard. In the same house there is a stain on the floor which is said to be still damp after over 300 years. According to tradition this is either consecrated wine or blood spilt by a priest in his haste to escape from Cromwell's men. Blood stains appear in an upstairs room at Church Farm, Ryhall, and the house is also haunted.

Some ghosts are immediately recognisable by the people to whom they appear, and they show detailed knowledge of events which have taken place since their deaths. Sir George Villiers lived at Brooksby Hall, where his second son, also called George Villiers, was born in 1592. Young George later became a court favourite, and was made Duke of Buckingham in 1617. Some ten years later his father's ghost, or 'daemon', as it was called, appeared to 'an aged gentleman, one Parker' and asked him to warn his son to avoid the company of a certain person who would otherwise bring him to death and destruction. The name is not given in the account, thought Parker must have been told; perhaps the person was Charles I himself. Parker ignored the summons, since he thought it unlikely the haughty Buckingham would believe him, but the ghost appeared for a second time and repeated his request with some feeling. On hearing Parker's objection, the ghost provided him with a secret (again unspecified) which would authenticate the message to Buckingham. On this, Parker went to the duke, who was at first sceptical. Although he was amazed when he was told the secret he refused to heed his dead father's message. After the conversation the ghost again appeared to Parker and thanked him for his efforts. It then gave him a dagger, and asked him to go once more to Buckingham, to show him the dagger, and to tell him that he would die by it if he did not change his ways. He also told the luckless Parker that his death would shortly follow the duke's. Buckingham still ignored the message, and six weeks later he was stabbed to death at Portsmouth by John Fenton, a naval lieutenant who had served in his campaigns and seen the results of his catastrophic leadership. Parker died soon afterwards.

More ghostly prophecies were made in what is known as 'Lady Betty Hastings' Vision'. The account was written by a daughter of Dr Kirkland of Ashby (for whom, see page 195), who had it from her mother. Lady Elizabeth Hastings was a member of the family which once owned Ashby Castle. She was the daughter of Theophilus, the ninth Earl of Huntingdon, and Selina, who later founded a nonconformist sect known as the Countess of Huntingdon's Connection. Among many other possessions the family had two adjoining houses at Ashby. One was called 'The Palace' (later 'the old place') because a king of England had spent a few days there on a visit to one of the earls. Mary, Queen of Scots, was detained there for a time. The other house was built later, with a communicating door. Lady Betty's circle included two aunts, Lady Ann and Lady Frances Hastings, a cousin, Miss Wheeler, and a friend, Miss Hotham, the sister of Sir Charles Hotham. Lady Betty and Miss Hotham, as readers of Voltaire, were sceptical about heaven and hell, despite Lady Huntingdon's religious zeal.

Lady Betty and Miss Hotham made a mutual promise that the first to die would, if possible, return from the country whence no traveller normally returns to bring news as to whether life after death really existed. Much later, Miss Hotham died, and she appeared after death, carrying a small candlestick and wearing the nightgown she had worn when the pact was made. She told a shocked Miss Betty that the glories of heaven and the torments of hell really existed, though she neglected to specify which she was experiencing herself. However she made several prophecies: Aunt Frances would die six weeks from then, and Aunt Ann would not long survive her; Betty would marry a widower who had children but would 'not live comfortably in the married state'; she would 'cross the water' with her husband, on which occasion the voyage would be dangerous, the ship driven to a distant shore and the people on board given up for lost, though they would eventually reach safety. Lady Betty told all this to Miss Wheeler, but could not bring herself to pass on a final prophecy, though she promised to commit it to paper, to be read after her death.

Lady Betty did not tell her aunts of the fate foretold for them, but they did die as predicted. Her marriage, to Sir John Rawdon, later first Earl of Moira, came about as forecast, her first child being born in 1754. So did the perilous sea voyage. After her death, no manuscript with the final prophecy was found, but a son- or brother-in-law of Miss Wheeler's committed a murder as a young man, and was committed for life to an asylum. The full story was related by Miss Wheeler to Mrs Kirkland, who told her daughter, who wrote it down. It is here published for the first time.

Prominent historical personages sometimes appear as ghosts. Dick Turpin has been seen at Pickworth and John o' Gaunt at Leicester Castle. Lady Jane Grey haunts the White Tower in the Tower of London and also Bradgate Park, where she appears in a spectral coach every New Year's Eve. Another version of the story says that Christmas Eve is the time, with coach and passenger going either to the church in Newtown Linford or to the ruined house in the park before disappearing. A third variant is that the four horses are headless, and that Jane carries her head on her knees.

Another coach with headless driver and passenger is seen in a lane called Marsick Close between Tilton and Halstead. The richly-dressed passenger is thought to be Sir Everard Digby, who was beheaded in 1606 for complicity in the Gunpowder Plot. He and his family owned Tilton Manor House, where lights are seen flitting from window to window at dead of night, and a ghost is said to have been bricked up in a wall. The family also owned North Luffenham Hall, which is haunted by the ghost of Sir Everard himself. One woman visitor claims that she was pinched by it. A coach and horses with a headless driver is seen driving at full gallop at

Thistleton Gap, and a similar equipage is seen at midnight between Croxton Kerrial and Branston. The ghost, this time with head, of a passenger killed in a stage coach crash was seen as recently as 1973 at Stocks Hill, Manton. A headless man on horseback is said to jump the hedge at Preston near where a windmill, demolished in 1926, used to be. The spot is aptly named Ghost Hollow. A headless pedestrian is seen on a footpath in the fields between Barrow-on-Soar and Quorn, and there are two headless figures at Ibstock. One rides by Clap Gates on the way to Kelham Bridge, and is thought to be the ghost of a local man who fell into the ditch one dark night while attempting to close the gate and broke his neck. The other is an unexplained female figure walking with head under arm near the Melbourne Road cross-roads. Another woman with her head under her arm walks Teigh Hill. Yet another headless female figure haunts Saddington Tunnel on the Grand Union Canal. It is said that a woman was once accidentally decapitated while travelling through on a boat.

The strange case of a woman from Bottesford was related in the *Leicester Chronicle* in 1874. Some twenty-five years earlier she had died in Leicester Royal Infirmary while undergoing an operation for breast cancer. She was afterwards seen in her house, dressed in white, with blood running from her breast. The latch of her bedroom door was heard to rattle. Bells rang and other unexplained noises were heard at the house in Wymondham of the surgeon who had operated on her. The parson and the policeman were called – apparently the surgeon thought it wise to seek help from both the ecclesiastical and secular arms – but nothing was found.

A draper called Sammley lived during the early eighteenth century in a house near East Gates, Leicester. He was once mayor of the town, and later an alderman. His wife died in 1727 and was later seen at the house on several occasions, dressed in silk and satin, and with a pallid face. She terrified the servants by shaking their bed-curtains and waking them up at night. The vicar of St Martin's was called in. He confronted the ghost and asked questions of it, to which he received answers. Afterwards the hauntings stopped, but there is no record of the dialogue which took place.

Many ghosts are thought to have walked because they had been treated unjustly in life. According to tradition a large field a mile north of Scraptoft is haunted; it was previously the village of Hamilton, which was deserted by or cleared of its inhabitants. One local man never passed a certain tree there without taking off his hat as a mark of respect. Horses grow restive, and one rider felt something 'beginning to lean up against him' and his mount, and only with difficulty disengaged himself.

In 1981 at the Barge Pole Restaurant, Bowling Green Street, Leicester, mutterings were heard in a previously disused cellar, a coffee machine switched itself off, keys went missing, and people felt something invisible brush past, or sensed something watching them. It was later discovered that someone had been imprisoned in the cellar, perhaps without just cause, in 1749.

Premises at Leicester St Martin's, shared by Age Concern and the City and County Rent Office, were long felt to be subject to strange phenomena. Miss Margaret Hoghton said: 'I have very often sensed someone standing behind me, only to turn round and find no one there. Heavy breathing has been heard in the deserted upstairs room, pillows and pens have gone flying, and one of our cleaning ladies says she saw the ghost of an old man through a hole in the skirting board. She later found out the hole didn't exist, and a painter working here one day had a rather nasty experience when a lady passed underneath his ladder and disappeared into thin air. He couldn't speak for about ten minutes afterwards, he was so shaken'. During the course of work in one of the cellars in 1984 the bones of a large man, a small woman and a dog were discovered. A pathologist judged the bones to be at least a hundred years old, and they were buried in Gilroes Cemetery. It remains to be seen whether the strange phenomena will now come to and end.

The death of a miller at Kibworth from a cruel prank caused his ghost to walk. During a party at the Coach and Horses he was downing quantities of gin for a bet. To try to make sure he lost, his companions gave him double measures. He still drank them off, and won the bet, only to fall unconscious. He was later pronounced dead, but there was a suspicion that he might have been buried alive, because noises were heard coming from his coffin. Perhaps those who heard were too frightened to do anything, so the burial went ahead, but the miller's spectre was seen subsequently.

Those who died by their own hand were thought not to rest easily, and the ghosts of suicides are seen at various places, including Snelston. A young boy was frightened in 1975 by a bearded figure in old-fashioned clothes at the Volunteer public house, Loughborough. A search of the premises produced no one, and research after the incident revealed that suicide had once occurred on the premises. The pub owes its name to having been used as a recruiting centre during the Napoleonic Wars. In 1980 a ghostly figure was seen gliding down the platform, carrying a lamp, at Rothley Station. Perhaps this was connected with a signalman who died there in 1936, though people are not sure whether his death was by suicide, by accident, or in an effort to save the life of another person. Another Rothley ghost is not only seen but sometimes spoken to at a public house, The Woodman's Stroke.

Lady Aslin died by drowning. She was a country girl who agreed, against her own better judgement, to marry the unsavoury Goisfried

Kibworth Mill in 1939
(Photograph by courtesy of *Leicester Mercury*)

Aslin, lord of Whitwick Castle in the time of King John. The marriage was followed by a brief period of happiness, after which connubial calm began to pall for Aslin. He reinstated his boisterous companions, and not only resumed the orgies carried on before his marriage, but compelled his young wife to join in. Full of revulsion, she made a desperate bid to escape, by swimming across a deep, dark pool behind the castle. She drowned in the attempt, and her ghost haunted the vicinity for the next 750 years. It was last reported in the 1960s.

Victims of murder seem to have been particularly liable to haunt the scene of crime. Agnes Clarke (for whom, see page 195) was murdered at the Blue Boar in Leicester in 1613. Not only did her spirit haunt the inn, but when it was demolished in 1838, and the name transferred to new premises in Southgate Street, the ghost followed. The second Blue Boar has now given way to a traffic underpass, and the ghost is seen no more. Another public house, the Drum and Monkey near Whitwick, is haunted by the ghost of a man who was murdered there. A private house in a village a few miles east of Leicester – the vague description, given in 1874, was no doubt to deter the curious – was haunted by the figure of a man wearing a long coat, knee breeches, white stockings and a straw hat. Noises were also heard, as if a person laden with chains were moving about. Local people said that the house had earlier been an asylum for the insane, and that a wealthy inmate had been murdered for his money. During the course of alterations the skeleton of a tall man was found buried in the garden, and re-interred in the churchyard. The ghostly activities then stopped.

Both murderer and victim haunted the old rectory at Swithland. In the 1780s the twenty year-old daughter of the rector was sent down a day before the rest of the family to ensure that the house was ready for its return. This was most unwise, for the butler was not only fond of the bottle but subject to fits of madness. In the night, while both drunk and insane, he broke into the young woman's room and hanged her from her own bed-post. As sobriety and sanity began to return he realised the enormity of his crime and cut his own throat. The two bodies were found next day by the returning family. Subsequently the spectre of the butler appeared with dripping throat, uttering hoarse cries of anguish. The spirit of his victim, called the 'Grey Lady' from the colour of the dress habitually worn, was often seen. Indeed, she was sometimes taken to be a guest at a rectory garden party, unremarked save for her old-fashioned dress. When the old rectory was demolished the Grey Lady was seen walking away towards the church, head bowed, carrying a stone slab, but then appeared no more.

A servant girl was once strangled at Manton Old Hall, and strange noises are heard there on occasion. Papillon Hall at Lubenham has a remarkable record of strange happenings. One of the family from which the hall took its name, David Papillon, died in 1762. He was known as Pamp, Old Pamp or Lord Pamp by local people, who feared him greatly. They believed that he could 'set' or 'fix' people who offended him. There is a story that he disapproved of the way in which some men were ploughing, so he 'set' them in such a way that they were unable to move hand or foot until he released them at the end of the day. If any villager suffered a misfortune he blamed the influence of Old Pamp, and people made a cross in their dough when baking or in the mash when brewing beer to avert his evil eye. Before his marriage he kept a mistress, probably Spanish. She was not allowed to leave the hall at any time, but took her exercise on the flat leads of the roof. She died in 1715. There is was no record of her death or of her place of burial, but the skeleton of a woman was found walled-up during alterations at the hall in 1903. Before dying the woman uttered a curse that ill-fortune would befall any owner of the house if ever her shoes (in fact, a pair of silver and brocade slippers and a pair of pattens) were ever taken off the premises. Consequently, whenever the house was sold the shoes were handed with the title deeds to the new owner, except in 1866, when the shoes were taken away to Leicester. The new family was awakened at night by the crashing of furniture and the slamming of shutters, but on investigation found everything in order. The shoes were brought back, and the noises ceased, but the house changed hands again, six years later.

The new owner foolishly lent the shoes for a year-long exhibition in Paris, but life became so intolerable that he and his family had to move out of the hall until the shoes were returned. The next occupant, who took over in 1884, was so determined to avoid trouble that he had a fireproof cupboard with a padlocked metal grille constructed so as to keep the shoes securely. However, despite warnings, Captain Frank Belville, who arrived in 1903, had the shoes removed to his solicitor's office during alterations. Accidents immediately befell the building workers, and one of them was killed by a falling brick. The men refused to work. After Belville himself had sustained a broken skull in an accident with his pony and trap the shoes were hurriedly brought back. Despite this experience Belville agreed to lend them to Leicester Museum for an exhibition in 1908 or '09. While they were away he fractured his skull while out hunting, and the hall was set on fire during a tremendous storm of thunder and lighting. Three horses were killed, and some say that two men also died. Once more the shoes were brought back and this time Belville locked them behind their grille and threw the key into the pond.

The shoes were safe until the second world war, when the hall was used for billetting American airmen. On two occasions men who had taken shoes away were killed in action, though somehow or other the shoes were returned, except for one patten. In 1950, shortly before the hall was to be demolished, Mrs Barbara Papillon was able to take possession of the remaining shoes. No more has been heard of the curse, but some Lubenham people still remember tales of Old Pamp and his mysterious mistress.

Another hall, at Hinckley, stood in what later became part of the vicarage grounds. Tom Paul, who was 86 at the time, remembered in the 1880s a story told about it by his mother, who had lived nearby. She heard the cries of a child, who subsequently died, being flogged there. Its spirit haunted the place afterwards. A team of ministers assembled in the room where the flogging had taken place to conduct a ceremony of exorcism. After a series of prayers and readings from scripture the spirit was induced to enter a bottle, which was secured corked and thrown into the 'motts' or moats (originally fishponds). At night the spirit could be heard buzzing or humming in its bottle. A similar story is told of the pit near Lash Hill, not far from Burbage. A local man, whose name has not been recorded, played the fiddle at fairs, statutes and dances. On his way home late at night he always took out his fiddle and played himself past the spot so as to charm the spirits. A ghost at a large house in Twyford was conjured into a bottle which was buried in the cellar. This was afterwards filled up. For some reason the ghost continued to be seen in a room at the top of the house, so it was kept closed, and the door covered with sacking.

Platts Stile on the footpath from Wymondham to Edmondthorpe was haunted. Within living memory children were told not to pass that way after dark for fear they should have the feeling of being hit by a heavy money-bag. When they pressed for an explanation they were told that two men had quarrelled at the stile over money. They came to blows. One was killed, and his ghost haunted the spot and caused the sensation described. One man passing that way regardless was staggered by a heavy blow at the back of the neck. When he reached his friend's house at Edmonthorpe he found a big red mark there. 'Oh', said his friend, 'that would be the ghost of Platts Stile'.

Other fights have left a legacy of strange phenomena. Two brothers once fought a duel at Morcott Hall, which is now a boarding school, over a certain Lady Betty. Blood was spilt, and the stain could not be effaced, however much the floor was scrubbed. Eventually the boards were removed. The duellists' fate is not known, but the ghost of Lady Betty, a small crinolined figure, haunted the house at least until the 1950s. Another duel was fought at Skeffington Hall between John Skeffington and Michael Bray. In the early seventeenth century the two men managed to kill each other, in a room on the top floor. People sleeping there, though they see nothing, wake with feelings of fear and horror. In a further case an account of 1875 speaks of a house at Kibworth known for

Platts Stile, Wymondham

'upwards of a half a century to be haunted'. There, one man killed another in a quarrel, and ghostly figures were afterwards seen fighting, or the noise of fighting or of pacing footsteps was heard. The householder matter-of-factly referred to all this as 'the bogey'.

Such things are by no means confined to ancient halls. At a council house in Market Harborough several apparitions were seen in 1980. A child saw a lady with a lantern who attempted to tuck him in bed. On at least six occasions the figure of a young man was seen, clad in a khaki greatcoat and a round hat. Once the older son of the family, himself a soldier on leave from the army, was wakened in the night by the same figure. It beckoned to him, and he followed on to the landing. 'He could see his face, which no one had seen, and it had a cordite burn mark on one side of it. The ghost seemed to be wanting to tell him something but then he disappeared'. The case was reported in the *Harborough Mail*.

Perhaps the ghostly soldier had died on a far-off battlefield. Nearer to home, the Battle of Bosworth left the phantoms of a headless soldier and spectral horseman which have been seen on the site. On 14 June, 1949, a man and a woman who were out cycling stopped near Naseby and saw carts passing down an old drover's road, pushed by men in leather jerkins. They both felt apprehensive, and left as soon as possible. Only later did they realise that it was the anniversary of the Battle of Naseby, and only then did they broach the subject of what had been seen – to find they had both had the same vision. Naseby is, of course, in Northamptonshire, but after the battle the pursuit of the routed royalists spread over half Leicestershire.

Much more ancient battles were fought at Wigston. When Wigston Magna Cemetery off Welford Road was opened in the 1880s the grave-digger found a broken sword, smashed-in skulls and bits of armour and harness. His comment was: 'It was just as if a battle had taken place there'. Possibly it was an Anglo-Saxon burial site, and 6th century finds were made at Wigston in 1795. The Danes are known to have sacked and burned Wigston in about 876. The full story of those distant times may never be known, but some reverberation seems to continue from them. In August, 1981, a woman and her son travelling from Nottingham to Basingstoke with a car and caravan broke down at Wigston. Repairs to the car were to take two days, so the caravan was parked in a field called Heard's Close, opposite the cemetery. After the first night the woman told a local man: 'This is an evil spot. I heard shouts and shrieks, groans and clashing of metal, just as if a battle was being fought'. She added that she would take a strong sleeping pill for the second night. On the next morning she was asked whether she had slept. 'Yes', she said, 'but I was wakened by my son shouting "Get up, get up".' Half awake, she saw a youth with a deathly-pale face, dressed in a white robe, who then vanished. Her son was in the bunk opposite, still asleep. She looked out of the window and saw that dawn was breaking through a heavy mist.

A local woman saw in the same place, though not at the same time, what she described as a vision: 'As I looked out of the kitchen window towards the cemetery it was misty, and an army or large numbers of men with spears and shields and armour were walking or marching through the mist, but then they were gone as quickly as they had appeared'. It may be coincidence, but a man working the same ground, opposite the cemetery, was killed in a collapsing trench in September, 1983.

Ghost stories are still common, though tales of UFOs bid fair to displace them from the headlines. Little is now heard of witches, save the occasional glimpse of ceremonies concocted for pseudo-sophisticates. For many centuries they were not only believed in, but severely punished. As early as 1596 a woman called 'old mother Cooke' was detained in Leicester Guildhall for five days on suspicion of 'Witchrye', then 'removed to the Countrye gaiole, and was for the same arrayned, condemned and han-ged'. Twenty years later nine women were tried at the assizes for bewitch-ing John, the thirteen year-old son of a Mr Smythe from Husbands

Bosworth. Each woman, it was alleged, had a familiar spirit in the shape of a horse, a dog, a cat, a fulmar, and so on. The boy would utter the noise appropriate for whichever spirit possessed him, and he also had fits. The women were found guilty by the jury and were sentenced to death by the presiding judges, Justice Winch and Sergeant Crew. One report says that they were hanged, another that they were burnt in what was for the next two centuries called Women's Lane.

Later in the same year, 1616, James I passed through Leicester on a royal progress. He was interested in witchcraft and had written a book on it. When he heard of the case he personally questioned John Smythe, and also arranged for him to be seen by the Archbishop of Canterbury. The boy confessed to having told a pack of lies at the trial, and the king severely criticised the judges for accepting his evidence. The so-called witches were already dead, but five out of six other women who were awaiting trial on similar charges were released. The sixth had died in gaol.

There was nevertheless another spectacular trial in 1619, this time at Lincoln Assizes, but involving women from Leicestershire and Rutland. The case concerned Joan Flower of Langham and her two daughters, Margaret and Philippa. Joan had enjoyed a reputation as a witch for some time. Philippa, 'being lewdly transported with love for one Thomas

Simpson', had bewitched him when her advances were rejected. Margaret entered the service of the Duke of Rutland at Bevoir Castle, where she lived in as poultry keeper and laundress, but she was dismissed for pilfering. Joan therefore cursed the earl and his family, and with her two daughters and three other women, Anne Baker of Bottesford, Joan Willimott of Goadby and Ellen Green of Stathern embarked on a campaign of revenge by occult means. They first made a pact with Satan, pledging their souls in return for power and the aid of familiar spirits, then procured a glove belonging to Henry, the infant Lord Roos. This was rubbed by Joan Flower on the back of her familiar spirit, a cat named Rutterkin, then dipped into hot water and pricked with pins. The child died, in 1613. The same treatment was tried on the next-born, Francis, but merely caused illness, so his glove was buried in a dunghill, with the expectation that as it rotted he would decline. He died in 1620. His sister, Katharine, was also ill, but all six women were arrested at Christmas time in 1618 and taken to Lincoln Gaol to await trial. On the way or, according to another account, in the gaol, Joan Flower called for a piece of bread and butter, saying that if she was guilty God would strike her down as she ate it. She indeed fell dead after biting it, though she may have seized the opportunity to take poison, knowing the likely fate which awaited her.

The others were all tried, and found guilty. Margaret and Philippa Flower were hanged, though their fate cannot be verified, since records for the period at Lincoln have not survived. What happened to the others is not known. A number of contemporary publications, including a booklet and a ballad, tell the story. The monument in Bottesford Church to the sixth Duke of Rutland, who died in 1632, his two wives and children, bears an inscription, the only one in England which refers to sorcery. 'In 1608', it runs, the earl 'married Lady Cecilia Hungerford . . . by whom he had two sonnes, both which dyed in their infancy by wicked practise & sorcerye'.

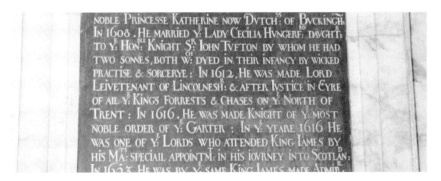

Part of the inscription at Bottesford Church

With such news in the air it is not surprising that all sorts of similar accusations were made. In 1620 the minister at Swithland, Gilbert Smyth, complained to the circuit judges at Leicester that Christopher Monk had claimed he was 'a Sorcerer and the meanes of the breakinge of his wives Arme and of his sons cuttinge of his owne throate'. Monk counter-petitioned to the king, but the outcome is not known.

In 1635 a woman called Agnes Tedsall was tried at Leicester Assizes on a charge of causing the death of Richard Linsey by witchcraft, but was acquitted. Fifteen years later Ann Chettle was arrested on suspicion of witchcraft and obliged to submit to an examination to reveal whether she had a so-called witch-mark on her body. This was any spot which did not bleed when pricked by a pin or needle. Four townswomen certified 'that they had diligently searched the said Ann Chettle from the crown of her head to the soles of her feet, and found her to be clear of any suspicion'. Two years later she was again in trouble, and a warrant was issued for her arrest on another charge, but the result is again not known.

Sir Roger Smith of Edmondthorpe died in about 1655. His tomb in St Michael's Church has alabaster effigies of his two wives. One, that of Lady Ann, has a red stain on the wrist. The local explanation is that she was a

The lower effigy is that of Lady Ann Smith, showing the stain on the wrist, at Edmonthorpe Church

witch who could turn herself into a cat. In this shape she was wounded in Edmondthorpe Hall by the butler, who struck at her with a cleaver. She was wounded in the paw, and blood was spilt on a kitchen flagstone. Lady Ann bore the mark on her wrists, and it was reflected on her statue. The bloodstain on the kitchen floor proved to be indelible. Eventually, some time between 1918 and 1922 the Countess of Yarborough, who then lived in the hall, had the stone taken up because the maids complained that however much they scrubbed it would not come clean. It was removed to J.W.Golling's workshop in Wymondham Main Street, where it was the object of considerable curiosity.

Another crop of witchcraft cases appeared at Horninghold in 1709, as revealed by the diary for that year of Rev. Humphrey Michel, Rector of Blaston and Vicar of Horninghold. The first, unusually, concerns a man, a labourer called Thomas Holmes. On 11 June a crowd of 500 people assembled to see him 'dowsed three times for a witch' in the Dungeon Pit at Blaston. he 'did not sink, but swam, though his hands and feet and head were all tyed fast together'. This was taken as a sign of guilt. In the same Whitsun week Elizabeth Ridgway and Jane Barlow were similarly ducked, and also failed to sink. Barlow, aged 40 offered to try the test again, in another pond, in an attempt to clear herself. She still floated, though 'Mary Palmer, her sister, a cripple from her cradle, almost 42 years old, was dowsed there for a witch several times, and though bound hands and feet, did not swim, but sank immediately, like a stone, before us all'. Next, a collection was taken and handed to a servant called Joseph Harding to take the same test as a sort of control experiment. He did so, and immediately and conclusively sank.

In August of the same year Frances Sharp, wrote Michel, was 'in all probability bewitched to death by one Widow Ridgway', presumably Elizabeth. Before dying Sharp stated that Ridgway had appeared to her in terrible shapes, and that she had lost a protective charm given to her by 'the white witch of Kibworth, one Clow', to be 'kept in her shift about her bosom'. Finally, in October, 'a wench of the Widow Barlow, a supposed witch', walked out of the church when Michel read out the text of his sermon from *Deuteronomy*: 'There shall not be found among you any one that maketh his son or his daughter to pass through the fire, or that useth divination, or an observer, or a witch, or a charmer, or a consuler with familiar spirits, or a wizard, or a necromancer'.

By this time, however, the official prosecution of witches was about to come to an end, if not the private persecution of them. The last recorded indictment for witchcraft at a secular court in England took place at Leicester in 1717. Jane Clarke of Wigston and her son and daughter were suspected of witchcraft and were publicly swum. They floated 'like a cork, a piece of paper, or an empty Barrel, tho' they strove all they could to sink'.

They had blood drawn 'above the breath' to take away their powers, and were taken to court. Despite the willingness to testify of twenty-five witnesses the grand-jury threw out the bill of indictment, and the Clarkes were set free. The crime of witchcraft was removed from the statute book in 1736. In 1760, perhaps for the first time, punishments were imposed on those assaulting witches after incidents at Glen (now separated into Glen Magna and Glen Parva) and Burton Overy. Two old women at Glen vehemently accused each other of witchcraft, and challenged each other to submit to the ordeal of swimming. They stripped, had their thumbs and big toes tied together cross-wise, and were thrown into a deep pool, with a rope tied round their waists. One sank immediately, but the other floated. They were both pulled out and, the guilt of the 'swimmer' having been established, she was invited to name her accomplices. She said, rather subtly, that at Burton Overy there were several old women 'as much witches as she was'. As a result, over the next few days, three of them were ducked in a gravel pit. Two of the men responsible were subsequently sentenced to be pilloried at Leicester, then imprisoned for a month, and twenty others were fined.

A similar incident was reported in 1776, and the writer's indignation is made very clear. After suffering for several years from 'a disorder resembling that which proceeds from the bite of the tarantula' a woman at Earl Shilton took it into her head that she had been bewitched by an old woman in the neighbouring village of Aston Flamville. These events followed:

On Thursday June 20, the afflicted person, her husband, and son, went to the old woman at Aston, and threatened to destroy her instantly, unless she would submit to have blood drawn from some part of her body [which was thought to deprive a witch of her powers], give the woman a blessing, and remove her disorder. The son (who is a soldier) drew his sword, and pointing it at her breast, swore, he would plunge it into her heart, if she did not immediately comply. When the old woman had gone though this ceremony, they went off. But on Monday last, the person not being cured, they collected a great number of people, and returned to Aston, pretending to have a warrant to justify their proceedings; then, with uncommon brutality, took the poor creature (who is 80 years age, and a pauper) from her house, stripped her quite naked, and, tying her hands and legs together, threw her into a horse-pond; she was then taken out, and in this shameful condition exhibited for the sport of the inhuman mob. As she did not sink in the water, they concluded she was really a witch; and several returned on the following day, determined to discipline her in this cruel manner till they should put an end to her life. The mob, however, was not sufficiently strong, so that she escaped for that time;

and it is hoped that some methods will be pursued to prevent a repetition of this horrid usage.

It is a pity that the outcome does not seem to have been recorded, but belief in witches certainly continued in the area. At Elmesthorpe a farmer complained in 1811 that: 'It is common almost everywhere amongst the women when they brew to make crosses to keep the witch out of the mash-tub and that the ale may be fine'; and he added that 'farmers and common people' were 'very great believers in old popular tales of ghosts, fairies, witches, and people and cattle being under an evil tongue'.

At Snelston a witch was reputed to run out and hang on to the wheels of carts as they laboured up Galley Hill, and at Twyford certain women if they were offended by a farmer could 'set the plough teams fast' in the field or make a waggon and horses immoveable on the road. They could also bewitch cows so that they gave no milk, or the cream in the dairy so that no butter came. For fear of this a naturally holed stone was kept in a dairy at Wymeswold, another village with a witch problem, since it was thought to forestall witchcraft. The stone was presented to Leicester Museum in 1852. Back at Twyford, some alleged witches were ducked, and nearly drowned. One farmer's wife always seemed to know everything, no matter where the servants went or what they did. The claimed that she turned herself into a cat and sat listening, or into a hare in the fields. While in the guise of a hare she was bitten by a dog, then as a woman was taken ill, and confessed to her witchcraft before dying. Still at Twyford, a man known as 'old Joe' did no work, but lived on hand-outs given because he was feared for his power to set ploughs and carts fast, and to make all the horses in a stable be covered with white lather at the beginning of the day. He could also bewitch scythes, so that mowers or reapers could do no work.

The witches of Twyford and South Croxton were eventually destroyed. They were accustomed to meet in a field by a brook, and they would travel down the brook as cats, floating in dough-tubs. People heard strange music at night, though they could see nothing. Early one summer's morning, a man coming over a bridge saw them all floating in a large wooden bowl, still in the shape of cats. He heard one say:

Tweddle away, bowl,
Day's drawing nigh.

Before they could 'tweddle away' the man threw a large stone and split the bowl. All the witches fell into the water, and were drowned.

Another centre for such activity was Tilton. The wife of a shepherd there, S----- H-----, – the initials were probably used because she was still living, or had close relatives living, when the account was written, in 1875 – was reputed to be able to transport herself by supernatural power, night or day, to a neighbouring wood. There, she would dance round a tree seven times, then strike it with a stick or wand, and flames would burst from it. She had two daughters, of whom the elder inherited the power, but did not wish to be a witch, so her mother performed some ceremony with her every Christmas Eve until she was twenty-one to avoid this.

Another witch, 'Old S-----', could ride the upper air to Tilton Wood, where she met her weird sisters. She could bring blood out of a tree by striking it with her hand.

At Smeeton Westerby several old women lived in mud houses. They were thought to be witches because whenever a hare was chased it ran towards their houses, and disappeared. Once a hare was pursued by a dog, and was in the act of jumping through the window of one of the houses when the dog managed to nip its backside with its teeth. The human occupant was not seen for several days, and was then found in bed suffering from a wound 'in the hinder parts'.

At Fleckney a garage now stands at the end of the main street. A wooden seat which stood on that spot until the late nineteenth century was known as the Witches' Seat, and only used by the old women of the village. A man once braved custom to sit on it. Shortly afterwards he was thrown from his horse, and suffered a broken neck. The place where he was killed was subsequently known as Witchcraft Corner, later abbreviated to Craft Corner. Bayard's Leap, a hamlet on the Lincolnshire-Leicestershire border, four miles from Sleaford, takes its name from another incident involving a witch and a horseman. The man was riding home from market when a witch barred his way. He spurred forward to ride her down, but she stepped aside and hit the horse across the rump with a broom. It took a prodigious leap, and jumped a huge, dense hedge, at least twelve feet high, then fell dead on the other side. The rider was saved, and to commemorate Bayard's Leap, removed the horse-shoes and displayed them in a glass case in a spinney where two roads meet. There are there to this day.

Until recent years, Leicester children living near the Newarke were afraid to pass at night through Rupert's Gateway, leading to the castle, because a witch called Cat Anna was reputed to lurk there. This seems to be corruption of Black Anna or Annis who lay in wait in her 'bower', a cave in the Dane Hills, for young children. Those she caught were scratched to death with her long claws, then their blood was sucked and their skins hung up to dry. As a poem by John Heyrick put it:

Where down the plain the winding pathway falls,
From Glen-field vill, to Lester's ancient walls;
Nature, or art, with imitative power,
Far in the Glenn has plac'd *Black Annis's Bower*.

. . .
'Tis said the soul of mortal man recoil'd
To view Black Annis's eye, so fierce and wild;
Vast talons, foul with human flesh, there grew
In place of hands, and features livid blue,
Glar'd in her visage; whilst her obscene waist
Warm skins of human victims embrac'd.

To be more precise, the Dane Hills were an expanse of rough, hillocky ground off Glenfield Road, Leicester, which remained partly open until after the second world war, when houses were built there. Part of the area, near to the present Convent of St Catherine, was known as Black Annis' Bower-Close. On Easter Monday a fair was held there, attended by the mayor in his scarlet gown and other officials, accompanied by the waits. In the morning there were various entertainments and sporting events, followed by a hare-hunt at noon. Originally a real hare was hunted, but later the hounds and huntsmen followed the trail of a dead cat soaked in aniseed. Traditionally, the trail ended at the mayor's door, so the hunt went in full cry throough the streets of the town. The custom was already ancient when it was first mentioned in the town records, in 1668. It seems to have fallen into disuse about a century later, though the fair continued. Even this was opposed, as the *Leicester Journal* reported in 1826: 'Within the last few years attempts have been made by the Proprietors and occupiers of the 'Dane Hill Closes' to put an entire stop to any diversion upon the Grounds during Easter Week'. Nevertheless the festivities continued at least until 1842, when the *Chronicle* noted: 'The Dane-hill fair was crowded with visitors, principally young people of the working classes, and the fields beyond the spot where the fair is held were also thronged with merry-makers'.

The same ground was used for family strolls, as one man wrote: 'As a child I remember walks to Black Anna's Bower, said to be a witch who lived in a tree somewhere near the present Dominican convent at Danes Hill'. In the twentieth century the area could still be reached on foot, though only by a narrow footpath, called 'The Black Pad'. In one of the mounds there was a cave, half-hidden by thorn bushes, with a stunted oak close by. Black Anna was reputed to have dug the cave with her own fingernails. She was also said to have been the same witch that warned Richard III of his fate (see page 13), and to have lived in cellars under Leicester Castle, linked to her bower by an underground passage. The delay in building on the Dane Hills was attributed to a suggestion that a witch was buried there, and another belief was that the area had been a Danish battleground, with the dead having been buried where they fell. Until recently, any particularly unpopular woman was referred to as Black Anna, and a spiteful one as Cat Anna.

Perhaps the lady has been unfairly treated. Robert Graves equates her with his 'White Goddess', deriving from the Celtic Anu or Dana. If so, she has connections with the ancient mother-goddess of many peoples, from India to Ireland, and she was benevolent before she was malign, nymph before hag.

The underground entrance to Leicester Castle, from Flower's *Views of Ancient Buildings in the Town and County of Leicester*

12. Calendar Customs

JANUARY

It was considered, and many people still keep up the custom, that the first visitor on New Year's Day should be a dark man. If necessary a suitable man from a house would go outside just before midnight on New Year's Eve so as to be let in immediately afterwards, preferably carrying a piece of coal. Women were regarded as particularly unlucky first visitors. Another means of bringing luck was to put a bag of money outside before the New Year and take it in afterwards and hide if for the rest of the year. A neighbour would leave on the doorstep on New Year's Eve a piece of coal, bread and a sixpence, which would bring warmth, food and money to the people in the house for the ensuing year.

Gifts were once offered on New Year's Day, both by individuals and institutions. The records of Leicester Corporation show items given and received. In 1602–3 the large sum of 60 shillings was spent to provide 'a new yeares gyfte' of twelve gallons of wine for the Earl of Huntingdon. In 1610–11 Mistress Elizabeth Haslewood sent to the town two corselets, a pike, a musket, a sword and a dagger. The mayor, Thomas Parker, gave the messenger five shillings and sent back 'a runlett of wyne and one suger lofe' for his mistress, at a cost of 31 shillings.

The great event in January was Plough Monday, the first Monday after Twelfth Night. As Thomas Tusser, who particularly associated the custom with Leicestershire, said: 'Plough Monday, next after Twelftide is past, bids out with the plough the woorst husband is last'. The children, as one from Mountsorrel recalled, 'celebrated it by dressing up in whatever outlandish garb we could muster, and visiting neighbours singing: "A hole in my stocking, a hole in my shoe, Please will you give me a penny or two".' The adults also celebrated, in a very large number of villages in both Leicestershire and Rutland, by a variety of rituals (see Chapter 6) and also plays (see Chapter 9). Stattis buns, otherwise called plum shuttles, were given to farmworkers at Oakham on Plough Monday. On the previous day, Plough Sunday, a plough was taken into the church for blessing at Great Easton, at least until 1978. St Agnes' Eve or Day (19 or 20 January) were favoured as being propitious occasions on which women could discover the identity of future husbands. The devices used for this divination included pins and prayers, twisted stockings and strange sleeping positions (Chapter 4).

Plough Sunday at Great Easton, 1978
(Photograph by courtesy of *Northamptonshire Evening Post*)

FEBRUARY

St Valentine's Day (14 February) remains very popular as a time for the
exchange of tokens of true love. Valentine buns, lozenge-shaped, with
currants and caraways, were once sold or given on the day. In Leicestershire they were made only at Melton Mowbray by the 1890s, but were
remembered at Knossington with the rhymes:

Goodmorrow, Valentine, I wish ye fair day,
The mice are at the shittles and we've come to scare them all away.

They were widely popular in Rutland, where they were also called Plum
Shuttles (pronounced 'shittles'). Householders customarily gave them to
children, as at Glaston and Market Overton; they were still being baked at
Uppingham in the 1890s, and the custom only ended at Ridlington with
the closure in 1915 of the last baker's shop in the village. To obtain a free
bun, or a penny in lieu, children went to likely houses and chanted:

Good morrow, Valentine,
A piece of bacon and cheese
And a bottle of wine.
If you've got a penny in your pocket
Slip it into mine.
We used to come at eight o'clock
And now we come at nine.

Shrove Tuesday is not a fixed date, because it is always the seventh
Tuesday before Easter, which is itself a moveable feast. On the previous
day, known as Collop Monday, eggs and fried collops (hence the name) of
bacon were eaten, together with any meat left in the house, so as to clear
the larder before Lent. On Shrove Tuesday a bell was formerly rung to
call the people to church to be shriven, that is, confessed and given
absolution. Eventually the same bell came to be seen as the signal to start
making pancakes, and it was called the Pancake Bell. School children were
usually given a half-day's holiday, and many adults also had time off work.
It was traditional day for sport. Children played at whip and top, and also
at shuttlecock and battledore, which was also played in the streets by
adults at Hinckley and Leicester. As late as 1878 some 'artisans, men and
women' were asked why they were playing and answered: 'Because it's
Shrove Tuesday'. On the following day, Ash Wednesday, the normal food
was fritters and fish.

The big event of Shrove Tuesday was at the Newarke, where there was a
fair, with oranges and gingerbread on sale. Cockerels, some tied to stakes,
others liberated, were used as targets for those who paid for six shies at
them with clubs. There were wrestling and single-stick (cudgel) bouts too,
but the main game was shinty, a form of hockey. Football was also played.
At a certain hour, one o'clock according to Throsby, three according to
Gardiner, the Whipping Toms arrived to clear the ground. These were

several 'stout fellows' with cart-whips and a handkerchief tied over one eye who were accompanied by a bellman. Until dark, they had licence to whip anyone found in the Newarke, subject to certain rules. They were not allowed to apply the whip above the knee, nor at all if a person were kneeling, nor outside certain boundaries, nor if a person opted to pay a small fine. Many chose to run the gauntlet, with all the skill and daring of men running before bulls. They took good care to wear strong knee-boots and to arm themselves with a stick to parry the whip-lash. Large numbers of spectators assembled at a safe distance to watch the contest, which went on for several hours, but the custom was not universally popular. The Vicar of St Mary's, who was known to be hostile, was once caught in the arena and forced to run the gauntlet of Whipping Toms from one end of the Newarke to his own gate, which he cleared at a bound. After several attempts to suppress the Whipping Toms the city fathers sponsored a private act of parliament, which was passed in 1846. The Leicester Improvement Act declared the 'custom and practice called Whipping Toms' to be illegal, and provided a fine of five pounds, a huge sum for the time, for anyone who played at 'Whipping Toms, shindy, football, or any other game' on any part of the Newarke on Shrove Tuesday, or who ever merely stood 'in said place with any whip, stick, or other instrument for playing thereat'. On the next Shrove Tuesday, in 1847, a large crowd assembled to pursue the sport. A full-scale riot ensued, but a very large force of police eventually managed to clear the area. Many arrests were made. So ended a custom which some dated from 1002, when the Danes were expelled from Leicester on Hoke Day (the second Tuesday after Easter), some from the time of John of Gaunt, some 350 years later. A plaque now marks the spot where the Whipping Toms held their sport. One sport still held in Leicester on Shrove Tuesday is pancake racing which is altogether more tame.

MARCH
On Mothering Sunday, the fourth in Lent, people were once expected to visit their mother church, which is to say the church in their native parish. They took the opportunity of visiting their own mothers, and later the festival became purely a family occasion. It was customary to eat a delicacy called furmenty (or frumenty or thrommery), which was made by par boiling whole grains of wheat in water, then straining them and boiling them in milk sweetened with sugar and flavoured with cinnamon and other spices. Another method was to bake wheat or pearl-barley, then boil it in milk thickened with flour. Sugar and dried currants were added, and sometimes egg. The dish could also be laced with spirits, if desired. Yet another recipe appeared in rhyme:

Take wheat and pick in fair and clean,
And do it in a mortar shene.
Bray it a little, with water it spring
Till it hulle without lesyng.
Then winnow it well, need you must,
Wash it fair, put it in pot.
Boil it till it burst, then
Let it down, as I thee kenne.
Take now milk and play it up
To it be thickened to sup.
Lie it up with yokes of eggs
And keep it well lest it burn.
Colour it with saffron and salt it well
And serve it forth, sir, at the meale
With sugar candy thou may it douse
If it be served in great lord's house
Take black sugar for meaner men
Beware therewith for it will burn.

APRIL

April Fools' Day is still ardently kept up, though many forget that the tricksters' licence ends at noon. An attempted fooling after that time can be rebuffed with this formula from Market Harborough: 'April's gone and May's a-coming, You're the fool for being so cunning'.

Palm Sunday, the Sunday before Easter, is known as Fig Sunday from the custom of eating figs or fig pudding at that time.

Easter often falls in April, since by a complicated calculation Easter Sunday is the first after the first full moon after 21 March, unless the full moon is on a Sunday, in which case Easter Sunday is the following Sunday. On the day before Easter Sunday, Holy Saturday, a holy fire of charcoal was kindled in the porch of St Martin's Church, Leicester, by burning glass and the light of the sun if possible, if not by steel and flint. The fire was blessed by the priest, and the lamps and candles in the church lit from it. A similar practice obtained at St Mary's, though in neither case did the custom survive the Reformation. A living tradition at Market Harborough on the same day is the service at William Hubbard's grave, which has been held every Easter Eve since 1807. Hubbard, a gardener, left one guinea in his will for the singers at St Dionysius to hold the service in St Mary-in-Arden's churchyard, where his grave is marked by a fine slate headstone. Although the interest on the legacy must be now only a few pence, the custom survives.

Easter Monday was another day for sport. At Cossington 'the lads and lasses of the adjacent villages' met on Shipley Hill 'to be merry with ales

225

Singing the hymn over the Hubbard grave on Easter Eve at St Mary-in-Arden, Market Harborough, c.1900
(Unpublished photograph by Sir Benjamin Stone, reproduced by permission of Birmingham Reference Library)

and cakes', and at Leicester there was a fair on the Dane Hills and the Fosse Road, following by trail-hunting (for which, see page 219). Hallaton Pie-scramble and Bottle-kicking (see page 127) is still held, and attracts enormous interest.

Another still-flourishing tradition is the 'Lane Setting' which takes place on Holy Thursday (the Thursday after Easter Monday) at Ratcliffe Culey, in the parish of Witherley. Since 1882 at a gathering in the bar of the Gate Inn a local firm, John Briggs and Calder, has auctioned one year's use of the grass verges along the lanes round the village for grazing or mowing. The money raised – the sum in 1983 was £148 – goes into parish council funds. Before the proceedings a song entitled 'Little Yellow Bird' is sung, and repeated afterwards to start a celebratory evening of song and story. Rather incongruously, it is a music hall piece which happened to take the fancy of a former auctioneer, the late John Briggs, but it has continued to feature at the Lane Setting. On the same day, Holy Thursday, there were fairs at Hallaton and Loughbrough, and Twyford Wakes were also held during April.

On St George's Day (23 April) or soon afterwards the great procession called 'Riding the George' used to take place in Leicester (see page 149).

226

MAY

'The first of May is a very fine day, So please to remember the Maypole Day': so runs a song which Mrs Agnes Harvey of Market Bosworth recalled in 1966 from seventy years earlier. From earliest times May Day was celebrated as a sign of the coming of summer and the renewal of vegetation, and traditional rites continued until recent years. A description of the May Day activities at Bradgate Park in the sixteenth century appears in 'The Tablette Book' of Lady Jane Grey's sister, Lady Mary Keyes: 'Then, when the merrie May Pole and alle the painted Morris-dancers, withe Tabor and Pipe, beganne their spiritelie anticks on our butiful grene laune, afore that we idel leetel Bodyes had left owre warme Bedds, woulde goode Mistress Bridget, the Tire-woman [lady's maid] whom our Lady Mother alwaies commanded to do owre Biddings, com and tells us of the merrie men a-dancing on the Greene'.

People went out in the very early morning to bring back green branches to decorate their doors and windows. The practice became such a nuisance in the eyes of Leicester Corporation that in 1551 it decreed that anyone breaking or cutting boughs would be fined one shilling '& ther bodies to pryson ther to remayn duryng Mr Mayer will & plesure'. The puritan city fathers also disapproved of dancing. Six morris-men were taken to court in 1599 for performing on 'Tuesday night in Whitsonweeke last'. Five were released on bail but the sixth, Edward Cheynes, was 'appoynted one of the three soldiers for [the quota for] Leycester and sent into Ireland'. In 1603 there was almost a riot over the corporation's opposition to a maypole 'unlawfully' set up in Southgate Street: the first of May fell on a Sunday that year.

Villages usually had a maypole, often a tall, straight tree such as a silver birch, brought from the woods and set up on the green. The maypole at Knossington was particularly imposing: it towered to a height of fifty feet. Some places had a permanent maypole, such as the one which still stands at Belton, near Loughbrough. During the 1890s the men of Shepshed once stole the thirty-foot pole and set off homewards with it. The Belton men were alerted and turned out of their beds – it was late at night – to pursue the offenders. They caught up by Carr Lane Brook, and after 'a bloody conflict' returned in triumph with their maypole. The incident came during a period of sharp antagonism between the two villages.

On May morning groups of singers went round all the houses. At Stretton the songs started at 9 a.m. At Cottesmore there were two special songs, a night song which mentioned the collection of greenery and a day song which greeted the hearers.

The maypole at Belton

We have been trav'-ling all the night And some part of the
day, And now we have re - turned a - gain And have
brought you a bunch of may. A bunch of may we have brought you And
at your door it stands. It's no-thing but a sprout But it's
well spread a - bout By the work of our Lord's hands.

I have a bag lies on my arm,
Is lined with silk and string,
And all we want is a silver piece
To line it well within.
Good morning all, both great and small,
We wish you a joyful day.
Good morning all, both great and small,
We wish you all good day.

Good morning, lords and la - dies, It is the first of May. Come
look at our fine gar - land That looks so fine and gay.

The cuckoo sings in April,
The cuckoo sings in May;
The cuckoo sings in June, July,
And then she flies away.

The cuckoo is a merry bird,
She sings as she flies.
She brings us good tidings
And never tells no lies.

The festival was very much in the hands of adults, but as tradition weakened it increasingly passed to children. The practice of plaiting a maypole with ribbons while dancing round it was introduced from the continent by John Ruskin in 1888, and was spread by teachers. At one time, as early school logbooks reveal, children had absented themselves from school in large numbers on May Day, which was perhaps one reason why the educational system attempted to assimilate the custom. Later, because of a swing in teacher opinion to the view the maypole dancing was too formal, too old-fashioned, it was dropped, though some schools carried on until the 1920s and '30s (Caldecott, South Luffenham, Lyddington, Newtown Linford, and no doubt others) and some even until the 1960s (Fleckney and Waltham-on-the-Wolds). As maypole dancing was dropped by schools it was sometimes taken over by village committees and voluntary organisations. Parades and processions with a girl or woman chosen as May Queen are still held, though not the unique Braunston practice of having two queens, one fair and one dark.

Another feature seems to have disappeared, the garlands and May dolls. At Ashby in the 1890s 'bands of girls, some hailing from adjacent villages, perambulated the town' on May Day, 'bearing miniature maypoles tastefully decorated with flowers'. At Barrowden even later a procession visited each house to bring luck through the May doll, which was also called a May Queen. Large number of flowers were carried, such as mayblobs (marsh marigolds), primroses, lady's smock, cowslips and even kingsfingers (a variety of wild orchid). Garlands were arranged in many different ways, the simplest being merely a bunch of flowers tied to the end of a stick. A hoop, mounted vertically on a pole, was used as a framework at Barlestone, Barrow-on-Soar, Bruntingthorpe, Cottesmore, Exton, Hungarton, Newbold Verdon, Oadby, Thurnby and Swepstone. At Oadby there was a doll in the centre of the hoop, called 'the lady'. The participants did not know why. Perhaps it was originally a representation of Our Lady; alternatively of the even older, pagan goddess, Flora. Mrs Madge Stacey (1898–1979) remembered setting out a six in the morning at Oadby and taking home 1/11d after a long stint of singing and collecting. She handed the money to her mother, who gave her a halfpenny back to spend on ABC biscuits, no doubt saving the rest for later treats. Some children were allowed to spend the money they collected at the local feast. At Swepstone several groups went round the village, each with what they called a maypole, 'comprised of a broomstick with a wooden hoop secured to the top. This was decorated with wild flowers, marigolds, lady's smocks, and of course ribbons. We sang, among other songs, the following:

Oh may - pole day is a ve - ry fine day,
Please re- mem-ber the may - pole. A - round the may-pole
we can trot, See what a may - pole we have got.
Dressed in rib - bons, tied in bows, See what a may - pole
we can show. With a jig and a jag and a
ve - ry fine flag, Please re-mem-ber the may - pole.
Let your mo - ney be great or small, We've got a purse that will
hold it all. If you have-n't got a pen - ny a
ha'-pen-ny will do. If you have-n't got a ha' - pen-ny, God bless you.

The singer was Mrs. E.M.Carter, who was born in 1910.

The garland consisted of two hoops fixed at right angles to each other at Gaddesby, Manton, Saxby and Whissendine. At Braunston there were three, and at Tinwell, two or three. Mrs J.Harvey remembered how things were organised at Tinwell between 1910 and 1915. The children were given the afternoon off school on 30 April to go collecting flowers, which were then kept in water overnight. On 1 May adults made up the garlands, starting at 5 a.m. Until 1910 the boys and girls had separate garlands:

The girls' garland was pyramidal and its framework consisted of three circular hoops secured to three broomsticks or poles; bunches of flowers were tied to the hoops and poles and a bunch of Crown Imperials always surmounted the garland. Slung on a long pole, the garland could be carried by two children. The boys' garland was spheroidal and was secured to the top of pole or broomstick, called the 'Maypole'; the two crossed hoops were covered with flowers tied to them and there was a bunch of Crown Imperials on the top.

The children moved off at eight o'clock or 8.30 a.m., with the girls leading and the boys following in a separate group. The procession stopped at each house in the village, with first the girls, then the boys singing:

Good morning, lords and ladies, it is the first of May,
We hope you'll view our garland, it is so very gay.
The cuckooo sings in April, the cuckoo sings in May,
The cuckoo sings in June, in July she flies away.

'Then followed other popular country songs; the boys' selection always included "The Farmer's Boy". The day was taken as a general holiday, the custom was very popular, and generous donations were made to the children'.

The ball formed by the intertwined hoops was called a 'May Bush' at Braunston and Ridlington, and the same term was used at Knossington. Mrs Vera Wright (born in 1907) remembers several rival groups at Frisby, each carrying a May Bush, which in their case meant 'a small branch of a tree gaily decorated with flowers and leaves'. The best bush inspired the best collection.

Other garlands were simply an arched rod of hazel or willow, as at Kibworth and Sproxton. Mrs Monica Turner remembers that at Stonesby and neighbouring villages the little girls went round collecting and asking for flowers for two days before, then on May Day, dressed in white, with flowers in their hair, carried a decorated arch of willow. They sang:

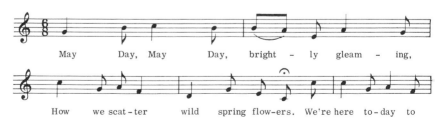

May Day, May Day, bright - ly gleam - ing,
How we scat - ter wild spring flow-ers. We're here to - day to

wish you well And wel - come in the may.

A flat basket (sometimes a laundry basket) or box or tray was filled with flowers at Barsby, Kibworth, Market Bosworth, Narborough, Newbold Verdon, Oakham, Scalford, Sproxton and Tugby. At Narborough this was called a 'May Box', and held a doll dressed as the Queen of the May. Such a doll was present in most cases, and sometimes there was more than one. Saxby had four. The doll was often covered with a net or muslin veil, and was only revealed to those who made a contribution. Gifts were often generous. The Dowager Duchess of Lonsdale at Cottesmore Hall always gave a half-sovereign and treated the singers to cakes and milk. More often the coins were halfpence or even farthings. Something, however little, had to be given, since it cemented the luck-bringing compact. Little is now heard of all this, though there are very strong, and often wistful memories.

Leicester Cheese Fair was held on the second Thursday in May, and also the second Thursday in October.

Once every three years the parish bounds were beaten at St Mary's, Leicester, on 4th May. The procession in some cases passed through houses which straddled the boundary. Other parishes had a similar custom, on different dates (see below).

On Old May Day (12 May) cattle-herds used to carouse at some low hills called the Shepherds' Tables, near Croft, to mark the turning out of their animals into the common pasture. The place took its name from shepherds' celebrations which were held there.

During the month of May, after the Sunday School Anniversary at Sileby, the vicar distributes oranges to the children under an ancient elm tree in the churchyard. The custom may date from a celebration of the victory at Waterloo in 1815. It lapsed at one stage, but was revived by the present vicar, Rev. R.J.Hunting.

Oak Apple Day (29 May) commemorates Charles II's escape from capture by hiding in the Boscobel Oak and his subsequent restoration to the throne of England. The rhyme, 'A stig and a stag, And a very fine flag, And a Maypole', was recited on 29 May, having transferred there from 1 May. In my schooldays at Newtown Linford between 1937 and 1943 every boy wore a sprig of oak in his button-hole and carried a nettle with which to sting anyone not conforming to the custom. Since all boys wore short trousers in those days their bare legs were an obvious target, though as with April fooling, only until noon. The customed was widely observed, but is now, I think dead. At Hinckley peals of bells were rung at the

233

church, and the ringers fixed oak boughs to the battlements and above the doors of important townspeople. On the same day, processioning o' beating the bounds took place at Ashby Wolds.

JUNE

Rogationtide is the fifth Sunday after Easter, and thus sometimes falls in May, sometimes in June. Whetstone bound-beating takes place on that day. At Barrowden the beaters of bounds were led by a band, and included every child capable of walking the distance. The parish provided a lunch of bread and cheese halfway round, and at certain points coins were thrown to be scrambled for by the boys as a way of impressing the vital topography on their minds. At Ashwell the parson and schoolmaster followed by their respective flocks, perambulated the parish boundary pausing at what were called treacle holes. Boys were set in them, given a symbolic good hiding, then a spoonful of treacle. In earlier times the hiding was real, and was intended as a powerful stimulus to the memory. Shepshed bounds were beaten on Ascension Day (40 days after Easter) but even in the late eighteenth century the ceremony, as Nichols sadly noted, was 'often omitted'. It lasted at Barrowden until 1913.

Whitsunday is the fiftieth day and the seventh Sunday after Easter. Whitsun week was once regarded as a general holiday by ordinary people, at least in Leicester, and was the main time for festivities arranged by clubs and friendly societies. These events continued in villages until recent times; for example, Belton Whit Monday Club Feast continued until the 1920s. Burbage Feast was on the same day, and Wymondham had a Singing Feast.

During the Middle Ages there was a solemn religious procession on Whit Monday from St Mary's to St Margaret's Church at Leicester (page 149), and in more recent times a secular pageant called the 'Riding of the Millers' was held at Hinckley (page 99). Sports, including horse racing, took place at Burrough Hill (page 115). An ancient custom, known as 'Selling the Wether', is still kept up at Enderby. In the case of meadows with joint occupiers at Desford, Nailstone, Ratby and Stanton-under-Bardon a day was agreed when everyone would turn out to mow the grass. After completing the work the mowers enjoyed themselves in 'wrestlings, footballs, cudgel-playing, and other athletic exercises', followed by music and dancing. In the late 1370s John o' Gaunt, Duke of Lancaster and Earl of Leicester, happened to pass the Ratby meadow while on the way to Leicester, and stopped to ask the reason for the festivities. They explained, and said that the traditional name given to their meadow-mowing day was 'Ramsdale'. John o' Gaunt joined in the merrymaking for a time, then summoned fourteen of the men to meet him at Leicester Castle. When they did so he presented them with a field at Enderby by the River

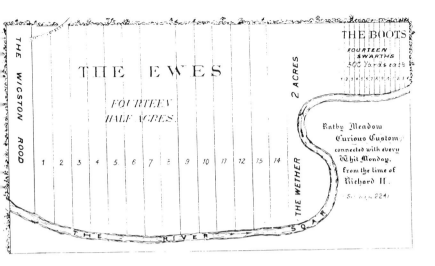

THE WICSTON ROAD

THE EWES

FOURTEEN
HALF ACRES.

1 2 3 4 5 6 7 8 9 10 11 12 13 14

THE WETHER

2 ACRES

THE BOOTS
FOURTEEN
SWARTHS
300 Yards each

THE RIVER SOAR

Rathy Meadow
Curious Custom
connected with every
Whit Monday.
from the time of
Richard II.

The Ewes, the Boots and the Wether, from Spencer, *Notes and Queries*

Soar, subject to certain conditions. The field was to be divided into fourteen strips of half-an-acre each, called 'the Ewes', and fourteen 'swarths' of 300 square yards each, called 'the Boots', together with a residual piece of two acres, called 'the Wether'. Each man had one of the Ewes and one of the Boots for his individual use; the Wether was to be held for the common benefit, and its crop of grass was to be sold to the highest bidder every Whit Monday to provide money for a feast. The ceremonies have varied over the years, but the auction continues to this day. It is held at the Nag's Head, Enderby. A crown coin is passed from hand to hand during the proceedings, and only the person who has it in his hand can make a bid. The money raised is still spent on a celebratory dinner.

On Whit Tuesday the Ancient Order of Druids held its annual feast at Sutton Cheney, which the children 'looked forward to as much as Christmas'. It was followed by the half-yearly Rent Day: 'After you'd paid your rent you'd go up to the village inn and you'd get a little loaf, a quart of old ale and a pound of cheese, and that was to keep you until the end of the week when you received your wages. It was an old custom which ensured that the landlord wouldn't take the last bit of bread out of the house'.

The Sunday after Whitsuntide is Trinity Sunday, which was the occasion of the Trinity Guild Feast at Leicester, and also the beginning of the village feast at Teigh. On the Thursday after Trinity the great procession of Corpus Christi Guild took place (page 149). Belton Horse Fair (page 142) is still held on the second Monday after Trinity.

235

Midsummer (24 June), also St John the Baptist's Day, is another landmark. The Crown and Thistle in Loseby Lane, Leicester, under a deed of 1626, still pays an annual rent of two pennies and a damask rose on this day. Narborough Feast and Fair were held on 23 and 24 June, and Whitwick had its wake on the Sunday afterwards.

JULY
This month, which falls between haysel and harvest, was a favourite time for feasts and wakes. These were held at Barrowden, Bisbrooke, Claybrooke, Empingham, Exton, Langham, Market Overton, Medbourne, Wing and Wymondham on the first Sunday after St Peter's Day, 29 June; at Shepshed on Old Midsummer Day, 5 July; at Braunstone and Glenfield on the Sunday after 5 July, and at Stretton on the Sunday after 6 July; at Frisby on the second Sunday in July; at Belgrave and Oadby on the Sunday after 10 July, at Cottesmore on the second Sunday after 11 and at Whissendine on the Sunday after 13 July; at Barrow, near Cottesmore, and Ridlington on the Sunday after 22 July, and at Belton and Seaton on the Sunday after 25 July. In several churches hay was strewn, and in some still is, at this time of year (see Chapter 3).

AUGUST
At Ashby Folville Church hay strewing began on the first Sunday in August, and continued until Christmas. On the Sunday after 15 August feasts took place at Ayston, Greetham and South Luffenham. These were to some extent replaced by the institution of August Bank Holiday, which was formerly on the first, now on the last Monday in the month. Harvest festivals are still held in this month, or early in September. The Harvest Supper seems to have declined, though it is still held at Laughton after the evening service on Harvest Festival Sunday. Melton Fair was held on the Vigil, Day (10 August) and Morrow of St Lawrence.

SEPTEMBER
Some places clearly chose dates after harvest for their feasts. These were held at Ashwell, Caldecott, Clipsham, Edith Weston and Morcott on the Sunday after 19 September, and at Burley on the Sunday after 26 September. Fairs were held on Michaelmas Day (29 September) at Hallaton, Hinckley, Husbands Bosworth, Kibworth, Lutterworth and Leicester (where the event spread over the three previous and the three following days in addition). This was also the time for hiring fairs (see chapter 8), which were held at Ashby on the first Tuesday after 21 September and at Melton and Oakham on 29. Others were held in November.

The Crown and Thistle, Loseby Lane, Leicester

OCTOBER
Feasts were held at Braunston, Lyddington and Ryhall on the Sunday after 10 October, and at Glaston and Whitwell on the Sunday after 11 October. Hallowe'en (31 October) was the day for callers and collectors, usually hooded or masked or with blackened faces, and carrying turnip lanterns. Hallowe'en parties are still part of the social calendar.

NOVEMBER
On All Saints' Day (1 November) children traditionally had a bonfire at Goadby. A peal was rung at Morcott on 5 November. Before their Bonfire Night festivities children went round collecting money and materials with their doomed effigy of Guy Fawkes, as they still do. There was a traditional collecting rhyme: 'A stick and a stake For King James's sake, And a bonfire, O'. A variant from Knossington, where the bonfire was made on Pinfold Hill, ran:

A stick and a stake for King William's sake,
And pray, Dame, give us a kid or a faggot.

The Guy Fawkes celebrations were zealously supported by ordinary people, and any attempts at curtailment were fiercely resisted. When the local constable, John Clapham, caused some Uppingham boys to be prosecuted for letting off fireworks in the street a mob besieged his house, broke all his windows and removed part of the roof. He retaliated by twice firing his gun at the crowd, which caused several minor injuries and one serious wound. This was in 1841, and the public bonfire was stopped the following year because of the 'scenes of riot and lawless dissipation'. By 1853 the bonfire was back, in the middle of the Market Place, and the owner of 'ten or a dozen large wagons containing waxwork figures' prudently removed them to Oakham before 5 November. In 1854, during the Crimean War, the Emperor of Russia replaced Guy Fawkes. After being 'ignominiously exhibited in effigy through the town on a pole' he was 'eventually consigned to the flames in the presence of many spectators'.

An anonymous writer at Wigston in 1869 somewhat regretfully reported that 'the fifth of November has come and gone without any effort being made by the poorer classes of the village to celebrate it in the manner that obtains in many of our large towns and villages – on the reverse, all was quiet and not a Guy was to be seen perambulating the place, nor the fire within whose vengeful flames his body was to be afterwards burnt, nor was the village street, as in a not far gone time, lit up with the fitful blaze of rolling tar barrels and swinging fireballs'. The reason, he suggested, was 'the war' being waged by the press, the pulpit and the school against 'ignorance and vice, and a latent stupidity not confined to the so-called lower classes of Wigston'.

The blazing tar-barrels abandoned at Wigston continued in use at Market Harborough, as part of the vigorous Guy Fawkes' celebrations which were tolerated by the police. A new superintendent, James Holloway, who took over in 1874, decided to institute a more rigid policy. He found some boys letting off fire-crackers near the church on 5 November, and took their names, warning them that they would be prosecuted. The news of this unprecented severity spread through the town, and a huge crowd turned out in the evening. The superintendent was greeted with a hail of squibs and crackers, then mud, mortar, dirt 'and other matter'. He was eventually dazed by a large brick, and forced to take refuge with his men in the Three Swans Hotel, which was besieged till midnight. The town was quiet the following day, when police reinforcements arrived from Leicester, but after these left on 7 November 'a great procession was formed headed by a band with the effigy of the Superintendent carried in front, the band playing "We'll run him in", from the opera, "Madame Angot", which was then very popular. The effigy was duly burnt and pandemonium was let loose with tar barrels galore. . . . Police reinforcements were brought over again from Liecester the next day but the people concerned having given vent to their feelings, the town resumed its normal condition'. On 24 November nine men were charged with 'making a great riot and disturbance to the terror and alarm of Her Majesty's subjects'. They pleaded guilty to the lesser charge of affray, and were bound over to keep the peace for twelve months. Pistols and guns were fired into the air over the bonfire held in the Market Place at Melton until the authorities intervened in 1860.

Feasts were held in November at Wigston (All Saints) and Tinwell on the Sunday after the first of the month, at Ketton on the Sunday after 11 and at Loughborough after 14. The Hambletons' feast was on the Sunday before 30 November. Martinmas (11 November) hirings were held at Castle Donington, Ketton, Loughborough, Market Bosworth and Sproxton.

St Clement's Day (23 November) was one of the several occasions scattered through the winter months when it was legitimate for children to go round asking for money, fruit or food. At Market Bosworth there was a 'gooding' chant:

St Clement's, St Clement's, St Clement's is here,
Apples and pears are very good cheer.
One for St Peter and one for St Paul,
And three for him who made us all.
Up with the kettle and down with the pan,
Give us some apples and we will be gone.

Barring out took place at Hallaton on St Andrew's Day (30 November).

DECEMBER

St Tibba's Day (14 December) was celebrated in Rutland, particularly at Ryhall, by fowlers and falconers whose patroness the saint is.

As well as on St Clement's Day the custom of gooding took place on St Thomas' Day (21 December), when it was also called 'gooin' a-Tummasin', and the participants were usually old women. The money and food collected were used for Christmas. The same day was known as 'Wass-ailing Day' at South Luffenham, where it was customary for the old women to be given a shilling or a quarter of tea.

Wassailing proper was singing. Rev. Aulay Macaulay wrote that: 'Old John Payne and his wife, natives of the Parish of Claybrook, are well known for having perambulated the Hundred of Guthlaxton for many years at Christmas, with a fine gewgaw which they call a 'wassail' and exhibit from house to house with the accompaniment of a duet'. He concluded: 'I apprehend that the practice of wassailing will die with this aged pair'.

Their current successors are carol singers. At Braunston this was once 'a great event', with the singers practising for a fortnight beforehand:

On Christmas Eve, when the clock struck midnight all would sing 'Christians awake' and other carols, and by the time they had finished it was time to go to work on Christmas morning. On Boxing Day carols would be sung in the two pubs, and money would be collected round the village for an evening ale party. One frosty Christmas Eve when a man brought his fiddle the strings broke one by one, and his language was considerable, to the merriment of all. On another dark Christmas, at two in the morning, the leader told everyone to creep home quietly; he then burst into song and promptly walked into a clothes line, which sent him flying backwards. The air became blue, and a voice from a window shouted: 'What's going on down there?' For a moment there was hush, and to a man they all struck up with 'Ark, 'ark, the 'erald angels sing'.

A home-made carol ran like this:

I 'ave a little whistle-bob made out o' 'olly tree,
The finest little whistle-bob that ever yer did see,
For it is a Christmas time an' we travel far an' near,
An' we wish yer good 'ealth an' a 'Appy Noo Year.

Others forms of music were provided by handbell ringers, both on Christmas Eve and New Year's Eve. Charlie Wilson of Empingham was a member of the team of ringers which visited Normanton Hall every Christmas until it was burnt down in 1925. I myself remember the ringers at Glaston. The waits played at Leicester and the mummers were out in many towns and villages (see Chapter 9). The Devil's Knell was rung on the church bells at Oakham on Christmas Day.

At Christmas the fare was once much more modest than it now is. Children's stockings would include perhaps only apples, oranges and sweets. Mrs A.G.Hall of Coalville expected only a few nuts, a small chocolate bar, an orange, an apple and a penny. Mrs Ellen Smith remembered that at Wymeswold in about 1910 she would receive a sugar mouse, and that breakfast on Christmas Day traditionally consisted of home-made pork pie. This was also the case at Burbage, and no doubt elsewhere. Rabbit was often eaten for Christmas dinner. Another delicacy was mince pigs, pasties filled with minced pork, in the shape of a pig. These were favourite presents for absent members of the family, and were made in various sizes, large for adults and small for children. Currants were inserted as eyes.

Decorations were often home-made. A holly bush was hung from the ceiling, or a garland made of two wooden hoops intertwined at right angles, trimmed with coloured paper and tinsel. Glass baubles, trinkets and a few small gifts were tied on. The children scoured the fields for holly and mistletoe.

On St Stephen's Day (26 December), now called Boxing Day, there was a custom of holding up hands and spoons in remembrance of those who were absent. In 1614–15 Alderman Robert Heyrick wrote to his brother in London that:

'We were busy wth hollding up hands and spoones to yow, owt of porredge and pyes, to the remembraunce of yowre gt lyberality of frute and spice, which God send yow long lyffe to contynew, for of that day we have not myssed anny St Steven this 47 yeare to hve as many gastes as my howse woolld holld, I thank God for yt'.

On Innocents' Day (28 December) children were allowed to play in the church at Exton,

On New Year's Eve (31 December) church bells ring out the old year, and ring in the new. Formerly, the bells would be muffled for the old, and ring unmuffled for the new. At Ridlington the ringers were afterwards given hot dough cake and elderberry wine. At Leicester revellers see in the New Year in the Town Hall Square. Parties are widely held, as part of the ritual for ensuring good luck, health and prosperity in the coming year.

Appendix

Lyingham

(Annotations by Ralph Penniston Taylor)

The following is a scurrilous poem about certain inhabitants of Wymondham, Leicestershire in the eighth decade of the last century; it is anonymous and was published in Rome in 1879, probably first appearing in the village not long afterwards, just when there is now no way of knowing, but from knowledge handed down copies came by post to the principal characters featured in the satire as well as to other villagers. As one would expect, its advent caused more than a stir and it is related that after reading the caustic composition, certain of the recipients – no doubt those who had some connection with the 'characters' – promptly burned their copy, either in disgust or anger, or both. Others, however, were not so rash and may even have found the poem apt and amusing: although no copy of the original publication (possibly a 32 page paper bound booklet) has come to light, we must thank these others for hand-written transcripts do still exist, albeit in varying states of completeness and with slight variations and omissions.

The version which follows is the most complete and, except for the sub-headings taken from a later typescript, comes from a carefully hand-written copy made by two ladies of Edmondthorpe in December 1889 – one dictating, one writing down. Nothing should be read into the date of April 1st although it has been suggested that this may have been deliberate and that the composition may have been executed with 'tongue-in-cheek'. If there is any deliberation in the date it is more likely to be by way of emphasis on the part of the author towards the subjects of his poem. The hate and venom contained therein is too deep to allow of any humorous intention as suggested by the first theory.

Identification of many of the 'dramatis personae' has been possible through careful study of the text and by comparison with records of the time, but not least of all by members of an older generation – who knew, or knew of, the persons depicted – passing on their knowledge in various ways.

Allowance must be made for any 'over-embellishment' by the author because of his obvious hatred.

Although the author is anonymous, he was evidently well educated and – if we are to believe certain passages – a much travelled man. He was most certainly not a native of Wymondham and was able to see the village and its occupants through unclouded eyes; moreover, he did not like what he

243

saw. Several villagers come in for a lengthy lashing, but his 'bêtes noires' must surely be Edward Garnham – "Fromage", and Samuel Johnson – "Darkie Sam", against whom he directs the strongest invective.

Village mutterings have always implied that the poet was one of the schoolmasters – Grammar or National is never defined – and these would accord very well with the advent and departure of one, John Elkington: Appointed on 11th April 1877 to serve as Master of the National School, he took charge on 28th May, his wife, Eliza, helping out – particularly as needlework mistress. Before coming to Wymondham he was school-master at Covenham St. Mary, near Louth in Lincolnshire, a post he had held for only a comparatively short time.

During his short sojourn in the village, three of his children – there may or may not have been more – were baptised in the church: Oliver – who had been born at Covenham St. Mary on 10th January 1877 – baptised 28th July 1878 along with his brother, Lionel, who had been born April 21st 1878; and Geoffrey, born 16th July 1879 and baptised 28th September of that year. Around the time that Geoffrey was baptised the school governors were advertising for a new master: was this action precipitated by the appearance in the village of the explosive publication, or was John Elkington so disillusioned by the place and its people that he was desperate to relinquish an appointment which he must have felt to be disastrous? Perhaps the complaint made early in his mastership – August 1878 – by George Penniston about the treatment of his daughter contains a hint of the general feeling when that father extolled the virtues of the previous master, to the detriment of Elkington. Matters certainly did not improve and the deterioration in relationships is very apparent when it can be noticed in the school accounts that, whereas up to 31st May 1880 he is always referred to as 'Mr' Elkington, the entry dated 31st August of that year perfunctorily states 'Elkington's salary £18-15-0' – a noticeable omission of the courtesy title 'Mr.'.

John Elkington left at the end of that Quarter, succeeded in the mastership by Matthew Henry Boden, a bachelor, who took charge of the school on 11th October.

Lyingham
or
Rustic Knaves at Home

"Injustice, hate, uncharitableness
Tri-equal reign among this evil crew,
Words cannot come to paint them bad enough
And as they sink in sin they rise in vice.
To instruct such fools no art can ever reach,
No care improve them, and no wisdom teach."

Rome
Printed for the Author
1879

Preface

The following lines have been thrown together with the object of bringing the dastards with whom they deal to a sense of their degraded position. Refined satire would be lost on these obtuse clod-hoppers, who, though vicious and cunning, revengeful and treacherous, are yet idiotic and brutally ignorant. Their pachydermatous hides are impervious to weapons which are effectual with men of education and refined susceptibilities. This poem is adapted to their narrow intellects and coarse feelings and the wretched engineers of Lyingham are thus "hoist with their own petard."

The condition of such persons, morally, socially, and physically is paintful to look upon, in each point of view they are equally degraded. To endeavour to instruct them would be to cast pearls before swine. Neither honest nor manly, they are proud to loaf about the pot-house, muddling their sufficiently stupid brains with beer and gin and glorying in their depravity.

Fromage and his contemptible associates will now be able to appreciate the following fable, putting themselves in the viper's place. "A viper came into a smith's shop, and while trying if there was anything to eat, bit a file; in reply, the file scornfully said, "Why, o foolish one dost thou attempt to injure with thy tooth me, who am accustomed to gnaw every kind of metal?"

Lyingham
April 1st 1879

246

Notes

[A] This foolish old man is best dismissed with an epitaph recommended to his admirers:

"As Father Adam first was fooled,
A case that's still too common.
Here lies a man a woman ruled;
And Satan ruled the woman."

[B] He is evidently ignorant of the doggerel:

"All play and no work
Will make Jack a ragged shirt."

[E] And when the earth shall now be shovelled on him
If that which served him for a soul were still
Within its husk 'twould still be dirt to dirt.

[D] Weasel ap Fromage, a feeble youth.

[E] It may be remarked that this vulgar black man is too contemptible for notice. The common bug is an ignoble and repulsive insect, yet it is offensive, and is squelched accordingly. Compare with Cimex-lectularius in an olfactory sense.

[F] The natural course for a member of the "Donkey Dragoons." Rustic admirers call them "cavalry"-soldiers treat them cavalierly. Their only medals are those won for fat oxen and porkers.

"Mouths without hands, maintained at vast expense,
In peace a charge, in war a weak defence.
Stout once a year they march, a blustering band:
And, ever but in time of need, at hand."

[G] M–W ⎱
[H] A–W ⎰ Consult a Latin Dictionary

[I] M–E. A street dancer, and acrobat.

[J] This term might be predicated of anyone in a similar independent capacity – it is, so to say, an *ex officio* epithet.

NB *In the copy from which this is taken there is no note 'C', nor does an identifying superior letter 'C' appear in the text. Also, there is only one superior letter 'E' in the text, but two letter 'E's appear as above. As this apparent anomaly – or copyist's error – cannot be checked, her rendering is here printed.*

LYINGHAM

'Twill strike each stranger with complete amaze,
To learn that even in our modern days,
An English village holds a crew so vile,
As ever did Dahoman soil defile.
And shelters in its mud-built hovels drear
A horde of rogues and knaves to Satan dear,
Who peck their neighbours' faults with vulture bill,
And strive to make each failing greater still.
'Tis of Lyingham I sing, and sundry clowns
Who dwell in that most decayed of towns,
Whence truth and honour have long since been fled;
Where vulgar vice uprears its filthy head;
Where dastards seek to brand their neighbours' fame,
And pour their foulness on each honest name;
Where sland'rous gossip and foul fiendish lies
Are hourly spread to grieve the good and wise;
And scandals talked of all, both rich and poor,
How this one's a thief, and that one's a boor;
Where fawning traitors speak with pleasant smile,
But yet beneath their ample cloak the while
They grasp a dagger ready drawn to pierce
The upright mind with coward blows and fierce.
Where rogues because they're old, sick and obese,
May lie and swear and swindle as they please;
Where lawyers, like wrap-rascal "Sneaks" astound
By "Allegations falling to the ground";

Sneaks: not identified.
Where stupid ruffians, ignorant and blind,
Loud curses hurl at each enlightened mind,
And love each hoary sinner who would stay
The march of progress and improvement's way.
O Muse!, to whom each morn my vows I pay,
Grant me thy kind assistance now I pray;

And freely my reluctant pen inspire,
For much its theme doth need poetic fire.
And thou!, O truth, for once on Lyingham
Descend; unmask each rogue; expose each sham,
And on that God-forsaken village shower
Thy light, and rend the moral clouds that lower
Around the place, and make the good despair
Of justice, and of laying evil bare.
The upstart tradesman make to know his place,
And show his shame upon his brazen face.
Rebuke the clown, whose pedigree's his till,
His till which do usurious profits fill;
And sting with well-deserved scorn the backs
Of mud-born farmers and of rustic quacks.

☆   ☆   ☆

The Village
This dismal village stands in Bumpkinshire
Bumpkinshire; – Leicestershire
That fertile county farmers all admire,
Where bullocks, sheep and hogs do much abound,
With yet more hoggish tillers of the ground;
Where freely, too, the cunning foxes rove,
And feed the joyous sport that hunters love.
The straggling village and its clownish band,
Its dingy houses crumbling as they stand,
Its mud-built walls, its dirty, ill-kept green,
Where sorry curs and squalling brats are seen,
Its vulgar roisterers in their foolish glee,
Its hideous hags so ready for a fee,
Its easy maids who know not virtue's name,
And hold of little worth their virgin fame;
No forms of tedious courtship they require,
But ripely yield to each expressed desire;
Its boorish farmers, like Churchwarden Jim,
Churchwarden Jim: James Samuel Morriss, farmer; of 'Acacia House'. Church-
warden 1877 – 1883. Born c1853 at Brompton, Kent, the son of Hugh Morriss
and Rebecca Elizabeth Williams who were married in Wymondham in December
1849. Both Hugh and Rebecca were descended from the Craven family.
(What fun it is to watch him sing a hymn).
Its poachers, like the grey-haired villain Brown,
William Brown:
That oft-convicted rogue and perjured clown,

249

And – what is even here a foul disgrace –
Its pot-house kept by Henry Tallow-face;
Henry Tallow-face: said to be Henry Perkins, but there is no mention of such a
person in contemporary records. There was a Henry Burton, born in 1856, who,
with his mother, Jane, kept "The Three Horseshoes" about this time.
Where round the bar the village rascals stand,
And daily ripen for the gaoler's hand –
These are poor subjects for poetic lay,
E'en though reluctant Clio guide the way.

☆ ☆ ☆

Nor can the village boast of Nature's charms,
Although it lies 'mid large and fertile farms.
Around it rise no purple tinted hills,
Nor through its fields meander sparkling rills;
The dreary calm that broods o'er all around
Is never broken by a pleasant sound;
No gladsome birds e'er sing at eve or morn;
No fragrant flowers the cottage plots adorn;
No odours sweet are waft on summer breeze;
No pleasant shadows fall from stately trees;
No saints, but many sinners in it dwell;
And strangers brand it still with curses fell;
For from fair July till leafy June
There always is some foolery full in tune;
And altogether 'tis a wretched spot
Where no sane man would wish to cast his lot.

☆ ☆ ☆

The Factions

Two hostile bands the place divide and mock
The laws – though not in turn – by deeds that shock
Those who on Time's slow-measured justice wait,
And honour still the Law Courts of the State.
But sooth to say, one loses faith in "Law"
For years and months are gone since first men saw
The slow "Latrator versus Bulbus" [A] case
Latrator: a bawler or brawler; a barker: most likely alluding to someone named
Barker; not identified. Bulbus: Doctor Henry Douglas MRCS, LSA, born 1817 at
Woolsthorpe, Lincolnshire; he lived in Chapel Lane and was a member of the
Committee elected to supervise the re-pewing of the church in 1873.
In public converse take its tiresome place,
And Bulbus and his minions riot keep,
And fools applaud, and baffled justice weep.

☆ ☆ ☆

250

The Bulbus faction is a horde of knaves,
Whose fit condition would be that of slaves
In some Siberian mine, where cowed by chains
And knout, they'd have foretaste of future pains.
Unfit the rights of honest men to hold,
Their minds are cast in lowest brutal mould.
They deal in tricks, deceit, and lies alone,
And truth and honour are to them unknown.
A rabble rout of crones, small dirty boys,
And rascals whom no honest work employs.
Inured to deeds of shame, a dastard's race,
They are the plague and curse of all the place.
They form a numerous band, so I'll not seek
To name each name, and of each knave to speak;
But from the crowd of meaner rogues select
A few, who all the villainy direct;
And guide the actions of the lower sort
Who to old Bulbus lend their hired support.

☆ ☆ ☆

Dramatis Personae
No1 Cameleopard

Distinguished by his height among the throng
Of cads and rascals as they sneak along,
The youth Cameleopard we first behold;
Cameleopard alias Lying Jack: John Day of Wymondham House; born c1851,
married c1875; described as an Architect; the son of William Day.
A silly goat from an old lecher's fold
With lanky limbs, and tip-toe shambling gait,
With face emasculate and addle-pate.
He seems of intellect almost bereft
And much I tremble for the little left.
In Lyingham he's known as 'Lying Jack'
And oft'ner than his face he shows his back.
He knows not courage, nor doth truth admire,
Nor yet to aught that's noble doth aspire.
His sole ambition is to fish and shoot,
And seems a squire to every rustic brute;
A squire indeed!!! this knave and greedy ass,
Who meanly saves his cash and rides 'third class'.
Go reader, mark him well as he descends
To tops and marbles, and his coppers spends
On sweets, the while he plays at knuckle-down
With muddy street-boy and bucolic clown.

A critic, too, the booby fain would be,
Although he, alas, mis-spells two words in three.
Methinks it were more fit were he at school
Instead of 'Governor' – this noisy fool.
John Day was a 'governor' of the newly constituted Grammar School.
He yearns to hold the rank of village squire;
And as each cad some greater cads admire,
In Lyingham are some who in him see
A 'gentleman' and bellow loud with glee,
When with his dog and gun, a perfect guy,
They mark his long, lean figure slinking by,
Or watch him fishing in his saucer pond,
The pond: now filled-in, lay in the field south of, and belonging to, Wymondham House.
Where hapless little fish are held in bond.
In winter, too, on that same pool he skates,
And boldly braves the wrath of angry fates;
For well he knows no dangers him attend,
E'en though the ice should give, and he descend,
For, like a cork, that empty head would float,
And nothing would be damaged but his coat.
In Spring he shoots the luckless half-score rooks
Which in his trees have sought safe breeding nooks;
Though marvellous it is a bird so wise
Such bare and scrubby trees should e'er entice.
At cricket, too, he often tries his chance.
But in the game he does not much advance;
Becoming ciphers ever grace his score,
And of 'duck-eggs' he now has goodly store.
At football with a borrowed ball he'll play,
But when he bursts it, quite forget to pay.
Thus in its season, he each sport enjoys, *B*
But chiefly in folly his time employs.
The reason why, it is not hard to find,
Naught else but foolishness befits his mind.
Ever swift to obey the call of wrong,
He heedlessly floats with the crowd along.
A vain and empty blabber void of shame,
Who only speaks, his folly to proclaim.

                              ☆ ☆ ☆

A funny tale I'll here relate of Jack,
How once he tried to mount a fiery hack:
It happened thus: Jack thought he'd like to ride,

And so, with boots and spurs, and whip beside,
One day to Pieville town he gaily went,

ieville: Melton Mowbray

And to a posting-house his footsteps bent,
"I want a horse", says he to ostler small,
O'er whom he towered so aspen like and tall;
The ostler grins, and from its stall with speed
He brings for Jack a gaunt and fiery steed.
He helps him up, and with a cunning leer
The fiery steed he sends on its career.
Around the yard it flies with furious pace,
And terror quick o'erspreads Jack's beardless face:
The reins fall from his hand; he grasps the mane,
And Clings with might, although he clings in vain.
His hat falls off; his riding-whip he drops;
His steed rears high, and on the ground Jack flops.
O reader! I will spare you all the rest,
But from that dreadful day, by fear oppressed,
Jack loathes the sight of all the equine race,
Save one poor ancient trooper, slow of pace,
Which from its former honoured place cast out,
Now drags the chariot of this silly lout.

☆ ☆ ☆

But now enough of him; let him return
Into his mud-born friends, like them to burn
With helpless rage, and wish he'd ne'er been born
Than thus stand forth, a butt of public scorn.

☆ ☆ ☆

No. 2 Ted Fromage

A little chandler now demands my song,
Who stands forth prominent amid the throng
Of lying knaves and sneaking rogues who prowl
In Lyingham, and look with envious scowl
On all who high above their level rise,
And seek to glut their hate with sland'rous lies.
This little sneak – Ted Fromage is his name,

Ted Fromage: Edward William Garnham, born in Melton Mowbray 11th August 1829, the son of James Garnham a horse keeper. His shop is what is now Wymondham Art Studio on Main Street. He figured prominently in local affaris from 1864 until his death in 1899 and very often acted as Chairman at Parish Meetings. He, along with William Mann, James S. Morris, William Day and John Day, could always be relied upon to propose, second and vote for one another whenever the opportunity should arise.

Is known both far and wide to mocking fame,
And scorned by high and low on every side,
From self-contempt saves him his own thick hide;
In rain on him falls keen the lash of scorn,
For each sarcastic thrust as praise is worn.
Nor can he see the stains upon his name
Nor feel the pain of well deserved shame.
A graduate in gossip's vilest school,
He loves the lies of every knave and fool,
And all that's base, or works another harm,
Has for his obscene mind resistless charm.
His life is one foul page of actions base,
And all are stamped upon his vulgar face.
A mean, contemptible, ignoble wretch,
He's hardly worth the trouble of a sketch,
But yet, like him, contemptible are fleas,
And these whenever found we crush or squeeze.
So Ted, in language which he comprehends,
Shall be pilloried with his worthless friends.
A few short lines will show his sordid life
And trace his course, with sneaking knavery rife.

☆ ☆ ☆

A proud and happy boy was little Ted
When by the hand his ostler father led
Him first from home to learn the grocer's trade,
And study roguery of every grade.
From early youth in well contended mood
At call of every customer he stood;
He sold a pound of tea, or swept the shop,
With humble grace, a counter-jumping fop.
At Pieville he his knavish life began,
And there for years his mean career he ran.
From that fair town to Lyingham he came,
And printed o'er a grocer's shop his name.
He throve and prospered, and increased his trade,
And step by step he rose in social grade;
Until at length his sweet success to crown
He spoused the daughter of his master Brown.

*Thomas Brown, draper and grocer, died 1869. Ann Brown, daughter of Thomas and
Elizabeth, married Edward William Garnham at Wymondham in 1855.*

Since then full five and twenty years are gone,

*This would make the year to be 1880; perhaps the author was applying a little 'poet's
licence'.*

254

And mighty wonders they for him have done.
For now the ostler's son one scarce would know
In Ted, with self-conceit and pride aglow.
He his own merit sees, and hence his pride,
For he sees more than all the world beside.
See how in church he prays and sings so loud,
That his cracked voice resounds above the crowd.
And then with folded hands upon his paunch,
He sternly looks around, prepared to launch
Fierce wrath upon each trembling little boy,
Or girl, whose childish movements him annoy.
At church he's always late, and never fails
To place his hat upon the altar rails.

Edward Garnham was a Churchwarden from 1871 until 1882. The so-called 'upper-crust' of the village were wont to sit in the choir stalls at this time.

Methinks such sacrilage ought not to be,
Especially from such a cad as he.
In smooth black coat besmudged with greasy stains,
A blustering, little demi-god he reigns.
Behind his narrow counter all the week,
And though an humble man exceeding meek
When in another's power he finds himself;
His love of rule exceeds his love of pelf.
Of Bishops and of sheriffs much he speaks.
And fondly, hat in hand among them sneaks;
Looking as if he were expressly cut
To be the joker's ridicule and butt.
He loves to see his debtors humbly bend,
And to his pompous legal threats attend.

It is related that he was the type of man who, knowing a person owed a debt or rent would, upon encountering that person in some public place, raise his voice and, for the benefit of all within earshot, remind the unfortunate of that debt.

For Ted is fond of calling on the laws,
Although of late he oft has lost his cause.
With pride he daily serves out soap and teas,
With sugar, pepper, arrowroot and cheese,
And longs, with Gladstone, tyrant heads to punch
And with his heel the Grammar School to scrunch.

This attitude is somewhat contradictory, as in 1877 William Day proposed, James S. Morriss seconded, that E.W.G. be a Representative Governor of the Grammar School. These two, plus William Mann, were the only three who voted for E.W.G. Thomas Bennett was elected on this occasion. Nor did this apparent antipathy prevent him from permitting his son Thomas to go there in 1865.

Some years ago old Fromage lost his spouse
Whose wedded life had been on long carouse.
In doggerel verse poor Ted his grief expressed,
And tried to show that he was much distressed.
*His wife, Ann, died 4th July 1875, aged 44 years; the epitaph on her gravestone
reads thus:-*
"To gaze upon the loved in death,
To mark the closing beamless eye,
To press dear lips and find no breath
This, this, is life's worst agony.
But God, too merciful, too wise,
To leave the lone one in despair,
Whispers while snatching those we prize,
My kingdom come ye'll meet them there."
But soon his thoughts in other paths he turned,
And for a grim old dame with lust he burned;
For not content to lead a single life,
He searched the village through to find a wife.
And soon he found the ancient widowed dame,
Whom Lazy Jim maternally doth claim.
*Lazy Jim was James Samuel Morriss; his widowed mother was Rebecca Elizabeth
Morris of 'Acacia House'.*
He daily visits this old female's home,
And oft on Sundays they together roam.
For amorous feats they seem too dry and old;
About the time the poem was written Edward would be 50 and Rebecca 55.
Yet sundry little tales of them are told.
Ah, Fromage! moral censor, fie, for shame!
To play erotic tricks with your old flame!
　　　　　☆　☆　☆
A secret friend of Bulbus and his band,
Within the lists at length Ted took his stand,
And cast aside the flimsy veil of lies
Which long he'd held before his neighbours' eyes;
But from his sneaking ways he could not soar,
And right scurvily in the fight him bore.
Recall, O Muse, that famous hour and day,
When home in triumph, from the ill-fought fray
Old Bulbus and his drunken minions came.
And set the village rowdies all aflame.
The needy ruffians met them on the green,
And there began a most amusing scene.
For moved by hope of coppers and of beer

School Lane (now called Church Lane), Wymondham, c.1900

Some wave old petticoats and hoarsely cheer,
While others from the chariot loose the steed,
Assume its place, and forward dash with speed
Adown the village street, and at their gates
Deposit Bulbus and his worthless mates.
Oh! what a din there was of old tin cans,
Of penny whistles, and of frying pans,
As aged crones on high bore dirty flags,
And rascals clothed in funny hats and rags
Loud bellows as the cortége onward sped,
Cheers for fat Bulbus! cheers for sneaking Ted!

       ☆ ☆ ☆

By knaves from fools collection then was made,
And with the proceeds tea at Vir's was laid;
Vir: William Mann, then living at the Manor House.
The borrowed benches scantily were spread
With washy tea and beer, and loaves of bread;
And filthy scoundrels of the basest sort
Did there with ugly harridans resort.
And while they drank the slop and wretched beer,
They yelled and whooped and roared forth cheer on cheer,
For Sneaks, that foolish goggling clerk and slow,

257

Who in his day has oft been brought to woe;
For brazen Bulbus, chief of perjured quacks,
Who honours vice, but every virtue lacks;
For Vir, whose narrow brow and vacant stare,
His idiot mind and hoggish soul declare;
For craven Ted, who knows not honour's name,
And whose mean presence bringeth nought but shame.

☆ ☆ ☆

Since then it seems Ted's prosperous day is o'er,
For kindly fortune smiles on him no more.
And thought he all his peddling vigour strains,
A worthier man upon his custom gains;
Who, free from all officious meddling ways
Amply deserves success and prosperous days.

Ted's competitor: Arthur Johnson, born in 1852, son of Richard Johnson (from Garthorpe) and Elizabeth Talton.

But 'mid harassing fears and thoughts that tease,
Poor Ted enjoys neither content not ease.
And oft by faith in tales of gossip low
He has, of late, been brought to grievous woe;
With bitter wrath and fury oft he burns,
And oft his precious goods he spurns,
And vows on all a vengeance swift and dire
Who dare oppose him, or withstand his ire.
Yet there are none but laugh to see the fun;
For Ted is dreadful only as a dun;
And, poor muck-worm, provokes but mirth and sneers,
Wherever and whenever he appears.

☆ ☆ ☆

Reflect, O Fromage, change thy sneaking ways!
Repent thy worthless course, thy mis-spent days!
Though slow, the hour is surely drawing nigh,
When all thy tricks and knavery shall lie
Unrolled to view, and every hope be o'er
Of blotting out thy long disgraceful score.

Edward William Garnham died 23rd May 1899 aged 69 years

☆ ☆ ☆

No. 3 Lazy Jim.

Lo! next a clumsy village fop appears,
Inanely grinning as he struts and leers.
See how he rolls and swings from side to side,
And turns half right, half left at every stride.
His trade is farming – idleness his whim,

And hence his neighbours call him "Lazy Jim"
Lazy Jim: James Samuel Morriss.
This idle yokel well the proverb proves,
'Indolence hand in hand with drunk'ness moves."
For search broad England and you will not find
A fellow more lazy, drunken and blind;
A vulgar clown, who idles time away,
With fools and parasites the live-long day;
And drunk and maudlin, nightly seeks his den,
A slav'ring beast, the scorn of decent men.
This lout, whom such obscenities besmirch,
Shameful to say is warden of the church.
Ignoring honour and devoid of grace,
From year to year he crawls his dunghill race.
No noble thoughts inspire his sluggish breast;
No fair ambition breaks his clownish rest.
His turnips, swine congenial, and his mares
Engross his hopes and occupy his cares.
His daily joys are pipe and turbid beer,
Which his dull mind and craven spirit cheer;
When he with Darkie, Barge, and gaol birds twain
Their pewter pots in dogged silence drain.
Darkie: see below.
Barge: Robert Large M.R.C.V.S. Veterinary Surgeon, born c1829 at Branston,
Leicestershire, he died July 1896 aged 68 years.
'gaol birds twain': probably 'Jackal' and 'Raisins':
But quick in rage their clam'rous voices raise,
When on a gentleman they turn and gaze;
For then they feel their base and brutish state,
And in their own vile way they vent their hate.

☆ ☆ ☆

But though incredible it may appear
Besotted Jim loves something else than beer;
And woos a village Belle in boorish way –
Is actually engaged, the gossips say.
Oh shame! that it should ever be the case
That such a clown should kiss so fair a face.
Oh shame! that such an utter fool as Jim
Should clasp a waist so dainty and so trim;
For Jim's a man of nasty, clownish ways,
Of idle habits and of ox-like gaze;
And with his drawling words, so seldom wise,
Agree his foolish stare and funny eyes;

Timid and false, the scorn of friend and foe,
He never was known to return a blow;
But, full of knavery and ev'ry vice
His fav'rite weapons are cards and dice.
This weak, false-hearted knave, whose ill-taught mind
No thoughts of honour, truth, or wisdom bind,
Strove hard, of late, to glut his spiteful ire,
By dragging down his neighbours to the mire,
Where deep he wallows with his shameless friends,
And deeper daily in the slough descends –
(And heaven knows, they must be deep indeed
In filth, when even ladies are not freed
From foul remarks and scurrilous abuse,
Sprung from their dastard minds and brains obtuse).
In vain he strove! and on his own head recoiled
The wretched scrawl whereon his friends had toiled;
For soon before him lay the obscene scroll,
Stamped with the meanness of each swinish soul;
And each foul epithet and sland'rous name
Therein served but to show their depth of shame;
Then writhing 'neath the hand that thus laid bare
The craven deed, and charged him with his share,
He fain with brazen lies would have concealed
The mean conspiracy he feared revealed,
And flung away the offered chance to prove
His innocence, and all reproach remove.
Full well he knew his guilt; full well he knew
That fair investigation he must rue.
And so he cast aside, like sulky boy,
The chance a guiltless man had grasped with joy;
And bade that low-bred butler out of place
His lawyer, try if he could mend the case.
The pettifogger tried, but meanly failed,
And then against his stupid client railed.
Since then, whene'er in public place Jim shows
His face, but look at him, how red he grows.

☆   ☆   ☆

O wretched man! forsake thine evil ways,
And from the dust thy voice for mercy raise;
And call upon thine injured God to hear
Ere shameful death cut short thy vile career;
For thou dost play in life a loathsome part
With obscene tongue and craven, sland'rous heart.

No. 4 Bobby Barge

A hideous fellow rascal next I sketch,
Ill favoured Barge, that mean degraded wretch;
Bobby Barge: Robert Large – see above.
That dastard, drunkard, and of evil life,
That faithless brute who beats his foolish wife.
His wife: Ann, born c1825 at Normanton on Trent, Nottinghamshire.
Although in many distant lands I've been,
No uglier ruffian have I ever seen;
Not even 'mong those wretched Bulgar slaves,
Of whom the Liberal Gladstone fondly raves.
What wonder then that little children flee,
When Barge's whiskered, whiskied face they see,
As onward shuffling with unsteady feet
He flounders walrus-like along the street,
Or lolls at Fromage's door to swear,
And glares on passers-by with idiot stare.
A rural 'vet' by trade is red-nosed Bob,
But yet he very seldom gets a job,
And chiefly spends his time in drinking gin,
And boldly practising adult'rous sin.
He has seduced a simple farmer's wife,
And twixt the foolish spouses planted strife.
He shares with nigger Sam this faithless dame,
Nigger Sam: Samuel Johnson, see below.
The farmer's wife: not identified.
And makes no secret of the wanton's shame,
But boasts that through the open door he leaps,
While craven Darkie from the window creeps;
When each in turn the silly doxy leaves,
Who with such loathsome brutes her intrigues weaves.
But Barge loves drink past all on earth beside,
Nor seeks his filthy, drunken ways to hide.
See him besotted with the fumes of gin,
His substance wasted, and his life a sin:
And mark him rev'lling at the pot-house bar,
With boon companions till the morning star.
A raving sot, heedless of all control,
Defiled in body and depraved in soul;
Then reeling home besmudged with filthy stains,
Debased in morals, and devoid of brains.

✩　✩　✩

Oh Barge! beware, and while there yet is time,
Redeem thy wasted years of vice and crime
And pardon for what life has been implore,
Lest mercy's gate be closed for evermore;
And awful anguish curse thy dying day,
When Satan's demons claim thee for their prey.

☆ ☆ ☆

No. 5 Joe Shaker

Joe Shaker, that good shepherd, next behold,
Joe Shaker: Joseph Bennet, a shepherd.
Well noted for his love of dirt and gold;
In person filthy and in habits mean,
Insanely hating all things neat and clean,
He stands declared a miser and a fool,
A fitting butt for scorn and ridicule.
Good luck that he will never take a wife,
For he would surely blight her hapless life:
Of love he does not understand a line,
And his most fitting consorts are his swine.
A den of filth and foulness is his house;
His larder would not tempt the hungriest mouse;
And if his soul is grimy as his skin,
What evil case poor Shaker must be in!
A mangy cap, clumsy shepherd's crook,
A rusty beard, a foolish, knavish look
Distinguish him e'en 'mong the dirty lot
Who once protected Bulbus and his cot.
His beard – a field for Barge's vulgar fun –
Is rusty – well, as rusty as his gun:
And if to wash it he should ever try,
What hosts of ugly vermin then would die.
A steadfast pilgrim of the wrong is he,
With heart and soul for senseless villainy,
And, silly fool, must lend his feeble aid
To ev'ry scheme by coward ruffians laid.
He lately had his dastard friends to screen,
By taking all the blame of scrawls obscene.
No one, of course, regards the flimsy veil
Or credits all the statements of his tale:
For Weasel *[D]*, Jim, and Darkie had their share,
Weasel: A son of E.W.G.
Nor left the matter all to Shaker's care;
But with much time and labour did produce

The village green, Wymondham, c.1900

Main Street and the Three Horse Shoes, Wymondham, c.1900

263

Some vulgar nonsense, and some low abuse,
Ill-spelt, contemptible, their own disgrace,
And which but showed how wretched was their case.

☆ ☆ ☆

No. 6 Darkie Sam

Darkie Sam: Samuel Johnson. There were two persons by the name of Samuel Johnson living in Wymondham as contemporaries. The Samuel of this poem – Samuel Alexander Johnson – was born in New Providence, Nassau about the year 1853: He married Fanny Jane Kirk of Wymondham on Christmas Day 1872. By the time the poem was written they had six children.

A horrid odour floats upon the breeze,
And calls to mind a land beyond the seas:
For Sam, the local nigger's in the throng,
And as he passes lo! the scent lies strong.
A squat buck nigger is this darkie Sam, [E]
With skull as thick as any Leicester ram.
His nose is gay with gin, his mouth is vile:
His grinning face when he attempts to smile
Displays a row of fangs – O hideous sight! –
Which measures full a foot from left to right.
A thatch of matted wool protects his head,
Or rustic blows long since had laid him dead.
His legs enclose a far from graceful arch;
His back is stiff with clumsy yeoman starch:
For Sam's a member of the Bumpkin Corps,
A poor, untutored private – nothing more.
His views are very much confused and crude,
And rather dull and stupid is his mood.
But, good white people, do not look with scorn
On poor black Sam, a loafer all forlorn.
Despite his foul words, his valour's all a sham;
And queer tho' he looks, he's as meek as a lamb:
His fury he in valentines expends,
And foolishness in filthy pasteboard sends.
I do not take his part, or for him plead,
For crime and law have made his pocket bleed.
His life is hard – no roses for his bed –
And vulgar fists his nose have often bled.
From Ploughtown driven, with many a jibe and jeer,
Ploughtown: Oakham
Refuge he sought in his Lyingham dear,
And daily he loafs thro' all the village streets,
A pot-house sponge, ever looking for 'treats';

264

While poverty his naked home assails,
And with hunger and cold his offspring wails.
Sometimes on borrowed nag he rides to "Meet",
And looks, like Jim his friend, a guy complete,
In breeches, boots, and coat time-worn and thin,
And hat that matches fairly with his skin.
One day, seized with the nigger's love of show,
Poor Sam felt martial ardour in him glow:
'How fine to wear a helmet all of brass,
And coat with trimmings', thought this yellow ass,
'And hear a sword clank at my bulging heels;
What matter then though scanty be my meals?
A shabby lout I'll tarry here no more,
But straightway go and join the Bumpkin Corps'.
Such soldiering 'tis true is all a sham,
But, golly, 'twould be happiness for Sam,
E'en tho' he be a very raw recruit,
And tho' the sergeant call him 'stupid brute'.

☆ ☆ ☆

One day Sam heard that he must go to war,
And fight for England 'gainst the Russian Czar.
Now when the grievous rumour reached the place,
No warlike looks were seen upon his face,
But like a batman's cur he howled and whined:[F]
For Sammy was not easy in his mind,
He thought he saw himself a shapeless mass
In Turkey, lying on the gory grass:
But Oh! the thought filled Sammy's heart with fears,
And caused his whitey eyes to gush with tears.
Thus Sam, who often lets his passions rise,
And takes delight in black'ning rustic eyes,
And thinks a walking-stick a fitting tool
– Poor simple soul – with which to fight a duel,
Was filled with dread at thought of sword and lance,
And straightway swooning fell in craven trance.

☆ ☆ ☆

No 7 Weasel Fromage

Weasel Fromage: Charles Edward Garnham, born 10th October 1858 and died suddenly 11th April 1886, unmarried. This epitaph on his gravestone is also used on his father's: 'Lord all pitying Jesu blest, Grant him thine eternal rest'.

There's Weasel Fromage too, that slov'nly youth,
Ill-made, devoid of wisdom and of truth.
Weasel, with concience as his body, limp,

265

Quite proud to play the shameless spy and pimp.
He loves not waiting in his much shut shop,
Although he would be only about 18, the County Directory of 1877 describes him a
a 'clothier': probably his indulgent father set him up in business, but if, as the poer.
says, his was a much shut shop, then it is no wonder that some years later he was onc
more, assistant in his father's shop.
But far prefers in 'pubs' to smoke and slop.
The gossips say, that like his father Ted,
This simply ninny wishes he were wed,
But that he finds it hard to find a wife
To share the woes and follies of his life.
For maids are coy, and dread the Weasel's arms,
Wherein, indeed, they'd wholly waste their charms.
Yet there are some who might compassion take;
There's Vitula,*G* Canicula,*H* and Rake,*I*
Vulpicula, and others I might name
Whose ugliness a chimpanzee would shame:

Vitula			*little cow*
Canicula			*bitch*
	obviously women		*a word usually used to describe a man: perhap.*
Rake	*of doubtful virtue*		*the author here uses it in the sense 'as thin as c*
			rake'(?)
Vulpicula			*little vixen*

These are lone damsels, neither choice nor fair,
So, hapless Weasel, do not yet despair;
But let him vanish with this final sneer
And in his place let brother Ape appear.

☆ ☆ ☆

No 8 Ape Fromage
Ape Fromage: Thomas James Garnham, born 1857 and elder brother of Charles; a
bank clerk. He attended the Grammar School when old enough.
Of Ape old Father Fromage speaks with joy,
And boasts the triumphs of this darling boy.
At cricket, football, and at other games
Of which wide-trousered Ape some knowledge claims.
But Ape, the banking clerk so poorly paid,
Who must thro' dreary ledgers daily wade,
Is not a character to be admired,
E'en though he be by clerkly ardour fired;
Mean knav'ry sits enthroned upon his face;
And like old Ted he cannot feel disgrace.
His head is full of tricks and petty wiles,
And, ever grinning with meaningless smiles,

Wymondham House, c.1900, the home of John Day

The Village Green, Wymondham, c.1900, looking east

He gossips and meddles, tattles and lies,
And lets nothing escape his prying eyes.

☆ ☆ ☆

Such are these sneaking cubs of sneaking sire,
From whom all worthy men with scorn retire;
They'll never hold an honoured place,
But, like their father, crawl among the base.

☆ ☆ ☆

No 9 The Minor Rascals

The minor rascals thronging now appear,
Filled full with brutal ignorance and beer,
'Tis scarcely possible that one could view
Elsewhere in England such a dastard crew
As these who close behind their leaders crowd,
And boast their coward deeds in accents loud;
Who courage only in their numbers find,
And fight when twenty are 'gainst one combined.

☆ ☆ ☆

See at their head the brutish Jackal stand,
Jackal: not identified
The vilest craven of that loathsome band.
Mark how, with hang-dog look and staring eye,
He swings his heavy bludgeon up on high,
The picture of a slobbering artisan,
Whom 'twere foul calumny to call a man.

☆ ☆ ☆

Next Raisins comes, that dirty, evil scribe,
Raisins: William Rayson, a labourer, born in 1837: at the time the poem was
written was unmarried and had a room in the house of Thomas and Sophia James.
Who wrote the letters of the Bulbus tribe;
A hideous wretch this scribbling Raisins is;
His voice is something 'twixt a croak and hiss;
His slouching gait reveals his dastard soul;
His shifty eyes his coward heart unroll;
He looks exactly like a hoary rat,
Which lives in constant terror of the cat.

☆ ☆ ☆

These twain with fellow rogues did once combine,
And on an Autumn evening, bright and fine,
Forth rushing from the filthy, bawdy house,
Where Bulbus and his crew held vile carouse,
Attacked an unarmed man on his own ground,

268

While loud their yells and curses echoed round.
Among the brutes who this great deed performed,
And though they kept the hut from being stormed
Were 'Punch' the poacher, and the 'witness' Brown,
Punch and Brown: not identified.
Who thought their deeds most fittingly to crown,
By striking on the ground a fallen man –
And then, the dastards, ah! how they ran.

☆ ☆ ☆

Jackal and Raisins soon had cause to rue
Their deeds; for, ta'en from 'mid the filthy crew,
In dock before the Magistrates they stood,
A pair of dirty rogues of sullen mood.
Their fellow-ruffians hoped for their release,
And were prepared to hail them home in peace,
When rumour told them, shocking to relate,
That 'Fourteen days' was Jack and Raisins' fate.

☆ ☆ ☆

A smith there was, grim Toss-pot, now away,
Toss-pot: not identified
A parasite who drank while fools would pay.
His place another holds, a 'killing' swain,
Whose mouth is full of words obscene and vain.
The 'killing' swain was Edward Hayes; in his twenties, living with his sister and unmarried, had taken over the family smithy in Edmondthorpe Road from his mother Jane; Toss-pot could well have been employed by Jane during her widowhood until such time as Edward could take over the business.

☆ ☆ ☆

Then there is old meddlesome 'Pinafore John',
Pinafore John: John Johnson, shoemaker, born in 1848 the son of Richard and Elizabeth and brother to Arthur, mentioned above.
Who by day and by night toils ceaselessly on,
And scarcely will leave his much loved last
To snatch his frugal and scanty repast,
But fills his shops with boots that will not sell,
And shoes that will not wear, as buyers tell.

☆ ☆ ☆

There's Billivir, that farmer rude and hoar
Billivir: William Mann, nephew to 'Vir', who, although living with his uncle at the Manor House, farmed for himself. In 1888 he married Charlotte Cobb who had been living at the Manor House for some years; she was sister-in-law of his uncle William. He later lived at "Mann's Farm".

269

Whose old crock trots behind, and walks before,
While with his stick old Billi measure keeps,
As onward sluggishly the creature creeps.

☆ ☆ ☆

There's cobbling Jerry, prolific and grim,
Cobbling Jerry: George William 'Jerry' Hickman, son of Vincent, a shoemaker; born in 1841.
There's grateful Bell-ringer with one wooden limb,
Bell-ringer: Aaron Crowson
Then there is a wretched dealer in fowl,
Samuel Goddard: born in 1855, the son of William Goddard and Sarah Stafford.
Whose mother yclept the Lyingham ghoul,
Devised the wondrous form of rags and hair,
Which once was foolish Barge's daily care.

☆ ☆ ☆

But hold – enough of rascals low and base –
They may amuse, but still they must disgrace.
So now from Bulbus and the worthless band,
Who round that bloated centre-figure stand,
My Muse recoils, and leaves them to despair,
With all their evil characters laid bare.

☆ ☆ ☆

My space is short, and shorter still my time,
And narrow limits must confine my rhyme,
But many other themes for verse remain
In Lyingham; and though I must refrain,
Perchance some rustic poet will arise
And tell how – dreadul in aesthetic eyes –
In Chapel Lane a dreary building stands,
A temple surely made by careless hands.
The Congregational Chapel
This chapel where old Sector crows so loud,
Sector: (one who cuts): Henry Munday, one of the 'big-wigs' at the chapel. A tailor and draper by trade of Market Overton in Rutland: born in 1816.
Is but a cock-pit for the pious crowd
Of those whose Independence knows no bounds,
While Vulpus is the fox and they the hounds.
Vulpus: William Fox, minister of the chapel; born in 1829 at Papplewick, Nottinghamshire
Poor Vulpus! how unhappy is his fate,
Thou luckless butt of sinners small and great!
Dost thou recall the day when thou first came
To rowdy Lyingham, a preacher tame,*J*

270

A servant, bound, as told, to preach and teach;
And Lundi rose and made a furious speech?
Lundi: Henry Munday
Right glad am I to see this happy day,
And hope that 'ere for ever you may stay;
For know you're the right man in the right place,
  much am pleased to look upon your face."
Thus Lundi spoke, and sympathetic gazed,
And all around their chosen pastor praised.

☆ ☆ ☆

Then, leaving Vulpus to his weary fate
This future poet might with ease dilate
On lighter themes, and for his verses claim
An ancient mariner of hardy fame,
Who now no more the restless seas doth rove,
But lies secure in anchorage of love –
A quiet man who fills his glass and smoke,
And sometimes, too, be likes a little joke.
Then with his dog my sympathies all go,
'Tis hardly fair to treat the creature so.
The bard might then relate in pleasant strain
How daily one may meet in Chapel Lane
Fair L.P. or skittish, sly Sar'Anne,
L.P.: not identified Sar'Anne: said to be Sarah Ann Parker, but no mention of such
a person in contemporary documents.
With winsome looks the young 'Grammarians' scan,
And with their comrades passing to and fro,
Little Galateas, smile as they go.
Then though his efforts would be useless quite,
He might expose in all their foolish light
The silly pranks of one who tried in vain
To shoot a rook, by only broke a pane.
Then, too, he might describe a tiny wood
Where oft when ev'ning's shadows dimly brood,
A rustic Venus lingers at the gate,
And waits in local lingo for a 'mate'.
But now I must refrain though themes arise
In endless order and most motly guise;
And with each line but grows the fertile field
Which Lyingham people for satire yield.

☆ ☆ ☆

Bibliography

A. Works specifically concerned with Leicestershire and Rutland

W.Andrews (ed.), *Bygone Leicestershire*, Leicester and Hull, 1892
J.C.Badcock, *The History of Fleckney*, Fleckney, 1980
J.D.Bennett, *Discovering Leicestershire and Rutland*, Alyesbury, 1973
C.J.Billson, *Leicester Memories*, Leicester, 1924
       Leicestershire and Rutland: County Folk-lore, 1895
       Mediaeval Leicester, Leicester, 1920
S.N.Boase, 'Humberstone Gate Pleasure Fairs in the late Nineteenth Century', pp.16–25 in *The Leicestershire Historian*, 1979–80
J.Bourne, *Place-names of Leicestershire and Rutland*, Leicester, 1981
J.Brownlow, *Melton Mowbray, Queen of the Shires*, Wymondham, 1980
J.Buchan, *Thatched Village*, 1983
P.Buttery et al., *Oadby 1880–1980*, Oadby, 1980
Bygone Leicestershire, Leicester Mercury Special Issues, 1983–5
D.Campton, *History of Belgrave*, Leicester, 1927
E.C.Cawte, 'Ploughboys at Sproxton', pp.124–5 in *English Dance and Song*, Winter 1969; 'Seasonal Customs in Leicestershire', p.16 in *English Dance and Song*, Spring 1972, and p.56 in *id.*, Summer 1972
M.G.Cherry, 'The Plough-Monday Play in Rutland', pp.195–9 in *The Rutland Magazine*, Jan. 1903 – Oct. 1904
V.B.Crowther-Beynon, 'Notes on some Edith Weston Institutions', pp.176–80 in *The Rutland Magazine*, 1905–6
J.Curtis, *A Topographical History of the County of Leicester*, Ashby-de-la-Zouch, 1831
A.Cutting, *Leicestershire Ghost Stories*, Blaby, 1982
C.Dainton, 'George Smith of Coalville', pp.569–77 in *History Today*, Vol.XXIX, Sept. 1979
Deacon's Leicestershire, Rutland and Northamptonshire Court Guide and County Blue Book, 1890
C.Edge, *Popular Belief in Leicester*, unpublished B.A. thesis, Leeds University, 1965
B.Elliott, *Stories of Oadby*, Oadby, 1982
M.Elliott, *Leicester, a Pictorial History*, Chichester, 1983
C.Ellis, *History in Leicester*, Leicester, 1976, 3rd ed.

273

I.C.Ellis, *Records of Nineteenth Century Leicester*, privately printed, 1935

A.B. and S. Evans, *Leicestershire Words, Phrases and Proverbs*, 1881

I.M.Evans (ed.), *Charnwood's Heritage*, Leicester, 1976

T.Featherstone, *Legends of Leicester in the Olden Time*, 1838

J.B.Firth, *Highways and Byways in Leicestershire*, 1926

W.G.D.Fletcher, *Chapters in the History of Loughborough*, Loughborough, 1883

M.Forsyth, *Talking about Leicestershire*, Leicester, n.d.

P.Foss, *The History of Market Bosworth*, Wymondham, 1983

W.Gardiner, *Music and Friends*, 3 vols, 1838–53

J.Goodacre, 'Lord Macaulay on the Leicester Parliamentary Election of 1826', pp.24–7 in *The Leicestershire Historian*, 1980–1

'Wyclif in Lutterworth: Myths and Monuments', pp.25–35 in *The Leicestershire Historian*, 1983–4

S.E.Green, *Further Legends of Leicestershire and Rutland*, Leicester, 1974

Selected Legends of Leicestershire, Leicester, 1971

S.E.Green and J.Wilshere, *A Short History of Leicester Markets and Fairs*, Leicester, n.d.

B. Greenwood, 'Narborough Memories', pp.206–7 in *The Leicestershire and Rutland Magazine*, Sept. 1949

J.E.Harrington, 'Mountsorrel Childhood Recollections', pp.11–15 in *The Leicestershire Historian*, 1978–9

T.Harrold, 'Old Hinckley', pp.326–38 in *Transactions of the Leicestershire Architectural and Archaeological Society*, vol. VI, 1882–3

'Heywood', *Local Legends*, Loughborough, 1934

W.G.Hoskins, *Essays in Leicestershire History*, Liverpool, 1950

Rutland, Leicester, 1949

Touring Leicestershire, Leicester, 1971, 2nd ed.

P.E.Hunt, *The Story of Melton Mowbray*, Leicester, 1979, 2nd ed.

T.F.Johnson, *Glimpses of Ancient Leicester*, 1891

W.Kelly, 'Ancient Records of Leicester', paper read before the Literary and Philosophical Society of Leicester, 1851

Notices Illustrative of the Drama, and other popular amusements . . . extracted from the Chamberlains' Accounts and other manuscripts of the Borough of Leicester, 1865

Royal Progresses and Visits to Leicester, Leicester, 1884

The Leicester Chronicle and Leicestershire Mercury Local Notes and Queries, column published between May, 1874, and October, 1875

P.H.Lloyd, *Anecdotes of Bygone Leicestershire*, n.d., n.p., 3rd ed.

The History of the Mysterious Papillon Hall, Leicester, 1978, 2nd ed.

B.Lount, *George Davenport, Leicestershire's Notorious Highwayman*, Fleckney, 1983

A.Macaulay, *History and Antiquities of Claybrook in the County of Leicester, including the Hamlets of Bittesby, Ullesthorpe, Wibtoft, and Little Wigston,* 1791

A.Mee, *Leicestershire and Rutland,* 1967 ed.

K.J.Morton, 'Highwaymen in Leicester', pp.141–3 in *The Leicestershire and Rutland Magazine,* June, 1950

A.B. de Mowbray, *Knossington,* Reading, 1898

J.Nichols, *Antiquities of Hinckley,* 1782

       History and Antiquities of the County of Leicester, 4 vols, 1795–1815

G. Paget, *The Flying Parson and Dick Christian,* Leicester, 1934

G.Paget and L. Irvine, *Leicestershire,* 1950

R.M.Paisey, *John Ferneley (1782–1860), his Life and Work,* Leicester, 1984

R.Parkinson, *A General View of the Agriculture of the County of Rutland,* 1808

A.T.Patterson, *Radical Leicester: a History of Leicester, 1780–1850,* Leicester, 1954

A.J.Pickering, *The Cradle and Home of the Hosiery Trade,* Hinckley, 1940

W.Pitt, *A General View of the Agriculture of the County of Leicester,* 1809

D.Prestidge, *Tom Cribb at Thistleton Gap,* Wymondham, 1971

N.Pye (ed.), *Leicester and its Region,* Leicester, 1972

N.Pevsner, *The Buildings of England: Leicestershire and Rutland,* Harmondsworth, 1977, 3rd reprint

R.Read, *Modern Leicester,* 1881

Records of the Borough of Leicester, ed. M.Bateson, H.Stocks and G.A.Chinnery, 7 vols, London, Cambridge and Leicester, 1899–1974

Rutland Local History Society, *Oakham in Rutland,* Stamford, 1982

       Uppingham in Rutland, Stamford, 1983

       The Villages of Rutland, 2 vols, Stamford, 1979

J.Simmons, *Leicester: The Ancient Borough to 1860,* Gloucester, 1983, 2nd ed.

       Life in Victorian Leicester, Leicester, 1971

F.E.Skillington, *The Plain Man's History of Leicester,* Leicester, 1950

       '60 Years of Leicestershire Farming', pp.3–8 in *The Leicestershire and Rutland Magazine,* Dec. 1948

C.Smith, *Frisby before 1914,* Frisby-on-the-Wreake, 1975

E.Smith *Memories of a Country Girlhood,* Wymeswold, 1983

D.Sneath and B.Lount, *The Life of a Victorian Poacher: James Hawker,* Fleckney, 1982

E.E.Snow, 'Leicestershire Cricket', pp.128–30 in *The Leicestershire and Rutland Magazine,* June 1949

       'Rutland's Place in the History of Cricket', pp.105–9 in *Rutland Record,* no. 3, 1982–3

J. and T. Spencer, *Leicestershire and Rutland Notes and Queries and*

Antiquarian Gleaner, 3 vols, Leicester and London, 1891–5

J.Stevenson, *A Family Guide to Charnwood Forest*, Wymondham, 1982

J. and A.E.Stokes, *Just Rutland*, Uppingham, 1953

E.Swift, *Inns of Leicestershire*, Leicester, n.d.

'The Leicestershire Mummers' Play' pp.34–40 in *The Leicestershire and Rutland Magazine*, Dec. 1949

M.Tanner, *Crime and Murder in Victorian Leicestershire*, Blaby, 1981

D.Tew, *The Melton to Oakham Canal*, Wymondham, 1984

J.Throsby, *The History and Antiquities of the Ancient Town of Leicester*, Leicester, 1791

The Memoirs of the Town and County of Leicester, 6 vols, 1777

K.Varty, 'Reynard in Leicestershire and Rutland', pp.1–8 in *Transactions of the Leicestershire Archaeological and Historical Society*, vol.XXXVIII, 1962–3

B.Waites, *Exploring Rutland*, Leicester, 1982

S.Watts, *A Walk Through Leicester; being a Guide to Strangers, containing a Description of the Town and its environs, with remarks upon its History and Antiquities*, Leicester and London, 1804

D.T.Williams, *The Battle of Bosworth*, Leicester, 1973

J.Wilshere, *Leicestershire Weather Sayings*, Leicester, 1980

The Religious Guilds of Mediaeval Leicester, Leicester, 1979

William Gardiner of Leicester, 1770–1853: hosiery manufacturer, musician and dilettante, Leicester, 1970

P.F.Woodford, *History of Kibworth and Personal Reminiscences*, 1939

J.Wright, *The History and Antiquities of the County of Rutland*, 1684

V.Wright, *As I remember them*, Frisby-on-the-Wreake, 1977

B. Other Works

H.W.Barley, 'Plough Plays of the East Midlands', pp.68–94 in *Journal of the English Folk Dance and Song Society*, vol. VII, no. 2, 1953

W.G.Bond, *The Wanderings of Charles I*, Birmingham, 1935

J.Brand, *Observations on the Popular Antiquities of Great Britain*, 3 vols (ed. Ellis), 1849–53

G.Burton, *Chronology of Stamford*, 1846

B.Bushaway, *By Rite: Custom, Ceremony and Community in England, 1700–1880*, 1982

E.W.Cawte, A.Helm and N.Peacock, *English Ritual Drama*, 1967

T.Cooper, *The Life of Thomas Cooper*, 1872

G.Deacon, *John Clare and the Folk Tradition*, 1983

T.F.Thistleton Dyer, *Old English Social Life as Told by the Parish Registers*, 1898

D.H.Farmer, *The Oxford Dictionary of Saints*, Oxford, 1982

C.Fiennes, *The Journeys of Celia Fiennes*, 1982

Folklore, Myths and Legends of Great Britain, 1973

W.Forster (ed.), *Pit Talk*, Leicester, n.d.

A.B.Gomme, *The Traditional Games of England, Scotland and Ireland*, 2 vols, 1894–8

C.Griffin, *The Leicestershire and South Derbyshire Miners, 1840–1914*, Coalville, n.d. (1981)

Charlie Hammond's Sketch-Book, ed. C.Fry, Oxford, 1980

James Hawker's Journal: A Victorian Poacher, ed. G.Christian, 1961

W.C.Hazlitt, *A Dictionary of Faiths and Folklore*, 2 vols, 1905

A.Helm and E.C.Cawte, *Six Mummers' Acts*, Ibstock, 1967

W.Henderson, *Notes on the Folklore of the Northern Counties*, 1879

C.Hole, *British Folk Customs*, 1976

       English Traditional Customs, 1975

       Witchcraft in England, 1977

M.Howell and P.Ford, *The True History of the Elephant Man*, Harmondsworth, 1982

W.Hutton, *The Life of William Hutton*, 1816

P.Kennedy, *The Folk Songs of Britain and Ireland*, 1975

R.A.Leeson, *Travelling Brothers*, 1980

R.W.Malcolmson, *Popular Recreations in English Society, 1700–1850*, Cambridge, 1973

W.Marshall, *The Rural Economy of the Midland Counties*, 2 vols, 1790

S.P.Menefee, *Wives for Sale*, Oxford, 1981

H.Michel, 'Diary of the Rev. Humphrey Michel', pp.371–80 in *Transactions of the Leicestershire Architectural and Archaeological Society*, vol.I, 1866

C.Morsley, *News from the English Countryside, 1750–1850*, 1979

       News from the English Countryside, 1851–1950, 1983

R.Muir, *The Lost Villages of Britain*, 1982

'Nimrod' (Charles Apperley), 'Remarks on the Condition of Hunters, the Choice of Horses and their Management', pp.216–43 in *Quarterly Review*, vol.XLVII, 1832

G.F.Northall, *English Folk Rhymes*, 1892

I. and P.Opie, *The Lore and Language of Schoolchildren*, 1977

R.Palmer, *A Ballad History of England*, 1979

       Everyman's Book of British Ballads, 1980

       A Touch on the Times, Songs of Social Change, 1770–1914, Harmondsworth, 1974

M.Palmer, *Framework Knitting*, Princes Risborough, 1984

J.Richardson, *The Local Historian's Encyclopedia*, New Barnet, 1974

R.Samuel, 'Mineral Workers', pp.1–97 in R.Samuel (ed.), *Miners, Quarrymen and Saltworkers*, 1977

J.Simpson, 'Multi-purpose treacle mines in Sussex and Surrey', pp.61–73 in *Lore and Language*, vol.3, no.6, part A, Jan.1982

D.M.Smith, *The Industrial Archaeology of the East Midlands*, Dawlish and London, 1965

E.Swift, *Folk Tales of the East Midlands*, 1954

P.Underwood, *A Gazetteer of British Ghosts*, 1971

A.R.Wright and T.E.Lones, *British Calendar Customs – England*, 3 vols, 1936–40

Acknowledgements

I should like to thank for permission to reproduce material: Dr E.C.Cawte for the Ab Kettleby song from A.Helm and E.C.Cawte, *Six Mummers' Acts*, Ibstock, 1967, p.41, and for the Caldecott and Sproxton plays from his private collection; and Mrs Elizabeth Ruddock for the two Cottesmore songs from her article, 'May-Day Songs and Celebrations in Leicestershire and Rutland', p.77, in *Transactions of the Leicestershire Archaeological and Historical Society*, vol.XL, Leicester, 1964–5.

For assistance, these institutions: Anglian Water Authority, John Briggs and Calder, Auctioneers, Atherstone, the Harborough Museum, Radio Leicester, Leeds University English Department, Leicester Reference Library, Leicestershire Museums, Art Galleries and Records Service (especially the Newarke Houses Museum), the Lincolnshire Library Service, the Vaughan Williams Memorial Library at Cecil Sharp House, London, and the Women's Institute.

For help and encouragement, a large number of individuals, including: my publisher, Mr Trevor Hickman, who also with Sue Steel kindly took all the contemporary photographs, Mr O.D.Lucas (Wigston), who kindly allowed me to see a typescript of his memoirs and also offered many suggestions, Mrs Edith Carter (Swepstone) and Mrs Monica Turner (Thurmaston), who gave me May songs, Mrs Pat Palmer, my wife, Mr and Mrs G.H.Palmer, my parents, Mrs Joy Knight, my sister, Mrs Mabel Smith, my mother-in-law, and also Mrs Olive Snelson and Mr Geoff, Wainwright (Loughborough), Mr and Mrs J.Osband (Kirby Muxloe), Mrs D.R.Hayball (Sheepy), Mr J.Hipkiss (Sibson), Mr T.Vann (Belgrave), Mrs Stella Jones (Stocking Farm), Mrs I.Oakland (Blaby), Mrs Dorothy Sutton and Mrs Joan Underwood (Wigston), Mr Austin Sanderson (Kibworth), Mr Malcolm Elliott (Rothley), Mrs Dorothy Baker, Mrs Linda Hood and Mr Kenneth Bell (Burbage), Mr Michael Tanner (Sleaford), Mr Denis Baker (Coalville), Mr Sid Marnoch, Mrs Hilda Burbage, Mr S.D.Flinders, Mr Bill Measures, Mrs Boreen Davis and Mrs Evelyn Powell (Leicester), Mrs Vera Jones and Mr Jack Birch (Hinckley), Mr Jack Marshall and Norah? (Markfield), Mrs Gwen Ingham (Newton Harcourt), Mr David Sneath (Fleckney), Mrs Mavis Ward (Narborough), Mrs G.H.Hall and Miss E.Wilson, daughters of the late Charlie Wilson (Empingham), Mr C.D.Poster (Groby Community College), Mr A.P.G. Macdonald (Rutland Sixth Form College, Oakham), Mr E.C.Turner and Mrs Pauline Buttery

Oadby), Mrs Maureen Cruickshank (Beauchamp College, Oadby), Mr S.Hicks (Ashby Grammer School), Mr C.J.Kershaw (Melton Mowbray Upper School), Rev. L.A.Dutton (Ashby), Mr A.K.Bennett (Secretary, Leicester City F.C.), Rev. R.J.H Hunting (Sileby), Rev. K.Newbon (Braunstone), Rev.T. Dulley (Langham), Rev.P.Tambling (Glenfield), and Mr and Mrs Jack Lee (Coalville). I apologise if there are any inadvertent omissions.

Index

286